Counterinsurgency

Counterinsurgency

What the United States Learned in
Vietnam, Chose to Forget and
Needs to Know Today

DAVID DONOVAN

McFarland & Company, Inc., Publishers
Jefferson, North Carolina

LIBRARY OF CONGRESS CATALOGUING-IN-PUBLICATION DATA

Donovan, David.
 Counterinsurgency : what the United States learned in Vietnam, chose to forget and needs to know today / David Donovan.
  p. cm.
 Includes bibliographical references and index.

 ISBN 978-0-7864-9769-0 (softcover : acid free paper) ∞
 ISBN 978-1-4766-1921-7 (ebook)

 1. Counterinsurgency—United States. 2. Counterinsurgency—United States—History—20th century. 3. Vietnam War, 1961–1975—United States. 4. Vietnam War, 1961–1975—Influence. 5. Vietnam War, 1961–1975—Personal narratives, American.
 I. Title. II. Title: What the United States learned in Vietnam, chose to forget and needs to know today.

 U241.D66 2015
 355.02′180973—dc23   2014046218

BRITISH LIBRARY CATALOGUING DATA ARE AVAILABLE

© 2015 David Donovan. All rights reserved

No part of this book may be reproduced or transmitted in any form or by any means, electronic or mechanical, including photocopying or recording, or by any information storage and retrieval system, without permission in writing from the publisher.

Cover images © iStock/Thinkstock

Printed in the United States of America

McFarland & Company, Inc., Publishers
 Box 611, Jefferson, North Carolina 28640
  www.mcfarlandpub.com

This book is dedicated to the memory of
MSG Chalmers C. Humphries and
SSG Edward Ambrose, both of
Mobile Advisory Team IV-72,
Delta Military Assistance
Command, Vietnam.

Killed in the line of duty,
August 1969.

Table of Contents

Acknowledgments	iv
Preface	1
One—The Test: Five Questions	3
Two—The Program: Five Requirements	29
Three—The Campaign: Five Challenges	44
Four—Those Who Do Counterinsurgency: The Advisors	65
Five—Donovan's Dozens: Rules for Counterinsurgency	85
Six—Counterinsurgency Failure: A Dozen Ways to Do It	134
Seven—Counterinsurgency Program Organization: It Can Work in Its Specifics but Still Be Overwhelmed	157
Eight—Counterinsurgency and the Potemkin Village	179
Nine—The Soldiers They Send	197
Bibliography	207
Index	211

Acknowledgments

It is a rare book that is truly written alone. John C. Fischer of Temple, Texas; George C. Gandenberger of Bridgewater, NJ; John C. Haseman of Grand Junction, CO; Kenneth C. Jacobsen of Charleston, SC; Ray Mullen (deceased) of Bangkok, Thailand; Alejandro D. Murphy-Lugo of Fajardo, PR; Daniel P. Reimer of Rock Hill, SC; Tucker Smallwood of Los Angeles, CA; Richard M. Stanley of Austin, TX; William Treadway of Georgetown, TX; and Richard W. Webster of Jacksonville, IL are all former advisors with experiences gained in the counterinsurgency environment. Each submitted one or more written experiences relevant to counterinsurgency and they were each gracious enough to allow me to edit their submissions and include them as the "Lessons Learned" vignettes of this book. I thank them for their help.

My wife, Susan, did her usual service as first editor, and that help, also as usual, was invaluable. My thanks in that direction exceeds all others.

Preface

"Whence cometh this alarum and noise?"
—William Shakespeare; *Henry VI*

If you could feel the heat and sweat of the tropics; if you could hear the noise of battle and sense the fears, if you could put yourself on the other side of the world where you are the selectee of your government to advise and help a unit of foreign fighters defend their village; and if you and that unit are at this moment in combat but they are being slow to react, you might come close to understanding how I felt one day in 1969 in the Mekong delta of Vietnam.

The enemy were in a nearby tree line and had taken us under fire. Bullets were cracking around us and cutting leaves from the trees. We already had wounded, one man shot in the foot, another in the side. Everyone had gone to ground and the Vietnamese officer, my counterpart, had crouched behind a small dike with some of his soldiers. He was fixed in place, not taking the lead. I was an American infantry officer there to provide assistance when possible and leadership when necessary. Frustrated at my counterpart's performance, I ran toward him in a crouch intent on getting him to lead his men; but as I made my way a background program was already running in my mind. It asked, "What are you doing here? Is it worthwhile? Is it going to mean anything? The larger question underlying those was the one that came to virtually every American soldier: is our intervention here going to be worth the effort in the end?

Preface

I was in Vietnam because the United States had decided to assist an ally in fighting an insurgency stimulated and supplied from across international boundaries. The rights and wrongs of our intervention were a matter of vigorous debate and still are, but that debate was not mine. I was an Army officer trained in counterinsurgency and I was in Vietnam to lead a small advisory team in a remote village near the Cambodian border. We were doing counterinsurgency focused on two things: improving village security and encouraging local development.

Improving security meant improving the fighting skills of the local militia. They were poorly equipped and poorly led, neither of which helped their morale. Improving their fighting skills meant going into combat with them, fighting beside them, and learning first hand what it means to fight a guerrilla war. Encouraging development meant helping local officials with programs that could provide for projects meant to improve community life.

David Donovan serving as a U.S. Army advisor in the Mekong Delta of Vietnam, 1969–70.

The main enemies to security were the local guerrillas. The main enemy to development was a corrupt bureaucracy.

We finally made our assault that day back in 1969. When I couldn't get the Vietnamese officer to do anything effective, I knew any leadership was going to have to come from me. I signaled to my American teammate on the operation then he and I, waving and shouting at the others, began a maneuver against the enemy's tree line. The unit followed our lead, but the delay had allowed most of the enemy to slip away. It was not an

Preface

The Terrain: remote villages, tree lines along streams and canals, flat paddies and grasslands stretching north to Cambodia.

uncommon result, the reasons for which are complex and range from the military to the religious and everything in between. That is why counterinsurgency is such a complicated task. I know because I have done it.

Our being in Vietnam was a circumstance shaped by the cold war, which from the American government's perspective was a contest of capitalism and democracy versus communism and dictatorship. In terms of advertising, it was freedom versus chains. That kind of simplification rarely does justice to international issues and it did not to the war in Vietnam. In fact, the American policy on Vietnam was run through with complexities that blunted understanding and agreement; but for me those complexities had been distilled away the day I first landed on a dirt helipad outside the walled fort that was to be my home in the remote stretches of the Plain of Reeds. On that day the issues resolved to only two: duty and survival.

I was a military advisor in a counterinsurgency program aimed at the rural villages and hamlets of Vietnam. My five-man team and I were assigned to a village on the Plain of Reeds where we were far away from any American ground forces. In our district we were the only fixed representatives of

Preface

The Outpost: a mud fort on the banks of the major canal running through the author's district.

American military power and American aid. Five guys with M-16s, an 81mm mortar, a radio, and a jeep. We made our one-room team house in a mud fort, the headquarters of our local militia company.

Our mission was to advise our District Chief, local village chiefs, and local militia commanders on military operations that would promote security and on development projects that would improve the lives of the people. It was counterinsurgency, war of a kind that has binomial goals: defeat the insurgents on the battlefield and win the loyalty of the people.

I was an infantry officer trained in military assistance and counterinsurgency, but I was young and inexperienced. In the months that followed I learned a lot about living in a foreign environment submerged in a foreign culture. I knew about counterguerrilla and counterinsurgency operations from my training, but I learned a lot more by doing it and by making my share of mistakes. Years later I wrote about the experience in *Once a Warrior King* (McGraw-Hill, 1985).

The fifteen-year lag between the experience and the book was because I had returned to graduate school after my Army service and gone on to

Preface

The Village: no electricity or running water, a single street ending at the gate of the author's team's home fort. Like poor villages in many areas of the world, it was fertile ground for insurgents opposed to a seemingly uncaring government.

become a scientist and professor at the University of Virginia. After *Once a Warrior King*'s long gestation, I was grateful when it was published to good reviews, and seemed well regarded by readers in general; but I was surprised when over twenty years later, in 2006, it was the cause of my receiving an invitation to attend a symposium at the U.S. Army's Combined Arms Center in Fort Leavenworth, Kansas. The symposium was to be on security assistance to foreign countries including the training of indigenous forces, which is to say the training of foreign soldiers on their own soil by American advisors. It was part of what I had done in Vietnam and written about in *Once a Warrior King*; thus, the connection to my past.

To say I was surprised to get the invitation is an understatement. By 2006 I was a Professor of Urology and Professor of Cell Biology at the University of Virginia School of Medicine. Since the 1985 publication of *Once a Warrior King* I had spent most of my time deciphering the biology and pathology of the male reproductive system, so the invitation to Fort Leavenworth was a jolt. It stirred old memories and animated what I had

Preface

Afghanistan: The people, politics and terrain are different from southeast Asia, Latin America, and other places of conflict; still, as these U.S. Army advisors (seated) from the 501st Infantry Regiment in Khost Province, 2012, are doubtlessly learning, the issues in counterinsurgency remain much the same.

continued to carry as a background interest in military and foreign affairs. From that perspective I looked forward to attending the symposium.

It turned out to be very interesting. The symposium presenters spoke about past experiences in military assistance in Southeast Asia, Latin America, the Middle East, and Central Asia; but very quickly I developed a sense of disquiet. As one speaker followed another it became clear that much of what had been learned over the last one hundred years, going back well before Vietnam, about training, living with, and operating with indigenous forces had been forgotten. Institutional memory had failed. With each more recent advisory effort spoken of—El Salvador, Iraq, Afghanistan— it seemed that counterinsurgency planners and advisors had had to relearn lessons that we of a certain age had learned with our own sweat and blood in Vietnam. That was disturbing.

I thought of all the lessons-learned publications the Army had put out during the Vietnam War. What had happened to them? What about

Preface

all the handbooks, analyses, and reviews that had detailed the things done right and the things done wrong? Where were they? Many of the difficulties being mentioned by the symposium speakers were actually old problems that to my mind anyone working with indigenous forces, especially those involved in counterinsurgency, should have known about from day one. In answering a question about that point, then Lieutenant General David Petraeus, commanding general at Fort Leavenworth at the time but soon to be promoted and leave for his assignment as commanding general in Iraq, commented that once the cold war threats had collapsed back in the 1990s, the Army had "cleared the shelves" of its information on military advising and counterinsurgency. A new army design was in play; light, tight, and ready to fight; but it was an army focused on conventional land warfare, not the special warfare of insurgency/counterinsurgency. At the time the Army had adjusted to the perception of current need, but it had also discarded a large package of memory, which illustrates one reason for the observation that one of the most persistent lessons of history is that we do not learn much from history.

Recognizing the new demands in special warfare, the Army's Combined Arms Center at Fort Leavenworth had already been at work on a new counterinsurgency field manual under the leadership of General Petraeus. That field manual was published later in 2006, but it did not address the how-tos and what-ifs of counterinsurgency advising, *per se*. While the conference I was attending was not specifically about counterinsurgency, the subject was often remarked upon in its relation to the training of a country's local forces. As a result, when I returned home from the conference I began to think more broadly about my experiences from the past and about the fundamental aspects of counterinsurgency I thought not only the men and women in the military and those working in the foreign policy arena ought to know, but even the interested citizen ought to be aware of. To check and refine my memory, I began looking for what had already been written on military advising and counterinsurgency. The material available was actually plentiful but much of it was either fragmented, as in short articles in military journals, or encyclopedic, as in contracted Defense Department studies or tomes from the Army's Combat Studies Institute. The relevant material is there, I thought, but is anyone reading it? Apparently, not so much.

Preface

It seemed to me that a readable distillation of important points about counterinsurgency from a source independent of any governmental funding or policy agenda would be useful whether from the standpoint of military advising, diplomatic considerations, or a general interest in foreign affairs. Importantly, that distillation should include the fundamentals relevant to advisors involved in counterinsurgency, especially those important issues not often addressed elsewhere, and it should include real-life examples of how the specific points being made touch real human lives. Such a distillation follows.

It is a commentary based on a counterinsurgency experience of long ago followed by several decades of reflection. The opinions expressed are often unabashedly prescriptive, but that is where one ends up after a decade of observing counterinsurgency efforts that have cost the lives of thousands to little clear advantage for our country. Importantly, those opinions were sometimes aided in shading and clarity by the thoughts and writings of others. Where they were pertinent resources for a particular chapter they have been included in the list of "Relevant Readings" at the end of each chapter. Specific episodes from my own experience in counterinsurgency in Vietnam are included throughout the book to illustrate how the particular problem being discussed can really happen and have effect in real life. To broaden that point, a number of "Lessons Learned" vignettes from other former advisors in Vietnam are included to show that many others gained insights in that now antique experience. Those experiences are as relevant today as when they were freshly learned. Sadly, they have been available for decades, a repository of experience and knowledge apparently overlooked and certainly uncalled upon.

The inclusion of those lessons-learned experiences does not burden their principals with any responsibility for the book or imply that they agree with what is said in it. It does emphasize that the lessons of counterinsurgency have been learned by many, that all of us understand in a very personal way what those lessons cost in time, money, and lives, and that none of us believe they should have to be relearned from scratch as each new generation of leaders decides to undertake an adventure abroad.

It would be true to say that we are old now and that our experiences were long ago in a war that in many ways is unlike any since. At the same time, wars of insurgency/counterinsurgency share features in common, no matter the time or place, and we of a certain age and experience have had many years to wonder and resolve what it means to say that word, counterinsurgency. This book contains our reflections on it; I think they are important, especially at a time when counterinsurgency has become a prominent part of American foreign policy and is projected to remain so in the foreseeable future.

The discussions in this book are intended for those who think about counterinsurgency from a policy perspective as well as to those who do counterinsurgency in the field. It can also serve as a primer for engaged citizens interested in the complexities of counterinsurgency and in what is implied when counterinsurgency is called for as a tool of foreign policy. This book is not an academic tome dense with acronyms, citations, or the arcane nomenclature of the specialist. In fact, those have been avoided except where it becomes exceptionally difficult to proceed without them. Readers interested in more academic treatments of counterinsurgency will find books like *Counterinsurgency* by David Kilcullen (Oxford University Press, 2010) or *Learning to Eat Soup with a Knife* (John Nagl, Praeger, 2002) to be useful. Also, many technical elements of counterinsurgency are addressed in the Army's field manual on counterinsurgency, FM 3–24 (U. S. Army, 2006) and the Special Forces advisor's guide, TC 31–73 (U. S. Army, 2008).

In its fullest sense, counterinsurgency includes tactical combat advising and combat advising means those advisors must be authorized for combat duty. With that in mind and for simplicity's sake in writing, I have used the male pronoun when referring to military advisors in counterinsurgency operations. Nevertheless, much of what is said applies to trainers or advisors in more limited roles, male or female, whether they are involved in military or civil assistance. All the best to them all.

One

The Test
Five Questions

Carl von Clausewitz famously observed that war is politics by other means. An insurgency/counterinsurgency conflict illustrates that point well because it uses both social persuasion (politics) and organized armed violence (war) as tools to either gain or maintain control of the state. Insurgencies are by definition attacks on established governments; thus, counterinsurgency is the product of a government trying to maintain its power. Over the last one hundred years the United States has assisted other governments with counterinsurgency campaigns on multiple occasions, which is how counterinsurgency has become one expression of American foreign policy.

Counterinsurgency is often thought of only in military terms because the military has an obvious presence in the campaign and combat actions attract media attention. Still, the civilian side of counterinsurgency is extremely important. When done properly counterinsurgency is a joint military-civilian enterprise designed to overcome both the insurgents' armed threat and their political underpinnings. It requires not only military action, but program planning and action by civilian agencies of both the helping government and the helped. In the case of the United States, the State Department would be the primary but not exclusive agency of civilian activities.

The joint nature of counterinsurgency makes it a more difficult tool to employ than many give it credit for, a fault perhaps led to by counterinsurgency being thought of as "small war." In some ways that is an inapt description because counterinsurgency operations can become very large in terms

Counterinsurgency

of American diplomatic attention, military commitment over the long term, and drainage on the national treasury.

Vietnam, 1969

I was the leader of a Mobile Advisory Team and at the same time served as a District Senior Advisor in the Mekong delta. My five-man team and I lived in a village approximately 100 miles from the nearest American ground forces and were the U.S. part of the counterinsurgency effort in our district. On this particular day, I was standing at the edge of a thick wood line bordering a rice paddy. Behind me were more rice paddies and behind them the flat grasslands of the Plain of Reeds. In the distance water buffalo, once grazing, were now ambling away from the sounds of gunfire that had erupted near them. About five kilometers away across the flat landscape I could see the faint hint of a village, the indistinct brownness of thatched huts broken occasionally by the glint of a tin roof.

A few minutes before, the Vietnamese militia platoon I was advising had taken fire from the tree line in front of us. My major advisee or counterpart for the day was the commander of the platoon, and I had urged him to advance one squad to probe the tree line and to maneuver another to block the enemy's apparent escape route. I urged him to move quickly because the guerrilla units infiltrating from Cambodia were typically highly mobile. We would have to move fast if we were going to hold them in place for an attack.

We had not moved fast. My counterpart for the operation had previously proven to lack the gene for aggressive behavior and today had taken his time getting the blocking squad in position. By the time we had advanced to the tree line the only evidence of the enemy was the beaten grass where they had made camp, and a small, almost smokeless campfire.

Later that afternoon I discussed the operation with the counterpart and told him I thought he should have been more aggressive. I reminded him that this was the kind of thing he had to get right because the fight against the insurgents and their supporters from the north was becoming Vietnam's alone. Even now the American forces were beginning their draw down.

The militia commander smiled over the smoke of his cigarette and said he didn't think so. America and South Vietnam were allies against the communists, and with the Americans involved, the communists could never

One. The Test

win. He didn't say it, but I knew what he was thinking. "Why should I push my men to an unnecessary battle? Someone else will get a chance at it. There's no point in being too aggressive; the Americans will be here until we win."

Wrong. Three years later, after nearly two decades of effort, the last American units had left the country and three years after that Vietnam was in the hands of the communists. What my counterpart had either forgot or had never learned was that war potentiates actions and reactions. Results are magnified. A thing done or left undone can mean not a job gained or lost, but a life; not a house saved or burned, but a village; and, in the end, not a cause gained or lost, but a country. Every incompetence, every lack of intentioned pursuit of success has its accumulative effect and, uncorrected, they will lead to an ever-deepening or at least never-shallowing mire. When those deficiencies are a government's and when they prove immune to correction, even the best of allies will sooner or later wash its hands and say, enough. In time, that's what the United States said to the Republic of Vietnam and the results of a thousand inactions washed over that sorrowful land.

There is a lesson in that tale for any future U.S. ally in counterinsurgency: American patience has its limits. The lesson for America, having no claim on perfection herself, is that some friends are too incompetent to keep. This is not often admitted because it means acknowledging that good intentions have been frittered away for an ally who would not make the choices necessary for success. The reasons for this squandering of American effort are complex and are at the heart of why counterinsurgency is such a difficult tool to employ. The issues involved remain important because counterinsurgency is still being used by the United States in environments where the causes and cultures differ but the difficulties and dangers largely do not.

In the first place, a government the U.S. agrees to help might not be an icon of political rectitude; friendly governments are not always good governments. Still, when those governments have asked the U.S. for help in fighting off an insurgency, even when the policies and practices of that government likely have contributed to the insurgency, the U.S. has often responded with help. Those situations predict the requesting government will not be an easy partner in the counterinsurgency program, perhaps the leading reason why counterinsurgency is one of the most difficult of international enterprises.

The difficulty has at its roots the fact that people do not rise against their government without cause. They do not risk life and limb or family and fortune out of shallow discontent or transient pique. They rise out of anger at persistent grievances and out of a vanished hope that there will be remedy by any other means. In that light, most governments deserve their insurgencies, a truth that persists even if the insurgents are being guided and supported by outside influences hostile to American Interests.

The reality is that the United States' efforts in counterinsurgency have often aligned it with host governments that most Americans would find unacceptable for themselves. The only reason for American involvement might be that the insurgents are being led by those with a record of oppression and mendacity even worse than the host government's; the pages of history run red with the results from "liberators" like the Viet Cong, the Khmer Rouge and the Taliban. It is not in the human interest to allow governments with some elements of oppression to fall to insurgencies offering even worse.

With that history as a background, it is not surprising that American counterinsurgency officials have often found themselves frustrated with the governments they have been sent to assist. The problems that vex those officials might well be the things that instigated the insurgency in the first place, so it is not unreasonable to ask, if the host government is so ineffective or shows so little care for its people, why should the U.S. help it fight off an insurgency? Shouldn't America be on the side of the oppressed rather than the oppressor?

Of course it should, but the previously mentioned better-of-two-evils choice can be an important factor and there are commonly other national interests to consider as well. That means the American government must constantly be resolving the dissonance between its ideals and its interests. Traditionally, that resolution has been achieved by the U.S. lending assistance only as it also insists the host government undertake important reforms.

In the twentieth century, the United States pursued non-covert counterinsurgency operations in the south Pacific, in East and Southeast Asia, and in Latin America. In the twenty-first century, it has been engaged in especially extensive programs in Iraq and Afghanistan for a decade or more.

One. The Test

These counterinsurgency "small wars" in two different centuries have cost the United States hundreds of billions of dollars and hundreds of thousands of casualties either killed or wounded; but their ultimate outcomes have been either failure (example: Vietnam), qualified success of modest proportions (example: El Salvador), or results yet unknown (example: Iraq). Several counterinsurgency programs are still underway, the major effort in Afghanistan and a minor one in the Philippines for example, but there have been no American excursions into counterinsurgency that rank as unqualified successes, a fact that should cause sober reflection.

As each of America's counterinsurgency efforts has ended, policy makers have resolved to learn from the past and make better plans for the future. Those resolves have had little apparent follow through. Each new effort at counterinsurgency seems to require a relearning of lessons that were first acquired a half-century or even a century ago. Over and over again foreign policy makers and military leaders have appeared to be afflicted with what might be called *dysgnosis*: a failure to know (what should have been known).

Dysgnosis in counterinsurgency can be remedied, but not without an intentional effort. It requires the development of a national counterinsurgency policy independent of any specific engagement, and that policy should be made with a clear view of what conditions and practices are necessary for success. The policy should establish standards for undertaking a counterinsurgency program in the first place and for assessing that program's progress. It should also establish standards for American exit from the project while understanding that in the real world of strife and trouble exit standards have to be strong guides, not absolute boundaries.

Flexibility is required in counterinsurgency because each country and each insurgency has its own fogs and shadows. Each one is different from all others. For this reason, counterinsurgency operations cannot be treated in a one-size-fits-all manner; still, it takes a blind eye to the past not to value the lessons learned in counterinsurgency since 1899 when Major John J. Pershing was charged with defeating the Moro insurgency in the Philippines. That was an exercise of novices, but surely we have learned much since then. We have learned, but apparently as much as we have learned we have rapidly forgotten. It is not an uncommon observation that what we have are not lessons learned, but merely lessons observed. Given that thousands of former counterinsurgency advisors with experiences ranging over the last half-century form a broad repository of knowledge about war of this kind, it is hard to see any reasonable excuse for a current military structure not to be learned and ready for the counterinsurgency tasks of the future.

Why does any of this matter? It matters because American dollars and American lives are still being spent in counterinsurgency efforts that begin in confusion, proceed with uncertainty, and end with little benefit. A cogent example is Iraq, where after a decade of efforts that have included counterinsurgency, the net benefit to either the U.S. or the Iraqi people remains uncertain. As of this writing, after a ten-year effort in helping the Iraqi government and military through training, advising, financial support, and direct combat against a dedicated insurgency, the last American soldiers left the country and within a week of their exit, sectarian violence returned, an intense political controversy broke out within the government, and charges of autocratic tactics were made against the country's prime minister. After a further two years of sputtering conflict, the insurgents appear emboldened, Iraqi soldiers remain hesitant to take on a determined enemy, and the insurgency rises again. Whatever is happening in Iraq, for the American decade of effort, its name is not success.

This comes as no surprise to those who have said all along that the true measure of that outcome of the American adventure in Iraq will be the kind of government the Iraqi people have five or ten years after the American exit, not what is left behind on the day the last American soldier leaves the country. Will that government be a democracy, a religious oligarchy, or another strongman autocracy? Will it be a friend to the U.S. or a foe? The U.S. has now spent billions of dollars and thousands of lives on that country, yet the way forward is still pot-holed with ambiguity. Unfortunately, any uncertainty about Iraq can be expanded logarithmically in the case of Afghanistan where ethnic and religious prejudice, violence, and disdain for central government have been the characteristics of that country for centuries.

And who cares? The governments requesting American assistance should care because U.S. involvement is giving them a chance to survive. The underserved populations in the host country should care because improved security and government reforms can result in a better life for them and their posterity. Americans should care because American lives and money are being spent on programs that may or may not be effective.

One. The Test

Most of all, those who actually engage in counterinsurgency operations should care because it is their sweat and blood that are being expended.

Analysis of past counterinsurgency operations is an act of due diligence, but it is not a guarantee of future success. Counterinsurgency is not an objective science like physics where E always equals MC^2 or an endeavor like mathematics where two plus two always equals four. Rather, counterinsurgency is a combination of civil and military skills that sum to an art, and as in all art it requires an expertise and judgment that even when applied with skill can lead to variable results.

With its difficulties so great, its potential costs so high, and its historical outcomes so variable no counterinsurgency effort should be entered into without it having been submitted to a dispassionate evaluation of a number of key factors. For example, what are the important national interests being served? What are the strengths and weaknesses of the potential host government? Of its insurgents? Thus, The Test: five important questions that should be answered before making any commitment to join a host government in a counterinsurgency program. The answers to those questions will be the eventual determinants of success.

Question 1. What is the degree of popular support in the host country for its present government? It is important to know if the insurgency springs from a narrow segment of society, i.e. a specific tribe or specific region of the country, or if it arises from widespread disaffection among the more general population. That analysis should be hard-eyed and should harbor no illusions about the host government or its adversaries. It has already been acknowledged that insurgencies do not arise without cause. It should come as no surprise then when host governments almost always fail to meet the democratic standards of most European or North American countries. Whether that relates to the amount of government support among the population depends on many factors, so the significant subparts of this question are: is there support for the government, how much, where does it come from, and can more support be recruited with government reforms that are within the realm of the possible?

Vietnam, 1969

There were several guerrilla sanctuary areas in the remote reaches of my district, so the militia units my team mates and I advised often went into those areas searching out the enemy, attacking them when we found them, and destroying their caches of food, weapons, or other supplies. Once while on such an operation the platoon I was with had halted in a tree line at noon to take time for chow. I was working with two Vietnamese officers, the militia platoon leader and his superior from district headquarters. I was talking with the two of them as we ate our noon meal, a fish steamed in a banana leaf, when one of them asked me why I thought the U.S. was in the war. I knew the unspoken concern was the charge made by insurgents that the only American interest in Vietnam was hegemony. American imperialism. We wanted to rule over Indochina as the French once had.

My view was that the U.S. was supporting a friendly government because it wanted to have friends in the region aligned against the communists of the Soviet Union, China, and their allies. It hoped that such friends could be persuaded to agree on issues of common interest, but rule? No. Imperialism? No. My answer to the man's question was something like that and I added that the people of Vietnam ought to have the government they wanted, not one that is forced on them. That's what we were fighting for, no? The people of South Vietnam now had an elected government, I said. What did they think of it?

The two officers became uncomfortable. I had asked a question but had telegraphed no safe response. I couldn't have. I had no preconceived idea of what they thought and I really wanted to know. They shrugged and muttered platitudes. I could tell from the looks on their faces that they were no longer comfortable in the discussion.

I thought perhaps there was a political disagreement between them and were being too polite to say so to me. I tried to draw them out by repeating that they lived in a democracy. They could feel free to say whatever they wanted.

Well, not so much. The platoon leader made excuses and went off to check his men. The officer from district headquarters, who I knew the better of the two, glanced nervously around then quietly said that he couldn't talk about the government. Naïve me, I was flabbergasted. Why not, I asked, what about freedom of speech? That's part of what we're fighting for, isn't it? Use it!

The officer shrugged and with a bland smile looked off into the distance. He was uncomfortable because even in his not wanting to discuss the gov-

One. The Test

ernment he was revealing that the government was not as advertised. I already knew the Saigon government was corrupt and that the elections were faulty, but now a fundamental freedom was apparently inoperative. I was puzzled by the officers' response to my questions, but before I had time to think much about it, we were preparing to move out for the afternoon's operation.

We spent the afternoon sweeping the area, but found little other than a transients' hut tucked back in a tree line and a cache of rice. On the trek back to our village I found myself going back to that noon conversation. From my point of view, all of us, Vietnamese and Americans alike, were fighting to preserve a democratic government friendly to the United States. Yes, I knew that democracy was flawed, but now it seemed evident to me that the freedoms to think and speak freely were more curtailed than I had imagined, if not by law, at least by caution.

Surely, responsible people back in Saigon or Washington, D.C. know this is true, I thought. What did the American policy planners make of it when they made their assessments of South Vietnam? If the people don't feel free to discuss their government, what does freedom actually mean? What does democracy mean? What effect does the vague shadow of democracy have on the people's support for their government? How strongly could its security forces be expected to defend it?

I hoped for all our sakes that the U.S. had made an accurate assessment of the answers to those questions. My personal view was that the local people's support for their government was broad but thin. The farmers and fishermen in my district wanted to be left alone so they could work to provide for their families. They were not political and most of them would fall in line with whoever was in power. I didn't like what that might portend for eventual success.

In Vietnam, the national government was corrupt and widely ineffective. It needed to provide security for its people and improve the conditions of their lives at the same time it was fighting a major war within its own borders. That would be a challenge for any country, especially for an underdeveloped one, but unless a government can do those things, the cause is lost. American aid and American counterinsurgency programs can help only so far; in the end the host government will have to meet the aspirations of its people or fail. In Iraq, that outcome is still in question even though the American military mission has ended. Regarding Afghanistan, there are those who hope the outcome is at least still in question rather than being a foregone failure. Another view from those with perhaps more focus on the importance of Question One of The Test has concluded that a good outcome of the American effort in that country is extremely doubtful.

Question 2. What is the host government's willingness to make the political and functional changes necessary to increase its popularity? No one likes to say it, but international politics is about making useful friends, not necessarily nice ones. That being true, it comes as no surprise that the political leaders of governments requesting counterinsurgency assistance are often less than stellar characters. They often are more interested in the protection of personal interests than they are the salvation of democracy or some other political ideal and their personal interests commonly extend to those of their family, clan, or tribe, all of which depend on maintaining the status quo. The interests that need protecting can range from those that are deeply traditional to those that are about nothing but peculation; still, the more embedded those interests are in the country's history the less willing the government's leaders will be to make significant change. This is why the major aspects of counterinsurgency are political and economic, not military and it is why counterinsurgency efforts that focus primarily on military assistance are bound to fail in the face of a host nation's political structure that is resistant to change.

That resistance will not necessarily be direct or confrontational. It can be subtle or passive-aggressive and, like the insurgents' gunfire, sometimes hard to pin down. Previous U.S. experiences suggest that while a host government may agree to changes as a price for American aid, they may also make little effort to institute those changes absent continuous pressure to reform. Being alert to this potential for inaction is important because whether or not the U.S. can stomach the friend it has chosen will ultimately affect popular support at home (see Question Five) for the counterinsurgency effort.

Vietnam is an example of how a host government's lack of commitment to civil and military reforms led to an increasing dependence on American military help, a protracted war, and a decline in support for the effort from the American people. This same disquieting pattern was repeated in Iraq and eventually led to the U.S. drawdown. That lack of progress with government reforms is also in easy evidence in Afghanistan. In both countries, Iraq and Afghanistan, the willingness of the host government to make the changes necessary to hold the loyalty of its people remains in question. That's after more than ten years of war.

There is another aspect of this, which is for the U.S. to be clear that undertaking a counterinsurgency program with a host nation is not an open-ended obligation of nation building. Counterinsurgency has elements of nation building in it, but the host nation also has obligations to help build itself. That is why this question of the willingness of the host government to make changes is so important. A resistance within that government to make necessary changes predicts a low chance of success for the counterinsurgency program and it predicts a situation in which the U.S., even after a protracted period of assistance, will be left with what seems to be a continuing obligation help build a nation that refuses to help build itself. It should be clear from the beginning that no such obligation exists beyond that of the United States to its own security. An example of this danger is Afghanistan where conversations are now about how many billions of dollars for how many years must be promised to that government for it to sustain itself since it has always been and still is a land-locked, desolate country with no visible means of significant economic life.

Question 3. What is the host government's *ability* to make the political and functional changes necessary for success? This question of ability is tightly attached to Question 2 about willingness, but a question about ability is different. The host government might express a willingness to make changes, but impediments of people, culture, or infrastructure might militate against ability to make changes. What we by convention call a country may be only an amalgamation of tribes who hate each other, of religious zealot groups who hate each other, or of historically separate groups who still want nothing to do with each other. The U.S. should know what those impediments are and what their impact is likely to be on program success.

If the host government proves unable to make the changes required for success, there should be guidelines that illustrate the trigger point(s) for an American exit and there should be a contingency plan for how to achieve it. No host government is due continued American sacrifice if it cannot or will not make a vigorous fight for its own survival. That includes making the governmental changes necessary to gain popular support and the military changes needed to provide security for the population.

American policymakers and counterinsurgency experts should always feel the threat of the Saigon Syndrome—the strong being dragged down by the weak. The first symptom of that syndrome in American foreign policy is when the U.S. attaches itself to a host government unwilling or unable to institute effective change. Once the symptom is evident and adamant, the fulfillment of the syndrome is virtually assured unless the U.S. has an exit strategy governed by preestablished standards and current conditions.

Presently, the U.S. is being challenged by some for having agreed to leave Iraq after a decade of assistance and for having promised to leave Afghanistan on a date certain after an even longer struggle. Those governments' battles against sectarian insurgents continues, critics say, and the central governments remain weak. All true, but to all appearances, the Iraqi and Afghan governments remain either unwilling or unable to make the kind of changes needed for them to be more effective and, thus, better able to protect themselves against internal violence. There is no indication in either case that that situation will be different in another ten years, so at some point it is perfectly correct for the U.S. to say that it has done enough to try to help a host government. Counterinsurgency is not synonymous with an open-ended obligation to build, maintain, and permanently protect a foreign government no matter that government's own conduct.

Question 4. What are the U.S. interests in the host country and are they sufficiently important to require action? Are those interests motivated by sympathy or by practical strategic considerations? A widely held sympathy can drive American actions like humanitarian assistance, emergency responses, foreign aid, and the like, but sympathy alone should not be the cause for significant U.S. combat interventions, which an effective counterinsurgency operation would be.

Historically, only attacks against the United States or significant threats to important national interests have been the spurs to meaningful combat actions. In Vietnam, perceived national interests made us an ally of South Vietnam because North Vietnam was seen as a proxy for the Soviet Union and "Red" China. There was sympathy for a people being threatened with the rough boot of communism, but the expanding influence of the Soviets and China were also seen as threats to American security interests in Asia. Decades later an American administration took action against an Iraqi government that had gone rogue and was perceived to be a threat to a region thick with American political and economic interests. In Afghanistan, the Taliban government provided sanctuary for an al-Qaida terrorist group that had attacked the United States. When the Taliban would not relent, the U.S. took war action against it.

In each of those cases, a perceived threat to American interests was the stimulus for American actions, but in each of those cases the real risk to the United States was very different. With Iraq, for example, an American administration made an incorrect judgment about the threat being posed to its neighbors and to American interests. That judgment led to the U.S. making a preemptive attack on Iraq that through a course of events led to an insurgency the U.S. forces had to help fight for a decade before eventually withdrawing with the question of outcome still in doubt.

Iraq is an excellent example of why assessments of risk to American interests need to be made objectively and away from the heat generated by political idealism. Any romantic hope that American efforts to help a host country will naturally lead to that country's becoming an American-style democracy is simply naïve, especially if that country is from a vastly different cultural background. Such hopes cannot be used as a reason to engage in a counterinsurgency conflict. While some form of representative government might be generated—such things have occurred in South Vietnam, Iraq, and Afghanistan—that government is unlikely to function effectively or long in the absence of local traditions that include political compromise, the concept of individual rights and responsibilities, and a respect for the electoral process.

Question 5. What is the amount of American popular support for the government of the host country? Is it sufficient to support a sustained counterinsurgency effort? That effort will require the use of civilian and military advisors and those military advisors will likely engage in combat despite possible claims to the contrary. The American public has historically not been in favor of involving its soldiers in combat absent necessity, and support for that involvement rapidly wanes when necessity is no longer evident. The U.S. did not engage in World War II until it was actually attacked by Japan. The Korean War was initiated in an era of strong American anticommunism, but even there public support declined as necessity for the action

Counterinsurgency

became less evident. In Vietnam, initial public support decreased after it became apparent that a corrupt government in Saigon had a large appetite for American resources but a small appetite for making the internal changes necessary to win its own war. The situation was not helped by the American government's early dissimulations about war progress.

The effort in Vietnam failed in part because by 1968 the American public had wearied of supporting an ally that for too long had showed insufficient progress with governmental and military reforms. Further, the war there had gone on so long the average American no longer believed vital national interests were at stake. This pattern was repeated decades later in Iraq where governmental misfeasance remained a problem throughout the American military presence; further, in the early days of the conflict it had become clear that the feared Weapons of Mass Destruction supposedly held by the Iraqi regime had never existed. This only amplified a feeling among the American public that the war in Iraq was misbegotten in the first place and increased the doubt that American efforts in Iraq were truly serving a vital national interest.

While the American attack on Afghanistan was in response to an initial attack on the United States, the war there with its strong component of counterinsurgency has gone on long enough for much of the American public to be convinced that the Afghan government is hopelessly corrupt and unwilling to change. That puts the American counterinsurgency effort under threat because counterinsurgency requires time and money. In a world where impatient Americans are now seeing their own government afloat on borrowed dollars, there is little tolerance for the waste of either the time or the money.

Using the questions of The Test is a way to avoid foreign policy misdirection. It evaluates the commitment of both the U.S. and the host government to an enterprise that will in all likelihood turn out to be more complex and more protracted than either wants to imagine. Early consideration is crucial because once the counterinsurgency effort gets underway, problems of the moment will pop up like whack-a-moles. U.S. involvement with guns and goods will already be underway and it will be difficult to pack up and go home even if it is belatedly determined that the host government is not an appropriate receptacle for the American effort. Ask the questions early and get the answers; it can save a lot of pain.

One. The Test

The Test is important because it can help the government decide whether or not to engage in a particular counterinsurgency enterprise. Certainly, there are situations in which there is little or no opportunity for considering such questions. An example is the case of Iraq where a counterinsurgency effort was required subsequent to predisposing actions by the United States. In such cases, the willingness or responsiveness of the host government are rendered immaterial to the original commitment, but that kind of situation leaves U.S. counterinsurgency operatives, typically the advisors in the field, with a task even more difficult than usual. The advisors in those cases are not in the host country by original invitation, they are there because of a U.S. war against a previous regime. In such a case, the U. S has to support the present, installed regime no matter what the local people think, at least initially, and the counterinsurgency advisors get no erase key; they cannot get a do-over of the original events. They are where they are and they have to get about the business of solving the problems their role now presents to them.

The only prophylaxis for this kind of situation is for the American government to do its foreign policy planning and military preparations with an ever-rolling estimate of the situation that is taken seriously within the State Department and the military services. It is easy to wonder how much this has been the case when one considers that it has been predicted for many years that the major defense challenge for the U.S. and her western allies in the twenty-first century will be "small wars" sponsored by Islamic extremists. That challenge, taken seriously, means that by now our military services should contain a ready supply of men and women fluent in the languages and cultures of the Middle East and South Asia. Unfortunately, well after a decade of realizing the need for improved capabilities in the relevant languages U.S. military and civilian services still cannot meet the need, and the defense language schools are not being expanded. This is just one example of the separation between recognizing a need and taking that need seriously enough to meet it.

The problem is one of priorities. Making a major effort in the present to meet a need of the future is always difficult because it means making hard choices based on estimates that are never ironclad. In the present case, it means believing that the twenty-first century will be the era of small wars and it means preparing for that need in a world of great fiscal difficulty.

Counterinsurgency

Resources used in conducting small wars or in training for them are resources that in all likelihood will be subtracted from those used to prepare for a large war using conventional forces.

For military planners that begs the question, what if the predictions for small wars turns out to be wrong? Are there not nations with large armies who might pose a threat to the U.S. in the next ten years? Twenty? Fifty? When will that threat arise? From where? No one knows, so armored divisions still have to roll, infantry divisions still have to maneuver, and artillery battalions still have to fire for effect. Each of those requirements demands time, training, and money that are being competed for in an army strapped for resources, including manpower; thus, while small wars might be the expected threat of the twenty-first century they are not the only threats defense planners have to contend with.

It is a truism that the most dangerous threats come from unexpected directions. Proponents of conventional war capabilities can point out that Islamic displeasures will fade in importance should the U.S. face a major force like Russia or China in another cold war-like atmosphere. That grim possibility generates a tension within the military between the need to focus on counterinsurgency or, for that matter, unconventional warfare of any kind versus the need to prepare for large scale, conventional wars including nuclear options. This is a significant problem that requires constant attention, and application of The Test will help insure that resources committed to counterinsurgency will at least be used with a likelihood of success.

Adequate consideration of a potential counterinsurgency effort requires not only a timely answering of The Test's questions, but a correct answering. That means that the U.S. must have a fully engaged intelligence apparatus as a primary resource for administering The Test and that apparatus must have sufficient breadth and penetration in the host country to answer the relevant test questions. That task requires human intelligence, not just satellite observations or electronic surveillance records, and the intelligence reports developed must be heard without the distortions brought on by American idealism or political desires.

In many cases the intelligence required will come through the American embassy in the host country. There are components within every embassy, the economic section, the defense attaché's office, the CIA, etc., who are trained reporters of relevant information. Those components do best when they include individuals who speak the local language and who spend time in the countryside or urban areas developing information that is objective and reliable, not just the hearsay from around the embassy circuit. Intelligence, in the sense of coherent information about a country or situation, is more than the gathering of data points. It is about learned assessment. It is about avoiding the trap of quantifying a conflict without understanding it.

To that end, decisions about a counterinsurgency program must be based on a detailed understanding of the social and political environment in the host country. A counterinsurgency strategy is never better than the information used to make it, and that information encompasses a very broad range of subjects, certainly more broad than what most would consider conventional military intelligence. Military intelligence typically provides information that focuses on enemy forces; in counterinsurgency that focus shifts to providing intelligence about the population. The concerns and sympathies of the people are important to understand because that understanding is key to influencing the people, to gathering further intelligence from them, especially about the insurgents, and to gaining the peoples' cooperation in actions against the insurgents.

A strong intelligence capability is important to both counterinsurgency planners and operatives in the field. Planners need good, population-based intelligence to understand the factors behind the insurgency and to appreciate how deeply the insurgency penetrates across the society. They need the intelligence to foresee the kinds of reforms that will redress the population's grievances and to gauge the willingness of the host government in making those reforms. Counterinsurgency operatives, those advisors who do counterinsurgency in the field, need to understand the strengths and vulnerabilities of the insurgents, the strengths and weaknesses of the host government, and the needs of their local populations that can be addressed within the world of what's actually possible. As mentioned previously, the evaluation of program progress is critical and that, too, is an intelligence function though one played out in part by the advisors themselves.

Finally, while intelligence of all kinds can prove important in the counterinsurgency setting and full use should be made of modern technologies, including those of cyberspace, it is human intelligence that has made the greatest contribution to success. Human intelligence is that gathered from insurgent sources, ordinary citizens, agents in the population,

Counterinsurgency

reconciled former insurgents, and the like, and when done best it is high quality intelligence because it is fresh, specific, and unfiltered by layers of bureaucracy.

Objective reporting is important, but it is useless in the absence of objective hearing. Senior civilian and military staffers in embassies and in Washington must give reports from the field a dispassionate hearing whether those reports conflict with a current administration's desires or conform to it. In particular, progress reports from the counterinsurgency program must be made to serve operational needs only; they must not become tools of an administration trying to run a public relations campaign. If that happens, the reports will quickly come to be seen as politically tainted and will be discounted both in the United States and abroad. Counterinsurgency is a cooperative effort between the helper and the helped, but it is not a game. It is warfare in the field, in the village, and in the home. We have the moral obligation to get it right.

Relevant Readings

Brown, Donald M. *Vietnam and CORDS: Interagency Lessons for Iraq* (Fort Leavenworth, KS: School for Advanced Military Studies, 2008), 14–35.

Coffey, Ross. "Revisiting CORDS: The Need for Unity of Effort to Secure Victory in Iraq." *Military Review* March-April (2006): 24–34.

Collins, James L. *Vietnam Studies: The Development and Training of the South Vietnamese Army, 1950–1972*. Washington, D.C.: Department of the Army, 1991, 68–122.

Cooper, Chester L., Judith E. Corson, Laurence J. Legere, David E. Lockwood, and Donald M. Weller. *The American Experience with Pacification in Vietnam*. Vol. 1. *An Overview of Pacification*. Arlington, VA: Institute for Defense Analysis, 1972, 1–61.

Fore, Henrietta, Robert Gates, and Condoleeza Rice. *U.S. Government Counterinsurgency Guide. United States Government Interagency Counterinsurgency Initiative*. Washington, D.C.: Department of State, 2009, 13–21.

Gentile, Gian. *Wrong Turn: America's Deadly Embrace of Counterinsurgency*. New York: The New Press, 2013.

Hoffman, Bruce. "Insurgency and Counterinsurgency in Iraq" (an "Occasional Paper"), Santa Monica, CA: RAND Corporation, 2004.

Jones, Seth G. *Counterinsurgency in Afghanistan*. Santa Monica, CA: RAND Corporation, 2008.

Schwarz, Benjamin C. *American Counterinsurgency Doctrine and El Salvador: The Frustrations of Reform and the Illusions of Nation Building*. Santa Monica, CA: RAND Corporation, 1991.

Silinsky, Mark. "An Irony of War: Human Development as Warfare in Afghanistan." *Colloquium* 3 (2010): 1–16.

Two

The Program

Five Requirements

It will perhaps come as a surprise to some that the United States has now had over a century of experience in counterinsurgency. In some cases the campaign has been called for by predisposing U.S. actions (the Philippines in 1899, Afghanistan in 2001) and in others it has been a response to requests from foreign governments (Vietnam in 1955, El Salvador in 1981). The outcomes have varied from failure to limited success, which is a modest claim for a tool of foreign policy that has cost the United States so much in dollars and lives lost through death or disability. The previous chapter drew from that long experience in discussing the issues the United States or, for that matter, any nation should consider when deciding whether or not to engage in a counterinsurgency campaign. The Test was suggested because the answers to its questions, fully plumbed, are strong tools for predicting the campaign's success or failure.

If The Test has been applied and a decision to go forward has been made, the next questions to arise will be those about how the counterinsurgency program should be pursued. The United States' century of counterinsurgency experience strongly suggests five requirements be met in a counterinsurgency program. Each is discussed below with the help of relevant, real-life experiences.

Requirement 1: Manage Centrally

A successful counterinsurgency effort requires the involvement of civilian and military agencies working together under central management. During the war in Vietnam a variety of early, non-unified security and development programs proved inadequate to the challenge of making significant progress, but in 1968 the Civil Operations and Revolutionary Development Support (CORDS) program was initiated as a centrally managed, joint military-civilian effort to pacify the countryside.

Vietnam, 1969

My Mobile Advisory Team (MAT) operated under the CORDS program and was primarily charged with upgrading Vietnamese militia-like units responsible for village and hamlet security. Other elements of CORDS had primary responsibility for economic and social development activities, but MATs also engaged in development through civic action programs and small projects that could range from U.S. medical team visits to minor construction projects.

CORDS, the U.S.'s centrally-managed counterinsurgency effort with both military and civilian elements, was already in operation when I arrived in Vietnam in 1969 and continued until the end of U.S. military action there in 1972. Later evidence from both American and North Vietnamese sources indicated that CORDS was effective in pushing back the North Vietnamese-directed insurgency in South Vietnam. Ironically, the failure of that insurgency compelled the North Vietnamese to turn to their conventional army for an offensive that defeated the South Vietnamese army by main force. Despite the outcome of what had become a conventional war, the effectiveness of CORDS as a counterinsurgency program provides an instructive example of success in what otherwise must be rated a failure.

CORDS and MATs will be discussed in more detail in Chapter Seven, but suffice it to say here that counterinsurgency programs require U.S. civilian and military agencies to cooperate not only with their partner agencies in the host government, but with their colleague agencies within the U.S. government. Both requirements can be difficult. Government agencies like to operate within their own vertical hierarchies and they sometimes respond poorly when those hierarchies are cut across by interagency programs, especially when the agencies involved are from the separate military and civilian sides of government. To eliminate this problem, counterinsurgency programs require central management with a director of sufficient rank and impact to do the job effectively. Unfortunately, despite multiple attempts, it is not clear that this level of coordination and follow through was ever achieved in Iraq and remains a difficulty in Afghanistan.

There have been joint military/civilian teams focused on counterinsurgency in both theaters. Those teams are the Province Reconstruction Teams, but that they have ever been able to operate under a truly coordinated military-civilian command structure of any persistence is unclear. Further, separate counterinsurgency efforts have also been run by individual military units of the U.S. and other allied or coalition forces, which makes coordination even more difficult. The indigenous situations in Iraq and Afghanistan have been very complex, but that complexity is only intensified when the U.S. and its allies have multiple approaches to the counterinsurgency mission.

Requirement 2: Establish Security

Counterinsurgency programs face several challenges simultaneously. They must establish security to protect the people; they must expand development to improve the people's quality of life; and they must initiate government reforms to make the government more responsive to its citizens. The latter two depend on the first, which is why establishing security is the first goal of a counterinsurgency program.

Vietnam, 1969

My team and I operated out of a fort situated at one end of our village. I could look out over the fort walls to see the village on one side of the fort, rice paddies on the other, and in the distance the wide, empty spaces of the Plain of Reeds. On that side of the fort the view was unobstructed ... except for two masonry buildings sitting some distance away and across a large canal. One of the buildings was a school and the other a health clinic. Both had been constructed in the days before development assistance and military assistance were coordinated and were examples of what happens when development proceeds without security.

The buildings had been constructed across the canal from the rest of the village because it was thought the slight rise in the land there would keep them out of the high water during the rainy season. The fact that the lone pair of buildings across the canal could not be secured with the available forces had been ignored, the result of which was that by the time I arrived in 1969 neither building had ever been used and both were falling into ruin.

Larger problems had occurred elsewhere. Schools or bridges would be built, health or agricultural programs begun, or local markets improved, but when government forces would shift their attention or move away the insurgents would return and destroy whatever had been accomplished. This set up a treadmill of development failure that all were aware of. It was quite clear that transient security was as bad for development activities as no security at all.

One of the first aims of an insurgency is to destroy the people's sense of security, so it isn't surprising that problems like those I and others experienced in Vietnam have played out in other countries in more recent times. On the other hand, given that the results of lapsed security have been known for at least a half century, those kinds of failures still being suffered over and over again makes the counterinsurgency leadership seem exceptionally obtuse. Without security development fails, period; and security doesn't just mean security from insurgents. It means security from local bandits, thugs, gangs, or any other violent faction.

The need for security in the village is not generally a point where people disagree; how to achieve that security often is. A disagreement over how to best achieve security can arise from different opinions about the nature of the insurgency, its causes, its strength, and its likely persistence. Should the program focus on improving the constabulary or building up a regulated militia? What should be the role of the host government's conventional forces and where should they be deployed?

The answers to those questions and others will depend on what is needed to accomplish the four general tasks of security forces in the counterinsurgency environment. First, they must block the insurgents' access to the population, which is to say, provide security in the village. Second, they must disrupt the insurgents' military structure, which means kill or capture its leaders and fighters. Third, they must define and protect international borders, which is important because it will restrict the insurgents' access to external support and deny him sanctuaries in neighboring countries. Fourth, cooperating with other elements of the government, they must establish a climate of civil law and order. A government constantly charged with malfeasance and corruption will never hold a people's loyalty and security forces that contribute to the problem are a significant predictor of counterinsurgency failure.

Considering those four tasks, any host country can design a security program within its counterinsurgency plan. That program will have its priorities, the first of which must be to develop an army that is well trained, motivated to fight, and directed at protecting the people not only from the enemy, but, as much as possible, from the disruptions of war. Importantly, the army's officers must be dedicated leaders willing to engage the enemy. As in any army, the degree to which its officers fail to lead is strongly connected to the chances that army will eventually fail.

Second, it is helpful to have a regulated militia drawn from the local population. Local militia units should be trained to provide village protection through local patrolling and other light infantry operations. They work best when they are a daily presence in the villages where they and the constabulary are the constant evidence of government protection. To that end, militia units should be funded by the national government and regulated by it. Further, the units should be responsible to the national government, not to some local warlord or political group.

Finally, a properly operating constabulary or police force is vital to counterinsurgency efforts. In an insurgency, having a well-manned, properly trained, and properly acting police force is as critical to long-term success as are the conventional military forces. There is a tendency for U.S. counterinsurgency efforts to focus on shoring up the military of the host nation, which is understandable since the largest action element of the counterinsurgency intervention is typically the American military. This too often leads to situations where positive statements can be made about the improving status of the host nation's armed forces but an admission that the police forces still "have a way to go." Read that to mean that the police forces are still too poorly paid, too poorly trained, and too corrupt. This is a deficiency that can be deadly to the hopes of counterinsurgency success.

The military forces obtain security, the police forces are important in maintaining it. They should be trained to do their duties with attention to the legal rights and dignities of the people and with an ethos that does not condone corruption. Since a poorly paid police force is almost always a corrupt one, an important place to begin is to see that the police are paid salaries appropriate for their responsibilities and training.

Requirement 3: Expand Development

Insurgencies often find their best soil in the countryside where poverty is endemic and the government has likely had little presence or influence. To counter the insurgents' move, development programs typically focus on the host nation's rural areas. An effective way to do this is with development cadre, civilian teams trained to go into villages with programs fostering improvements in health, education, commerce or agriculture. Development cadre are armed if necessary and given appropriate weapons training if armed.

The development issues the cadre can work on in a village vary widely depending on local needs. A road may be built or repaired, a public water source installed, or an electrical generator and local wiring provided. A village school might be constructed or farmers might be given improved seed or breeding stock. The cadre might give classes on some aspect of public health, agricultural practices, or local government administration, among others. Projects undertaken depend on the resources available, but even small projects can make positive changes.

Well-trained cadre teams can be important assets to a counterinsurgency program, but poorly trained, dysfunctional ones will not. Especially in countries with a high illiteracy rate, recruiting and training of a properly skilled development cadre can be exceptionally difficult; thus, the use of development cadre in a counterinsurgency program depends on the situation at hand. Illiteracy is a problem in recruitment and training for many government agencies, the military, the police, and the education system among them; so something as mundane as a nation's illiteracy rate can have a significant impact on the potential for counterinsurgency success. It is the kind of thing that receives little attention in the first flush of war, yet it is one of the factors within the challenge of understanding the host country's manpower resources and needs (see Chapter Three).

Vietnam, 1969

My district on the Plain of Reeds was a poor one. There was no electricity, few sources for potable water, and no sewage systems. There were no roads save for one paralleling the Mekong River at one edge of the district and a branch from it that penetrated approximately fifteen kilometers into the interior. That branch ended in the village my team and I called home. Little had been done there in the way of development, so any effort my team made was seen as a bigger help than it probably was.

Our local village chief was really just a farmer with a third-grade education. He was not equipped, either socially or practically, to deal with government forms, copies in triplicate, or the concept of submission deadlines. He was a man of the canals and rice paddies where communication was eye-to-eye, obligation was by handshake, and time was as flexible as a reed in the Mekong.

Additionally, the government over him was so wedded to its cryptic bureaucracy that it could never find a boot and a bootlace at the same time. That only served to illustrate to the people that the government was either weak or disinterested. I was in no position to remedy the village chief's problems because my team's primary responsibility was to train and operate with the village militia; still, we tried to help on the development side where we could. On one early occasion I made our village chief aware of an aid program that could provide building materials for village projects. I urged him to submit an application for tin to repair the roof of the village office, which he managed to do, and when a pallet of new tin eventually arrived there were smiles all around.

Not long after that, the chief took on a larger project by applying for the tin, lumber, and concrete for making a new village market. The old market was an ad hoc assembly of stalls and open ground near the village center where there was no protection from the sun or rain. The village chief was pleased again when his application was approved and a new market place was built over the old. The new one had a concrete floor and a tin roof, and it was tangible evidence that the government had done something positive for the people. Smiles on the faces of the merchants and their customers told me and the village chief that we had done a good thing for the people and we had taken something from the enemy insurgents.

Development projects at the village level are a necessary tool of counterinsurgency because in an insurgency the ultimate place of victory is not on the battlefield; it is in the village. There the struggle is not for terrain or numbers of enemy killed, it is for the development of hope and for the loyalty of the people.

A successful development program requires administrative support by those who have been trained to provide it, yet another problem where illiteracy is high. Further, government officials must understand the word, efficiency, and they must have a sufficient understanding of their country's economy to provide regulations for it and to tax it without being destructive. Absent that sophistication, all development will eventually fail either from financial starvation or the dissipation of economic activity.

The U.S. in its assistance must be careful not add to the host country's administrative troubles, which it can easily do by presenting more ideas, plans, and programs than the host government can possibly absorb. No needy government is going to turn down money and material, but sudden flushes of it only lead to misallocation of resources, increased corruption, and even diversion of goods to the enemy. Thinking critically about program priorities can minimize the problem but the overarching question should be where can a *usable* amount of American resources be applied to maximum effect? Just as it had done in Vietnam, the U.S. has poured many more resources into the Iraqi and Afghan governments than could be absorbed with good accountability. As a result, billions of American dollars in both countries have vanished into the coffers of corrupt officials and contractors and into well-intended projects that added little to the overall goal of winning the loyalty of the people.

Requirement 4: Initiate Reform

To say that counterinsurgency programs should establish security and promote development is completely conventional. It is less often said that counterinsurgency programs must induce government reform, but the truth is that without those reforms any advances in security or development can become irrelevant. Host governments, including their military, are commonly inept, corrupt, or both, which makes government reform a critical target of counterinsurgency programs.

This is important because corruption can be pervasive. Government officials perhaps originally involved in only relatively modest venality are unlikely to suddenly become honest when a flood of money from American aid programs comes within their reach. Rather, they are likely to bring in family and friends to share in the bounty. That is how corruption spreads and stunts government action. It enriches the powerful and victimizes the poor. It is a cancer that metastasizes to all the organs of government and eventually eats its heart.

That being the case, it is astonishing in these current times to hear or read the occasional opinion from knowledgeable people saying that too much attention is being paid to corruption in the host governments. Even U.S. officials have said and written as much, offering the view that corruption in some countries is just a part of the culture. A payment made to an official for processing paperwork can be thought of as a "tip." One supposes then that so is the money that must be slipped to the customs guard to prevent difficulty at the border or the cash that must be paid to the policeman to investigate a break-in. It's just a part of the culture, no?

Yeah, sure. So is living with little food and bad housing just a part of the culture? Or is it a part of the culture like being used to sick children and having no education? Please! The counterinsurgency program will attack those aspects of "the culture" that lead to sick children, a lack of education, or poor living conditions; should it not also attack corruption? Corruption starves the people and feeds the insurgency. It is insanity to let it go on unaddressed and unpunished.

That is not to say that corrupt officials should have their hands chopped off in the public square. Corruption can be met initially by a sequence of disapproval, correction, and encouragement to understand its consequences. Eventually, however, it must be met with punishment. That being said, in the complex world of counterinsurgency some individuals guilty of corruption might be necessary assets to important program activities. In those cases, the flinches of purists notwithstanding, skillful diplomacy leading to behavior correction might be better than demands for formal punishment.

Vietnam, 1969

The pay system for local militia units was an arcane mixture of salary and allowances that was difficult to understand. Many uneducated village militiamen never knew if their monthly pay was correct or not and they could easily be taken advantage of. If a commander were so inclined, for example, he might keep a little of each man's pay with no one the wiser.

Counterinsurgency

Further, the village militia rosters were often inaccurate, and since validation of the rosters was rarely done, a unit commander might include a few extra names and collect the pay of those "ghost" soldiers. To reduce this kind of graft, U.S. military advisors were encouraged to attend payday formations and evaluate the local pay procedure. It was a task I got around to after several months on the job.

I did not look forward to it. Not only was my own understanding of the pay system uncertain, but the local militia commander had already proven to be inadequate by several measures and I was sure he was going to resent my watching over his payday routine. I was right. It turned out that he resented being watched, but it also became clear that he needed watching.

After crosschecking some of the men's pay, it appeared to me that the commander was withholding his men's firewood allowance, which was a part of the military pay system. I suspected that a couple of the junior officers knew what was going on because of their hesitance to answer my questions, but none of the men were complaining and it was apparently a payday as usual.

I said nothing to the unit commander until the next day when I raised the issue in private. I told him I thought there was a problem in the pay calculations for his men; perhaps he should correct that before the next payday. The commander feigned innocence and acted as if he was insulted that I should think such a thing might be true. I offered to go over the pay calculations with him or his executive officer. He refused, complaining that I didn't like him and was out to get him. At that point, I felt I had no choice but to report the incident to my Province Senior Advisor who would transmit the report to the Vietnamese Province Chief.

A couple of weeks later the militia commander was called back to the province town for a period of corrective training, but within week or so he was back, seeming somewhat chastened but deeply resentful. I had the sense that his graft was only temporarily abated and would await opportunity for resurgence once I was gone or would perhaps simply find another avenue even while I was there.

Corruption is difficult for advisors to address because it is hard to keep an effective eye on the enemy when you have to keep an equally close eye on your allies. It is easy to make the choice that you'll keep an eye on the enemy, he can kill you, and let someone else keep an eye on your ally

Two. The Program

who only wants to steal; but corruption in government gets much more complicated than skimming money from illiterate soldiers and it involves people more powerful than militia captains. High officials in the host government can easily be involved in million dollar schemes and in Iraq and Afghanistan they apparently have been. That is no way to run a war. Officials at all levels of the host government must understand that if corruption is not brought to heel, the U.S. will consider its commitments void. Short of that harsh penalty the U.S. risks falling once again to that Saigon Syndrome of the strong being pulled down by the weak.

Government reforms are not only about financial accountability; they are also about other aspects of program accountability and about repairing parts of the host government that are dysfunctional. Some elements of the military may not be performing properly or may have practices that violate the rules of war; government procedures might violate common standards of justice. Advisors have to face these difficulties, but since some changes will be more urgent than others, reform must be approached wisely. It is true that one cannot go in on day one, declare that all corruption must cease, and expect the declaration to stick. Corruption must be trimmed away carefully to insure that pruning does not kill the tree; still, the recognition must remain that corruption is a cancer. It destroys governments and if not cured will sooner or later prove the counterinsurgency program to have been for naught.

Requirement 5: Evaluate Progress

Like any other corporate task, counterinsurgency programs must be evaluated to document progress and reveal deficiencies. The evaluation tools must be relevant, accurate, and timely; and results must be comparable across time. This year's apples need to be comparable to last year's apples, not last year's crabapples.

One tool for program evaluation is the kind of progress report appropriate for statistical analysis. Those kinds of reports are important, but they risk missing information not easily reducible to a short-answer, quantitative format. Qualitative aspects of intelligence are also important and require not only experienced agents in the field, but appropriate reporting mechanisms.

Counterinsurgency

Vietnam, 1969

It was just after noon. I had been out on an ambush all the previous night, but with no results other than discomfort and boredom. At sunup I had returned to our fort tired, plastered with mud, and frustrated at having spent the night doing nothing but feeding leeches. After taking a cold-water shower under our water drum I had slept through the rest of the morning then had eaten a makeshift lunch before starting to work on my monthly Hamlet Evaluation System (HES) and Territorial Forces Evaluation System (TFES) reports.

The HES and TFES reports were computer printouts of questions relating to the development and security of the hamlets in my district and the combat readiness of the hamlets' militia units. From just looking at the stack of crisply folded computer paper sitting on the battered table in our rudimentary, non-electrified hut in a mud fort it was easy to suspect a disconnect between the people making the questions on that paper and the person in the hut answering them. The former seemed to be people in Saigon who, one guessed, had the idea that their questions would be addressed by district senior advisors (DSAs) with real capacities for giving answers that were as precise as the questions. That was not always the case. Some DSAs had fully staffed district teams, others did not. Some lived in districts with small geographic areas, other did not; some enjoyed ease of movement, others did not, and so on. These differences were not irrelevant to the accuracy of the reports, but there were no apparent adjustments to be made for them. My instructions were to answer every question as well as I could and turn in the reports on time. That's what I did.

I was a DSA with no district team. Actually, I was a MAT leader who one day was informed he was now also a DSA and that among his additional duties would the filling out the monthly HES and TFES reports. I quickly discovered that accurately answering the reports' questions would require information I did not have and was not likely to get. That being the case, my method of dealing with the questionnaires was to answer by best guess. Perhaps that should have bothered me, but it did not because I knew from conversations with other DSAs, all of them more senior officers than I, that some of them filled in their reports similarly. It wasn't that they didn't care, it was that in the warped world of remote, primitive outposts where everyone is overtaxed just to stay alive, fed, and somewhat sane, a multi-

Two. The Program

page, computer generated printout asking for more information than you can possibly get just doesn't seem that important.

It could be argued, and I am sure I did, that reasonable guesses from someone on the scene were answers enough for the intent of the HES and TFES reports. Whether or not that was true depends on the precision being imputed to those reports as they made their way up the chain of command. There were two other factors I suspected of being problems: Command influence and the desire for good counterpart relations.

Province senior advisors (PSAs) wanted their districts' HES and TFES scores to be improving over time. PSAs were full bull colonels and they could be quite clear about what they expected of their juniors. That alone could make a DSA worry about turning in HES and TFES reports with a persistently downward trajectory. Also, the Vietnamese Province Chief liked to hear positive reports. That made my counterpart, the district chief, an interested party; if my HES or TFES reports resulted in a downgrading of either our district or its militia units, he could be put in a bad light. That result could be bad for counterpart relations and life was hard enough without that being added in.

DSAs had to find the line between maintaining a good working relationship with their counterparts and turning in honest HES and TFES reports. From the policy evaluation perspective, honest reports were necessary; from the life-in-the-trenches perspective, effective counterpart relations were necessary. Finding the line between the two could be a constant struggle and distraction. I'm sure I did not do it perfectly because there were months when my counterpart was less than pleased; but when I thought my reports were going to cause him some difficulty, I tried to let him know ahead of time and to explain why my report came out the way it did. When the reports were going to make him look good, I tried to let him know that, too, though I always thought it better to let the good news come directly from his boss.

The point of that anecdote is not that life is difficult for an honest advisor. The point is that program progress evaluations can be affected by the contextual separation between the question maker and the question answerer (The HES questionnaire originally had 191 separate questions to be filled out by the DSA for each hamlet evaluated. That was later pared down, but, still, the average district had approximately 50 hamlets and the largest districts could have over a hundred. There was only one DSA and he had many other things to do). As already mentioned, progress reports can be tainted by command influence, but they can also be influenced by personal issues that tend to inflate estimates of progress. Some of those issues can be an evaluator's attention to the effects of poor progress reports on his own career, on the demands of his own ego, or on the opinions of his work that might be held by his fellow evaluators.

Planners and staffers of counterinsurgency programs should be aware of these issues and of their consequences when arriving at honest, effective tools for progress evaluation. The need for an honest hearing of honest results has already been discussed in Chapter One.

The five elements of The Program, manage centrally, establish security, expand development, demand reform, and evaluate progress are the broad basics of counterinsurgency. They are the bricks to be used in building a successful program, not the engineering details of how use them. Those details will vary depending on the insurgency involved and are rightly to be worked out by policy planners and representatives of the host government. Those basic elements of The Program are important, however, and are laid out here because too often the experts available in specific insurgencies get to the details of building a counterinsurgency program while leaving out one or more of the building blocks. Absent blocks or even poorly made ones lead to an unsound structure.

Relevant Readings

Brown, Donald M. *Vietnam and CORDS: Interagency Lessons for Iraq*. Fort Leavenworth, KS: School for Advanced Military Studies, 2008, 14–35.

Cassidy, Robert M., "Back to the Street Without Joy: Counterinsurgency Lessons from Vietnam and Other Small Wars." *Parameters* 34 (2004): 73–83.

Coffey, Ross. "Revisiting CORDS: The Need for Unity of Effort to Secure Victory in Iraq." *Military Review* March-April (2006): 24–34.

Collins, James L., *Vietnam Studies: The Development and Training of the South Vietnamese Army, 1950–1972*. Washington, D.C.: Department of the Army, 1991, 68–122.

Cooper, Chester L., Judith E. Corson, Laurence J. Legere, David E. Lockwood, and Donald M. Weller. *The American Experience with Pacification in Vietnam.* Vol. 1. *An Overview of Pacification*. Arlington, VA: Institute for Defense Analyses, 1972, 1–61.

Cooper, Chester L., Judith E. Corson, Laurence J. Legere, David E. Lockwood, Donald M. Weller. *The American Experience with Pacification in Vietnam*. Vol 2. *Elements of Pacification*. Arlington, VA: Institute for Defense Analysis, 1972, 218–36.

Heiser, Joseph M. *Vietnam Studies: Logistic Support*. Washington, D.C.: Department of the Army, 1991, 229–42.

Henrickson, Thomas H. *Afghanistan, Counterinsurgency and the Indirect Approach.* MacDill Air Force Base, FL: Joint Special Operations University Press, 2010.
Kilcullen, David. *Counterinsurgency.* New York: Oxford University Press, 2010.
Sepp, Kalev I. "Best Practices in Counterinsurgency." *Military Review.* May-June (2005): 8–12.
Silinsky, Mark. "An Irony of War: Human Development as Warfare in Afghanistan." *Colloquium,* 3 (2010): 1–16.

Three

The Campaign
Five Challenges

Counterinsurgency programs are fraught with problems seldom fully embraced by the "helping" nations, typically the U.S. and her western allies. From the history of such things, one can even get the impression that joining a counterinsurgency operation is a fool's errand because of all the ways things can go wrong. Typically, these are things that were never taken seriously in the original commitment. Why is that? In the first place, the host government is likely to be culturally different from its helping partner. In the second that government is likely to be under considerable structural and economic stress. The difficulties arising from those stresses only magnify the difficulties arising from any cultural dissonance and the summation of all effects is a partnership having all the qualities of a tar baby. Not only that, but the enemy will already be in place. He will already be a part of the local environment and be having some success, else the host government would not be making appeals for help.

With that as a background, the effort can reasonably be expected to cost the helping nation(s) much; the question then is will the reward be equivalent? In many cases, a reasoned judgment may be, no. Since the costs of counterinsurgency may easily exceed the potential rewards, senior American officials as well as advisors in the field should give full consideration to the real challenges in conducting a counterinsurgency program. Here are five.

Three. The Campaign

Challenge 1: Establishing the Identity and Purpose of the Program

Counterinsurgency efforts are usually long-term enterprises. When engaged in by the United States they cost American lives and drain the national treasury, yet the threat to the country is usually indirect, at best. In that setting, maintaining public approval for the effort can be a challenge. The challenge is made even more difficult by public perceptions formed by the news media's inevitable focus on what is dramatic, the battles, the bombs, and destruction. The less dramatic features of counterinsurgency, the training of local forces, the development programs, and the support for government reforms, among others, will carry less weight in the public's mind. That circumstance will eventually pose problems for any long, slow counterinsurgency process.

To an impatient public, long and slow are not positive features. In a country with a free press and free minds, there is little remedy for this problem other than achieving linear progress and reaching program goals at small cost in lives and material. History does not suggest this will occur. What then to do?

The first thing is to make the case early for why the counterinsurgency effort is in the American interest. The program needs identity, purpose, and freedom from American internecine "spin" treatments, none of which are well served by official fogginess about program goals and progress. Even in the face of declining public support the only constructive approach is to relay concise, realistic information with reminders of the important national interests at stake. If that approach cannot retain public support, the counterinsurgency program has root difficulties more profound than with those insurgents in the host country.

Challenge 2: Recognizing the Impact of Being American

Americans are pushy, impatient people. Even our friends agree with that; but what others can see as pushiness an American might see as determination and what others might see as impatience an American might see as goal orientation. The typical American sets goals and strives to reach them in a timely fashion because he or she sees existence as being played out in linear time. Objectives and opportunities come onto the time horizon, approach, and pass by like fence posts along a highway. An opportunity past is an opportunity lost; consequently, Americans tend to want things done now. Not tomorrow, now. In some other cultures, time is thought of in a more circular array. Opportunities will come again; there is no rush. Opportunities are not lost only delayed until a more propitious time. Fatalism takes hold, life goes round and round and what will be will be.

That kind of disconnect between two cultures (see Challenge 1, above) can leave an American gritting his teeth and complaining about lack of progress. It can also cause problems in a counterinsurgency program that supports what Americans think the host country *ought* to be rather what the host country *wants* to be. The Vietnamese man or woman, the El Salvadorian, Iraqi, or Afghan who has wanted his or her country to be a copy of America is a rare bird, and American advisors and counterinsurgency planners must understand the social and cultural conflicts this disinterest can present. Our being Americans has its baggage, and not understanding that can sometimes raise unnecessary impediments to program progress.

Vietnam, 1969

There was one road in my district. It penetrated some fifteen miles across the flat delta landscape from the banks of the Mekong River to the village where my MAT was located. My team was authorized to have an army jeep, an old M151, which during the dry season we drove on our solitary road to reach the hamlets spaced out along it.

Driving on that road was a risky business. It is a prime rule in irregular warfare that you should not leave a location and return to it by the same route. That is a basic counterambush procedure. In our case, we had no alternate route, and the lack of options always made us anxious when we were on the road driving home from a trip to one of the distant hamlets.

The only other counterambush tactic we could use on the flat, straight road was to go fast and keep an alert eye. Unfortunately, the road was also the main street of every hamlet along the way, so we had to slow for each one. We would have to slow as we neared the hamlet and the number of small, palm thatch houses began to increase. Adults and children would be out using the roadway as if it were their collective front yard. Pigs, ducks,

Three. The Campaign

and chickens would be ambling about looking for food and a water buffalo might be standing there as if he were prepared to take you on. I had ridden through these hamlets many times and each time I had managed to respect the local ways, which means that I had slowed our jeep despite my concern that going slow increased our chances of being ambushed. This time, my impatience got the better of me.

Sergeant Anderson, my light weapons NCO, and I were returning from an inspection of a militia post. For some reason, perhaps because of a recent increase in enemy activity, I was more worried than usual about the possibility of ambush; even so, we had slowed as usual through the first couple of hamlets. As we approached the third hamlet, however, my patience was diminishing. I was frustrated that no person, pig, or chicken in the roadway seemed to understand that Anderson and I needed to keep moving. My thinking had become," This is a road, dammit! Roads are for traffic, so outta the way!" And to give my impatience excuse, "How're these people gonna have development if they don't learn to stay out of the road?"

Underlying those gripes was the All-American thought that where I come from—where things are done correctly, of course—streets are for vehicles; people and pigs stay out of the way! It was the voice of frustration boosted by a spurt of attitude that said, "I know better than you." Not only did I know what was best for me, suddenly I knew what was best for everybody else; and my bringing up development was a way to give my impatience justification based on something other than fear. If these people are going to have development, I was thinking, they are going to have to learn what a road is for; and for that lesson there is no time like the present!

To the villagers, of course, the roadway was thought of more as a pedestrian thoroughfare than a road for vehicles. In fact, my jeep was the only four-wheeled vehicle in the district, so the villagers had reason for not exactly hopping out of my way. The occasional passing motorbike could weave through the playing children and wandering animals with no difficulty. Any other vehicle, including our jeep, was a rarity and was expected to fit in with the common usage. That usage was not as the street I wanted it to be and at the moment I was sure that needed to be changed. I knew better than the locals what was good for them, so I told Sergeant Anderson to use his horn and pick up speed.

Sergeant Anderson did as he was told. We picked up speed and Anderson started beeping a staccato warning with his horn. People began hustling out of the way and I leaned back in my seat congratulating myself on teaching this small lesson in modernity. That's when we hit the pig.

The jeep lurched and I heard a squeal. A young pig, probably a twenty-five or thirty pounder, ran from under our front wheels making me think we had bumped him. Wrong. He lurched for a few yards then fell over, his back legs kicking a time or two before going still. The "uh-oh" light went on in my head. This was trouble. Instant decision: Stop or keep going?

Stop. Take care of the problem now or risk having a worse one later. I knew that a pig was a thing of value. They were sources of meat and income, and in our district both were scarce; plus they and the ducks and chickens were the village's garbage dispose-alls, which was a reason they were allowed to wander about in the first place. I told Sergeant Anderson to stop the jeep and arm up. He was going to have to keep watch while I tried to deal with the problem.

Just as I stepped from the jeep an old woman hurried from one of the palm-thatch huts protesting angrily that I had killed her pig. She was right, but I was still holding to my high horse of roadway rectitude. Pigs shouldn't be in the street, I was still thinking, and it was time everyone learned it. I know, it sounds crazy; but I was an American and I knew best.

The attitude didn't last long. It started deflating as soon I saw the look in the old woman's eyes and heard the pain in her voice. I had killed her pig. Why, she asked. What was I doing? What had she done to me? She didn't have to tell me she was poor, but she did. She didn't have to say I might as well have robbed her, but she did; and the problem was, I knew she was right.

A crowd had gathered to watch all this and I quickly realized I was going to have to make this good. An elderly villager being treated badly by an American would be grist for the insurgents' mill and I could not let that happen. It would only cause trouble later on.

The fix for this kind of problem, to the degree that it could be fixed, was to treat the offended party with respect and see that they were compensated according to local custom. Sergeant Anderson was looking nervous, so I knew I needed to hurry. I apologized to the old woman and tried to explain why we had been in such a hurry. That didn't arouse any sympathy and didn't help with the price negotiations, either. By the time the episode was

Three. The Campaign

over it was I who had been taught a lesson. My American views about how "these people" had better change their ways to suit my views had had unintended consequences. In a small hamlet like this one, a couple of Americans and a jeep could easily play the role of a bull in a china shop and I had managed to do just that. My "better idea" had caused a problem, and I had been served an unpleasant dose of correction.

That incident is a trivial illustration of how Americans go wrong when out of frustration and impatience they ignore the customs and values of the host country, especially the customs and values of the common people. While they may be very different from that country's more westernized elites, they are the people who the counterinsurgency effort must attend to and they must not be steamrolled by ill-planned programs, by advisors with a bad attitude, or by American functionaries inattentive to local traditions.

In February of 2012 some books from the military prison library at Bagram Airbase in Afghanistan were disposed of in a trash incinerator. Some of the books were Korans and word somehow circulated among the local people that the Americans were burning their holy book. Suddenly, there were protesters at the gates. The Afghans' well-known xenophobia, always on alert, had found an excuse to break out. The crowds grew by the hour, emotions ran high, the tumult spread, and days of violence and death ensued, all over the burning of some Korans that to the Americans involved was purely incidental. To them, the disposal of worn, unused, or discarded books in an incinerator was likely routine. They were thinking like Americans. Then they hit the pig.

It is easy to point to the Afghans' behavior as an over-the-top reaction to the clearly incidental burning of some books. Yes, it might be agreed, in the best of all possible worlds, a holy book, whether Koran, Bible, or something else, if it is to be disposed of, ought to be disposed of in a manner respecting the traditions of the relevant religion; but the violent, vitriolic reaction of the Afghans to a minor incident, a religious *faux pas* at worst, was a far more serious violation of proper conduct than the unintentional pricking of a religious sore spot. That can all be true according to commonly accepted standards of behavior in the United States, but the point is that those commonly accepted standards of behavior are in many ways not in play in Afghanistan. The same may be true in other places of conflict, and

Americans have to recognize that wherever they are. Otherwise, they will let the impact of their being an American get in the way of progress.

Lesson Learned: The Most Important Thing You Can Do Is Listen

First Lieutenant George F. Gandenberger, team leader, MAT IV-30; Hoa Dong District, Go Cong Province (MACV Advisory Team 92), IV Corps Tactical Zone; 1969.

Being a good listener is one of the most important lessons taught to every new salesman, but in my experience it was an art generally ignored by the U.S. Army in Vietnam even though, in a sense, the Army had an idea to sell: Be on our side. For too long we didn't pay enough attention to the needs of the Vietnamese population and the local forces that could protect them. We concentrated on the military conflict through main force, attrition warfare, and didn't see that the drivers of the conflict might be a need for clean water, improved agriculture, functioning markets, and even an improved self-image.

I failed miserably with one counterpart because I didn't listen in the way I needed to listen. He was a young officer who must have screwed up somewhere because he had been made commander of a militia company in a miserable location surrounded by Viet Cong. Feeling put upon and lacking confidence, he refused to consider anything but defense. In the meantime, my advisory team was receiving direct encouragement from the IV Corps counterinsurgency director (J. P. Vann, see Bright and Shining Lie *by Neil Sheehan) to be more aggressive and take the night from the Viet Cong. Instead of helping the young officer to improve his confidence and performance, I wrote him off as a loser and he was soon relieved. I had been his advisor, the guy who was supposed to help him out, but I just accepted that he was a bad apple and didn't want to listen to his troubles. I didn't want to invest in him because time and energy were precious resources and I didn't have enough of either. Our experience together didn't do either of us any good.*

I got another lesson in listening the way I need to listen from the local village chief. This guy had the look of a slicked-back Ho Chi Minh, and more than once he became adamant about not cooperating with something I thought we should do. On one occasion, the medical folks at province head-

Lieutenant Gandenberger holding a captured AK-47 outside his outpost in Go Kong Province, 1969.

Counterinsurgency

quarters wanted my team's medic to inoculate all our villagers against cholera because the disease would break out in the village every year when the annual floods came. My team had a refrigerator that ran off of propane, so I soon had a refrigerator full of three thousand doses of cholera vaccine. That was fine with me, but, it turned out, not with the village chief.

A bit of background. Our village was in an area of Go Cong Province that had historically been pretty independent of the central government. The locals had the reputation of being rice pirates and tax evaders and were now pretty heavily infested with the Viet Cong; mostly, they said, because the VC taxes were lower than the central government's! My point is, the village chief never felt any obligation to do what the province headquarters said, and in this particular case he had a logic for refusing that was difficult to refute, especially by an American Army lieutenant who in a year's time would be gone and never again have to deal with the village's problems.

The village chief said, "Every year the water rises, every year the cholera comes, and every year the children die. But now if more children live, how does a farmer divide his small farm, maybe only four hectares of paddy land? We are farmers; where will all those children farm? If they have to learn something else to do, who will teach them?"

The chief had never been more than ten kilometers from his home village, but he fully understood the harsh realities of his local economy. Too many children were being born for the village to sustain, but with no medical methods of contraception being available, nature had always done the job through the norm of childhood mortality. For an American used to the attitudes and social supports available in the United States, that was a hard message to hear. On the surface, it seemed the village chief was coldly indifferent to the suffering of children, but he was faced with another reality: Too little land for too many people and all the consequences that implied.

The village chief got his way. I was left to wonder what the outcome would have been if years earlier the village chief or people like him would have been listened to by those planning counterinsurgency programs back in Saigon. Perhaps they would have thought more deeply about the real problems in the countryside and spent more resources on them rather than on trying to pound the enemy into submission.

On the positive side for listening, our villagers wanted a school for their kids. I listened to that and my team finagled the materials for them to build

Three. The Campaign

one. At its opening the locals held a big ceremony thanking us for our help. Soon, the village kids were learning to read, a positive outcome for something that took little effort on my team's part, yet it led to a lot of good will.

Of course, the need for listening goes both ways. Advisors have to listen, but so do their counterparts, though in either case it is sometimes hard to tell whether the failure to communicate is due to the failure to tell, the failure to listen, or the failure to understand what was told and listened to. Once my teammates helped start a local egg business. They purchased some chickens that had been brought in from the Philippines then scrounged the chicken wire and got the business started. When the first eggs were produced the village chief was informed of the success and he proudly invited the Province Ag Team out for a show and tell. Somewhere communication went wrong. When the Ag Team showed up they were feted not with fried eggs, but with fried chicken—the ones that should have been laying the eggs! Someone had not gotten the message correct either through not listening or not understanding.

Did I become a good listener? I don't know, but I did learn that my security depended on acceptance by the locals and I learned that it was their needs I needed to listen to. They could have pulled away at any time and let the Viet Cong have at us, but they did not. In fact, by late 1969 they were generally rejecting the VC as being bad for business and the guerrillas had been reduced to low-level banditry.

George Gandenberger is alive and well and prefers to leave it at that.

Challenge 3: Understanding the Host Country's Manpower Resources and Needs

American diplomats and military officials tend to deal with their like kind in other countries. In underdeveloped or emerging nations, the Americans' counterparts are typically the educated, westernized elites who can be quite different in culture and world view from the average person in the street and even more different from the person working in the rural byways. Understanding the country's relevant human resources versus those that are needed for a counterinsurgency program requires intelligence collected from the streets and those rural byways. For example, when considering the need for training of soldiers, public administrators, or government officers it is important to know whether the majority of the candidate population is literate, as is the case in Iraq, or illiterate, as is the case in Afghanistan. That information is critical when considering the potential difficulty of training an adequate government administration or an adequate army and it has a strong influence on the kind of administration or army the counterinsurgency program will attempt to build.

Also, host governments often depend on civil and military bureaucracies in which leaders are chosen based on the connections of family, tribe, or religion rather than merit. Such practices are outside the western norm and exacerbate the problem of removing poor leaders and replacing them with proven leaders without reference to social and sectarian distinctions. Broadening the base of the host country's government in this way can be complicated for many reasons, not the least of which is that people outside the traditionally favored groups often have had restricted access to education and social development. Manpower issues like these lead to problems in both the military and the civil service, and where personnel reforms do not occur, counterinsurgency operatives can expect a difficult time achieving success.

In the military, poor leadership leads to poor training in garrison and poor performance in the field. To remedy this, the counterinsurgency program must convince the host government's military to focus on proper recruitment and training of its officers and to reward performance with promotions based on merit, not lineage. The same is true for training and advancement within the civilian bureaucracy. Nepotism, tribalism, and sectarianism lead to a stagnant civil service more concerned about its perquisites than about operating a government. American civilian advisors can help by being persistent in their guidance toward administrative efficiency and their advocacy for training programs and proper personnel policies.

A host government's refusal to broaden its base or reform its policies to improve manpower resources is a signal of problems to come. Governments must inspire loyalty in their average citizens, not just in their elites. Security forces that fight primarily out of need for an income rather than from loyalty will almost always fall victim of those who fight because they believe fiercely in their cause. One insurgent anxious to die for his cause can have more impact than a company of government conscripts primarily focused on survival. This differential has been expressed in Iraq and Afghanistan on a regular basis, yet it is rarely confronted face on.

Three. The Campaign

One senses the degree of this problem when it is said that the host government's army is weak because it takes years to build an effective force, yet the insurgents are able to maintain an effective threat while giving their recruits only rudimentary training under poor conditions. The nut of the problem is this: successful insurgencies emphasize a fighter's endurance, his ability to accumulate skills with experience, and his willingness to die for the cause. To that kind of fighter, war is not about short patrols or safe billets. It is about a cause, not a sinecure. That is how insurgencies of the ants overcome governments of the ox.

Challenge 4: Managing Abundance

American assistance, if not carefully given, can overwhelm a host country's ability to absorb it. A country fighting an insurgency might well lack an effective bureaucracy due to the human resources problem mentioned above or to an engrained corruption that blunts much of any administrative effort. Such a bureaucracy cannot effectively manage its own affairs, let alone the new programs an American counterinsurgency program can bring with it. For the host government, trying to manage a surge of new programs can be like trying to drink water from a fire hose. It is difficult at best and can overwhelm the unprepared.

Vietnam, 1969

Long before I arrived in Vietnam my village chief had learned not to expect much from his government. His experience and that of others had been that the help offered from higher places in the government was rarely the help that actually arrived. Construction projects might begin but end up lacking critical items, school or medical supplies could go missing, or requests for repair parts could go unanswered. In short, the logistical system was inadequate, and that was due to a panel of problems spread across staffing, planning, corruption, or a combination all three.

Getting the supplies in country was not the crux of the problem. In fact, the quantity of supplies arriving at the country's docks, distribution centers, and military depots could overwhelm those responsible for the system's accounting and distribution. Still, critical supplies could sometimes be held back in army depots or provincial supply centers because senior commanders had no confidence that their supplies, once expended, would be replaced.

Counterinsurgency

That excess of caution had them holding supplies in reserve even if there were critical needs out in their units, a problem I saw after not being long on the job.

We needed sandbags and mortar rounds. The bunkered guard posts around our village were years old. Their sandbags were breaking down and the decay was weakening the bunker walls. Also, a couple of militia platoons in the district had exhausted their supply of 60mm mortar rounds, which they needed to help protect their outposts and to use in harassment fires along enemy infiltration routes.

When we requested the sandbags and mortar rounds, our province headquarters said we would have to wait because there was no transportation available. All their vehicles were being used for "more important needs." I knew that could mean anything from combat operations to helping the province chief's wife move furniture. Alternatively, it could mean that province headquarters wasn't willing to release the sand bags and mortar rounds to us in the first place.

Our inability to get the supplies was frustrating because I knew that the U.S. had provided the sandbags and mortar rounds to the Vietnamese supply system. The problem was that the Vietnamese government could not organize itself to deliver them. We were forced to get the sandbags brought out by an American Huey helicopter pilot who was coming nearby on another mission and we got the mortar rounds delivered by a U.S. Navy patrol boat. That got us our supplies, but it did nothing for enhancing the Vietnamese supply system. That sort of jury-rigging left rot in the system and probably contributed to later difficulties the Vietnamese armed forces had in fighting off the North Vietnamese invasion.

The logistical problems I saw out in a village in rural Vietnam provided a lingering illustration to me of how American counterinsurgency efforts are much more complex than sending American advisors to slog through jungles and rice paddies as they try to help a friendly government put down an insurgency. Counterinsurgency requires a logistical support system that has to be made operational in a way that does not overwhelm the host country's bureaucracy despite that bureaucracy's inadequate methods and poorly developed port and depot facilities.

That is not an easy task. A counterinsurgency program with its many goals and moving parts can send the host government's administration into a fog of confusion especially when the U.S. in trying to get its program off to a quick start sends too much too soon. When that happens, supplies sit on the docks rather than being sent on to whatever in-country depots that exist. Overwhelmed depots will end up sending supplies where they are not needed or accumulating the supplies that are needed. There will be blocks and deviations all along the supply pipeline, which not only means that supplies will fail to reach needy units or programs, it means that many of those supplies will end up on the shelves of the black market.

Building a proper logistical system requires the staffing of facilities in a way that will allow them to manage the relative abundance accompanying the counterinsurgency program. That logistical task entails everything from keeping accurate records of supplies received to effectively storing supplies to getting those supplies to their proper destination without loss or misdirection. Anything short of that will hobble the counterinsurgency effort because it leads to a waste of time, material, and, ultimately, lives.

Challenge 5: Maintaining Trust

A counterinsurgency effort will not work unless officials of both governments commit to an environment of trust and cooperation. To achieve this, both the American advisors and their counterparts should be educated about their responsibilities, the program design, and the methods to be used going forward. All should understand that progress will not be easy and that difficulties can be dealt with so long as communication remains open and trust in the program is maintained. Past experience shows that this kind of start will prove difficult to achieve. The lines of responsibility shown so clearly on organizational charts and the sensibility of programs described by senior officials in their briefings rarely survive the rumble and tumble of the field. Uncertainties will arise. Trust will be strained. Working through difficult situations will take effort, an effort that is part of every advisor-counterpart relationship.

An important challenge to trust and cooperation arises when the host government's bureaucracy operates outside the strictures of American rules and customs. Trying to change the behavior of the host country's bureaucrats can make them resistant to what they might come to consider "the American's program" rather than their program. Alternatively, they might truly be bewildered by their situation. One day they might be faulted by their superiors for not having adjusted to the new way of doing things and the next for not following the policies of the past. At the same time, they must face their American counterparts who expect changes to be occurring at all points and all times. Frustrated and resentful at being asked to operate beyond their capacity, those host-government officials can begin to suspect the value of the program and of the advisors who have recommended it. The advisors, detecting a lethargic response to their advice, can reciprocate by losing trust, as well. In that way, a cycle of disdain begins from which it is difficult to recover.

Vietnam, 1969

The Americans had been pushing land reform for years. Absentee landlords owned much of the country's tillable land, which left many rural peasants with little hope of ever owning land their families might have been farming for generations. Further, some of the agricultural land remained undeeded for a variety of reasons and the deeding process was going slowly. American officials had emphasized that it was important to the economy and to the concept of fair government for rural peasants to enjoy the possibility of owning their own land.

For my part, I was only vaguely aware of the land reform program and had heard nothing of it since joining my team. Had I been alert to the issue, after being in my district a while I would have guessed that much of the land was undeeded. The area had been thinly populated until the early nineteen fifties and now, in 1969, the farmers tilled their land mostly by right of their physical presence only. Few could actually prove ownership. At the same time, locally powerful families claimed large areas of the land which they rented to the local peasants. If asked, I would have agreed that land reform was a good idea; but, as is true with many government programs, the benefits obtained depend on how the job is done. So it was with land reform.

Early one evening my district chief came by and told me that our plans for the next day had been cancelled. He had just been informed that officials from province headquarters were coming out to deliver land reform.

Land reform? I had heard nothing about it. The district chief said all he knew was that some province officials were coming out by helicopter to

Three. The Campaign

deliver deeds for local farmers. He was to see that the farmers and local villagers were in attendance, but since the province officials would be bringing their American advisor, I should be there as well. Okay, I thought with a mental shrug, count me in.

The next morning, the district chief was out directing militiamen to mark off a large area using cord hung with small, yellow and red flags. By noon the villagers began arriving and were soon being shepherded into the square where they squatted to wait. Soon the square was full of farmers and villagers shaded from the sun only by their conical straw hats or cloth turbans. It was supposed to be a ceremony, but no one seemed in ceremonial spirits.

The government officials arrived as promised, but I knew none of them or their American advisor, a civilian. The senior official was a fair-skinned, well-dressed, middle-aged man with a condescending manner. All of that marked him as one of Vietnam's citified elites. His American advisor stayed in the background but he seemed pleased with how things were progressing.

After a short speech about the land reform program the senior official called individuals from the audience to hand them an official-looking paper, which the recipients accepted with handshakes and brief smiles. Soon, it was all done. The province officials and their American advisor got back on their helicopter and flew away, the strings of flags came down, and the farmers dispersed with their new deeds in hand. The ceremony was over, but the problems were only about to begin.

The deeds handed out had been generated back in the province town for undeeded lands already being farmed, but the deeds often did not match a farmer's traditional plot; rather, names seemed to have been filled in on some sort of template that assigned names to land with little requirement for accuracy. Since most of the farmers could not decipher the legalese of their deeds this only became evident long after the land reform officials had disappeared. As a result, no one paid any attention to the deeds and the only lasting effect of the boondoggle was the resentment of the farmers for having been dragooned for the exercise.

I later learned that the Vietnamese government had agreed to land reform only under American urging and had never pursued it with any vigor. The Saigon government had made an agreement without intent, exactly the kind of thing that strains trust between counterinsurgency part-

ners. Vietnamese officials had not trusted the wisdom of the advice of their American counterparts who were saying that the program was important. Now, I did not trust the Vietnamese officials because they had made a mess of things, at least in my district. It was a feeling shared by my district chief, though he might have blamed the grief on the Americans and their "better" ideas. Finally, the inconvenienced farmers didn't know whom to blame, so they probably chose to blame their local government. All in all, not a win for the home team.

Land reform was poorly done in Vietnam in part because Vietnamese officials did not believe it was as important as their American advisors said it was. They agreed to it in word only, not in deed. They doubted the program's importance and their lack of confidence in it led to a listless pursuit of the program's goals. Their advisors, in turn, saw that poor enthusiasm as a lack of cooperation. Similar situations can be found in any counterinsurgency scenario and undoubtedly has, up to and including Iraq and Afghanistan.

Developing and maintaining trust between counterparts is about the personal relationships that are the major paving stones of a counterinsurgency program. Those relationships can also be key to an advisor's survival. Both of those things are true whether the specific area of the program is about establishing security, improving development, or advancing government reform. It is true whether that advising is in the field, in garrison, or in the civilian environment. It is true whatever and wherever the insurgency.

Lesson Learned: Developing a Mutual Trust with Your Counterpart Can Save Your Life

Sergeant First Class Alejandro D. Murphy-Lugo, Light Weapons Advisor, 35th Ranger Battalion (MACV Advisory Team 74), Bao Trai District, Hau Nhia Province (MACV Advisory Team 43), III Corps Tactical Zone; 1964–1965.

Developing trust and respect with our counterparts was important because it was a matter of life and death. We were living together, eating

Opposite: Sergeant Murphy-Lugo with a Vietnamese Ranger counterpart in Hau Nhia Province, 1964.

the same food, and participating together in daily combat missions. Originally, I didn't know that I had a bodyguard assigned to me by the Ranger battalion commander, but I started noticing one of the Vietnamese soldiers staying close to me all the time and asking me questions about English words as he thumbed through a battered American dictionary. It turned out he had been assigned to be my bodyguard and had decided to use the opportunity to learn some English. That was fine with me; it was good to know he had a motivation to keep an eye out for my safety.

During one particular battalion operation three of my advisor teammates and I were separated to allow each of us to work with one of the four companies involved that day. On these types of operations, we typically stayed close to our company's lead elements so we would be there if contact was made with the enemy and our help was needed; so that's where I was, up close to the front. As we approached a Viet Cong controlled area my bodyguard told me the battalion commander had ordered him to have me move over to a nearby area until the lead squad had checked out the hamlet up ahead.

I was surprised because that kind of instruction had never happened before. I was even more surprised when I saw the other three advisors on the operation gathering in the same place. It turned out that all of them had bodyguards, too, and all of the bodyguards had urged their guy to stay in this area for a few minutes until the hamlet ahead had been checked out.

I was suspicious. None of us had ever been told to hold back from our units while we were out on an operation. What reason could there be for it? Were we being held back to keep us from seeing something? Worse yet, were we being set up for something bad? We all thought about ignoring the bodyguards; this was too strange and no one was giving good explanations. Still, we all trusted the ranger commander and each of us trusted his own bodyguard, so we decided to stay put.

Within minutes all hell break loose up ahead. Each one of us wanted to get up there with our units, but the bodyguards insisted we wait just a little longer. We weren't needed, they said. Things were going fine without out help. The firefight lasted about ten minutes, which is a long time if you're in the heat of it, then the word came back that we could move forward. The fight was over and the rangers had killed five Viet Cong and wounded several others. One ranger officer had been wounded.

It seems the Viet Cong had tried to ambush us, and by us, I mean the

Three. The Campaign

U.S. advisors, specifically. An informant had alerted our battalion commander beforehand, so he had ordered us held back until he could see what developed. As it turned out, the guerrillas had dug camouflaged firing positions in the hamlet with the plan of hiding in them until they could catch as many Americans as possible their trap. They would spring the ambush, kill the Americans, then slip away before any significant help came.

It was sobering to hear that plan because it made me realize that that first eruption of gunfire could have been the one that killed me or some of the other advisors. There were two things that saved us: The quick action of the ranger commander in thinking of our safety once he learned we were at specific risk, and our trust in the commander and our bodyguards.

After the action, the battalion commander confirmed to us what we had heard. He had held us back not only because he liked us and had a good relationship with us, but because we were too valuable to the battalion for him to lose. After all, he said lightheartedly, having advisors with his unit was like having a life insurance policy for it. We could call for air strikes, artillery fires, and medical evacuations and get it much faster than he could get that same help through Vietnamese channels. It's true that he wasn't going out of his way to save us simply because we all got along well, but it certainly didn't hurt.

Rapport runs both ways, and it was more than him liking and trusting us, we had to trust him, too. We hadn't originally understood his orders, but we knew him well enough to trust him. That was important. The lesson learned that day was that while in a combat zone, you need to be able to trust your counterpart and he needs to trust you. There are enough things to worry about from the enemy; you don't want to have a counterpart you have to worry about, too.

Alejandro Murphy Lugo retired from the U.S. Army as a command sergeant major in 1983. He later retired as a real estate broker in Fajardo, Puerto Rico, and is now a volunteer for the Disabled American Veterans.

Relevant Readings

Brown, Donald M. *Vietnam and CORDS: Interagency Lessons for Iraq.* Fort Leavenworth, KS: School for Advanced Military Studies, 2008, 14–35.

Coffey, Ross. "Revisiting CORDS: The Need for Unity of Effort to Secure Victory in Iraq. *Military Review* March-April (2006): 24–34.

Counterinsurgency

Collins, James L., *Vietnam Studies: The Development and Training of the South Vietnamese Army, 1950–1972*. Washington, D.C.: Department of the Army, 1991, 68–122.

Cooper, Chester L., Judith E. Corson, Laurence J. Legere, David E. Lockwood, and Donald M. Weller. *The American Experience with Pacification in Vietnam*. Vol. 1. *An Overview of Pacification*. Arlington, VA: Institute for Defense Analysis, 1972,1–61.

Fitzgerald, David. *Learning to Forget: U.S. Army Counterinsurgency Doctrine and Practice*. San Francisco: Stanford University Press, 2013.

Heiser, Joseph M. *Vietnam Studies: Logistic Support*. Washington, D.C.: Department of the Army, 1991, 229–42.

Hoffman Bruce. "Insurgency and Counterinsurgency in Iraq" (an "Occasional Paper"). Santa Monica, CA: RAND Corporation, 2004.

Schwarz, Benjamin C. *American Counterinsurgency Doctrine and El Salvador: The Frustrations of Reform and the Illusions of Nation Building*. Santa Monica, CA: RAND Corporation, 1991.

Silinsky, Mark. "An Irony of War: Human Development as Warfare in Afghanistan." *Colloquium,* 3 (2010): 1–16.

Four

Those Who Do Counterinsurgency
The Advisors

Counterinsurgency has been a tool of American foreign policy for well over a century, and that experience has shown it to be a tool of considerable complexity. The executors of counterinsurgency are the advisors, civilian and military, who are sent to assist a host government in putting down an insurgency. Military advisors can be assigned to work at any level of government, but at all levels their task requires a blend of blend of diplomatic skill and military expertise that is not a natural product of conventional military training. The quality of counterinsurgency advisors is critical because those advisors are the literal contact points between two governments. In distant places far from the seats of power they may become the only representatives of American policy and power; for any hope of success they have to get it right.

While both military and civilian advisors have important roles in counterinsurgency programs, it is the military advisors who penetrate most deeply into the host nation's countryside. They are the ones in the most isolated locations and the ones who face the most danger from the insurgency they have been sent to contest. For those reasons, the following discussion focuses primarily on military advisors. They often become the most extended expression of American foreign policy, and in that role they require talents very different from those typically valued in their profession.

Counterinsurgency

Vietnam, 1969

    I arrived in country as a young infantry officer having completed a course for military advisors at the Special Warfare School in Fort Bragg, North Carolina. I felt properly trained, so far as stateside training can do, and I thought I was ready for whatever assignment I was given. The reality was that training only provided a launching pad for an experience in which I still had much to learn.

    I was assigned to the counterinsurgency program called Civil Operations and Revolutionary Development Support (CORDS), a joint U.S. Army-civilian program under the authority of the Military Assistance Command, Vietnam (MACV). The MACV deputy for CORDS was a civilian serving on the general staff at a level equivalent to that of the general officer in charge of the conventional American forces in country. This mix of military and civilian efforts under a unified command continued down through the CORDS organization to the country's forty-four provinces where province advisory teams were made up of military advisors focusing on security concerns and civilian advisors focusing on development. The unified command structure was to insure that the security and development aspects of the counterinsurgency program were coordinated and directed toward the same general goals (CORDS will be discussed in more detail in Chapter Seven).

    Each province was made up of several districts, each of which had a district advisory team. Because of the small size of the teams and their increased security risks they rarely had civilian members, but they could utilize the development expertise available on the province team. Each province also had several all–Army Mobile Advisory Teams (MATs) that were typically assigned to militia units in specific villages or hamlets. Their mission was to upgrade the units' combat performance by living with them, training them, and fighting along side them in the field. Secondarily, the MATs were to work with their village chiefs to help with development projects. My initial assignment in Vietnam was to join a MAT out on the Plain of Reeds in the Mekong delta.

    MATs consisted of two combat arms officers (infantry, armor, artillery) and three sergeants who were a light weapons specialist, a heavy weapons specialist, and a medic. My teams' mission as described by my Province Senior Advisor in March of 1969 was "to advise and instruct (the militia units) in or near the village on field fortifications and barrier systems, requests and adjustment of indirect fire..., small unit operations with emphasis on night operations and ambush patrols, weapons employment and marksmanship..., emergency and preventive medicine, airmobile operations, ... administrative and logistical support procedures with emphasis on ... records keeping, pay and allowances, ... requisitions..., equipment maintenance, and field sanitation and hygiene. Additionally, (the team is) to assist the (militia unit) commander or village chief in coordinating the overall security of the village and to assist and advise the village chief in pacification and development matters." I thought that was a full plate, but a few months later I became the District Senior Advisor, as well. In either role, I was the senior American for miles around and had a strong influence on both military operations and local development projects. My team and I were the extended expression of American foreign policy, and it would have been hard for any training program to prepare a twenty-four year old junior officer for that.*

By 1969 most of the CORDS officer advisor slots were being filled by graduates of the advisors course I had attended at the Special Warfare School. That training had been practical with regard to military and civil operations, but it had also educated its proto-advisors about the language, culture, and religion of the people we were being sent to help. After an additional two-weeks of in-country training I and those like me were assigned to MAT or district teams, while many others were assigned as advisors to conventional Vietnamese army units, a different job but one with similar challenges and stresses.

The best advisors are those who not only have a professional expertise important to the program (combat tactics, engineering, etc.) but also have the specific training and personal qualities that tends to make them most effective. Both the training and the personal qualities are important because advisor duties differ in style and substance from conventional army duties. This suggests that advisors should be selected, not randomly assigned, and they should possess those professional and personal qualities known to be enhancing factors.

Counterinsurgency Advisors Should Be Selected, Not Randomly Assigned

In 1972 the Institute for Defense Analysis issued a report reviewing the American experience in Vietnam. That report noted that the job of an advisor requires he have "consummate skill, keen sensitivity, and constant awareness." Military advising, especially combat advising, is not a job for the faint hearted, the impatient, or the uncommitted. It is not for the hard-headed, the high-strung, or the hot spur who thinks there is nothing like a frontal assault whether it is in the field or the conference room. A counterinsurgency advisor must not only be competent in his military specialty and have the training necessary to be an advisor, but he must have the personal characteristics that allow him to function well in that role. An advisor has to be something of an anthropologist, psychologist, and professional diplomat while retaining the character and capabilities of a combat leader. Not everyone can pull that off, and filling out a roster of advisors is a case where an ounce of selection is worth a pound of random delegation. Advisors should be selected, not merely assigned. This has been known and written about by counterinsurgency experts for nearly half a century, and that American military forces still have personnel policies that ignore this wisdom represents a case of military dysgnosis, that failure to know what should have been known addressed in Chapter One, or perhaps worse, a case of knowing but failing to act.

Forty years ago Major General John Cushman, upon completing his tour as commanding general of the Delta Military Assistance Command in Vietnam said that the most relevant trait of an advisor was that he have "insight." To attain that, he said, the advisor must be intellectually curious and attuned to the culture he is submerged in. That kind of insight, he went on to say, comes from constant observation, reflection, and re-evaluation of previous assumptions, all of which help in making an accurate assessment of what's happening now. The best advisor, Cushman said, uses insight to see and report facts as they really are, not as he or his superiors want them to be.

Training, observation, and reflection are aids in helping the advisor be close to the people he serves with and to understand them and their culture. Properly focused, those attributes give the advisor insight and allow the development of a perspective that those without them will never have.

Vietnam, 1969

Living in a Vietnamese village helped me to understand the people's customs and to respect their way of life. This was a very different experience

Four. Those Who Do Counterinsurgency

from that of the American soldiers in conventional American army units. While I do not doubt that many of those soldiers and their officers worked hard to maintain good relations with the Vietnamese civilians and military forces in their areas, far too many showed a callous disregard for the people and their customs. This was a constant irritant and a significant problem wherever there were large American forces.

I once had occasion to be near the main base of the U.S. Army's 9th Infantry Division in the Mekong delta. I and one of my team mates were walking past one of the division's artillery batteries positioned near a busy road when I noticed a small group of American soldiers standing together and laughing at one of their fellows as he rode around on an old bicycle with a basket full of bread and vegetables. That soldier, a large, burly fellow, had taken the bike from an old woman and was making a big joke of it as he wobbled about like a clown and took in the cheers of his buddies. The old woman was standing in the road pleading for the return of her bike, but the soldier was ignoring her, which only prolonged her embarrassment in front of the other Vietnamese walking by. The Americans were large and boisterous, the Vietnamese were small and quiet, but all the Vietnamese were shooting sullen looks at the Americans. They knew that the old woman was suffering an outrage.

In Vietnam, as in any Asian country, the elderly are treated with respect, and to deal with them in any other way is a major breech of custom. Even in those soldiers' hometowns back in the States what they were doing would have been unacceptable and I was sure they knew it. What they really were doing was acting out their disdain for the Vietnamese and that culture's deeply rooted values. Those soldiers' act was not only offensive, it was dangerous. It was feeding the image of us all being rude, crude Americans bent on harassment and destruction. It was an image our enemies liked to make much of and one we too often fed.

I had seen all I needed. As the biker rode by me his chest somehow ran into the butt of my rifle, which surprised him, knocked him off the bike, and considerably roused his anger. I was not a member of the 9th Division and I was not in charge of this man and his buddies, but I ordered him to return the bike and let the old woman go on her way. He did as I said but with a mutinous glare that I thought was about to lead to trouble. Then one of his officers, a first lieutenant, walked up and ordered the group *to disperse. I protested to the lieutenant that his men's behavior was out of line and going to make trouble for everyone. Was that not obvious?*

Apparently, not to him. He said he had too many other things to worry about. He couldn't stop every little bit of his men's horseplay and it would be counterproductive if he tried. He could tell from my uniform that I was not a part of the 9th Division, so to him I was just another lieutenant who happened to be passing through this area. It was unlikely I would be staying around long enough to make trouble for him, so he didn't mind being frank: This was not something he was going to worry about.

The kind of soldiers I ran into that day at the 9th Division, officer and enlisted, were an anathema to counterinsurgency. Those men might have thought I and others like me were being overly sensitive or had "gone native," but the war all of us were engaged in depended more on the hearts of the people than the body count of a battlefield. Some of us respected the people we had come to help; we understood the struggles of their daily lives. Others did not, and they were always a threat to our cause.

Professional skills, cultural awareness, and insight are necessary to an advisor's success but by themselves they are insufficient to make success long lasting. Advisors also have to endure psychological and physical stresses, both of which can emerge from various sources. Psychological stresses include those that arise from the cultural adjustments required, so-called culture shock. It can be so profound as to make a person physically ill and unfit for duty. In some assignments, stresses can come from being under the hazards of war for twenty-four hours a day, seven days a week, with no relief for months at a time; and they also can come from the frustrations of dealing with counterparts who may be indifferent, inept, corrupt, or all three.

Culture shock and the unrelieved hazards of war can vary depending on the advisor's specific assignment, but the frustrations of dealing with corrupt or inept officials has been a consistent feature of American counterinsurgency efforts whenever and wherever they occur. That is not to say that all indigenous officials are corrupt or inept, but if host governments were supported by efficient civil administrations and well-led military forces, it is unlikely they would be having their insurgencies in the first place.

The physical stresses of an advisor's job can be especially demanding for those advisors in remote outposts where dietary restrictions, living conditions, and the demands of combat operations produce difficult physical stresses. All of those must be borne with enough energy remaining to function well in the non-combat aspects of the role. That is not easy when the job can be unrelenting in its requirement that the advisor be adaptable, capable of making independent decisions, and able to function despite his weariness and probable frustration. To meet that challenge even the most physically prepared and most fit of personalities need specific training to do the job at their best. Advisor duty presents many problems for which there is no "school solution"; but appropriate training will provide guides that point the advisor toward the best of the available choices.

Lesson Learned: An Advisor Has to Make Serious Cultural Adjustments

Staff Sergeant John C. Fisher, Light Weapons Advisor; Chau Thanh District, Dinh Tuong Province (MACV Advisory Team 66), IV Corps Tactical Zone; 1966–1968.

I guess the first thing that struck me about adviser duty was the fact that the village I was assigned to in the Mekong delta seemed to be a place pulled from the pages of ancient history. The houses were all wooden huts with roofs of bamboo, except for the few whose owners were well enough off to afford a few sheets of tin. The huts mostly consisted of one room where all the living, dinning, cooking and sleeping took place and all the floors were dirt. There was no running water or toilet facilities other than pits dug in the ground and the people bathed in the river up stream from their village because the pits drained into the river downstream. Of course, the village upstream had done the same thing, so go figure.

The bad water and lack of soap left many people with open sores on their bodies. For me that was deplorable; for them, it was life. Their diet consisted of rice and fish, rice and chicken, and rice and duck, usually with a few vegetables. To make things worse, I was the first adviser ever assigned to the Vietnamese unit I was advising and its commander spoke only a smattering of English. I had received no Vietnamese language training, so our communication was rudimentary, at best.

Counterinsurgency

Sergeant Fisher (center) with counterparts in Dinh Tuong Province, 1967.

The living conditions were dismal, so I used my Army NCO skills to scrounge some parts and make my own toilet and shower facilities. Then I ran an electrical wire from a nearby headquarters building, the only source of electricity in the village (and that jealously guarded) to my hut so I could at least turn on a light bulb. After that I settled in and life became a little more bearable.

Another cultural surprise to me was that the Vietnamese villagers, men, women, and children, were fascinated with body hair, at least a big, Texan's body hair. Vietnamese have little body hair, so to them, seeing me was like seeing something from a zoo. A person sitting next to me at a table might grin shyly and ask to feel the hair on my arms, but that was the least of it. Women and kids alike would come to my shower and peek over the board siding to see if I had hair all over my body, then they would go away wondering at the hirsute expanse of the big American. It's not that Army sergeants are shy folks, you understand, but I wasn't exactly used to that kind of full disclosure. In the end, you just had to get used to it and move on.

My formal introduction to military advising had been brief and had not

Four. Those Who Do Counterinsurgency

included any specific information about cultural differences. All I knew was that I was supposed to teach the local Vietnamese unit how to fight and to provide them with combat support when needed.

I learned very quickly that the unit I had been assigned to knew how to fight, they just didn't have the equipment to do it with. They had old World War II weapons and ammunition, of which the latter had been soaked and dried so many times it would often fail to fire. My unit patrolled the local waterways with boats equipped with water-cooled 30 cal. machine guns that even pre-dated World War II! So I had more scrounging to do: Weapons, ammunition, food, building materials, and just about anything else we needed.

Perhaps the thing that affected me most was the lack of medical care in the villages. I felt I had to do something about that, especially for the children, so I arranged for a medical civic action team to come out and give vaccinations. None of the parents or children seemed to have ever heard of vaccinations and at first everyone was afraid of them. I let them watch the big Texan take one of the shots with a smile, and after that they joined in without further trouble. I was having to take charge of all that because my Vietnamese unit's medic had had little training beyond what an American soldier would get in boot camp. He could wrap a wound, but that was about it.

The unavailability of local medical care even had me delivering a baby, which I had never done and not this one without considerable concern! I managed it by calling my advisory team's medic on the radio. He was miles away, but he talked me through the process, much to his apparent amusement. After it was all over I went outside and relieved myself of my last several meals.

As I got into my advisory duties, I learned how to survive where I was and to do my job despite the near culture shock I had had in the beginning. Despite the less-than-basic circumstances of their lives, I was struck with a deep appreciation for the Vietnamese people, especially those in the unit I was serving with. I have valued the experience ever since because it taught me the value, even the necessity of cultural adjustment when trying to help people from a very different background than your own.

John Fisher retired from the U.S. Army in 1985 and is currently the curator of the Hall of Heroes Museum in Temple, Texas.

Advisor Training Is Critical for Success

Counterinsurgency is a form of special warfare and should be respected as such. Without proper training the well intended can waste a lot of time and good will, which is why that training is so critical to success. Many Army and some Marine advisors of the Vietnam era were put through a six-week course at the Special Warfare School, Fort Bragg, North Carolina. That course focused on weapons and explosives training, counterinsurgency concepts and methods, physical fitness, intelligence operations, field-expedient engineering, the CORDS program, the Vietnamese military system, and Vietnamese language and culture. Some of those future advisors went on to a further eight or twelve weeks of language training. The advisor training provided advisors with an in-depth look at the how-tos, what-ifs, and what-fors of advising, including basic language skills.

The U.S. Navy also had a counterinsurgency school at the Naval Amphibious Base Coronado, Coronado, California for its "brown water navy" advisors. That course was thirteen weeks, total. Similar to the Army training, six weeks were devoted to basic weapons, field tactics, Vietnamese history and culture, and counterinsurgency theory, but an additional six weeks of Vietnamese language studies were a constituent part of the course. The Navy advisors also had one week of escape and evasion training.

Those were training experiences of long ago, but whatever the theater of operation and whatever the insurgency, such conflict-specific training should still be provided to counterinsurgency advisors. Less intense exposures do not sufficiently submerge the student in the topic and provide too little relevant information to be very useful. At a minimum, those officers assigned as counterinsurgency advisors should be qualified through an extensive course designed to fit them for the conflict at hand.

At the time of this writing the 162nd Infantry Brigade at Folk Polk, LA, has the mission of providing combat advisor training for the entire U.S. Army except Special Forces. The brigade's curriculum has shifted over time, but at one time it had a ten-week residential school for individuals, which was a substantial effort training male and female alike, officer and enlisted. That training did not focus on counterinsurgency as an aspect of special warfare, however, and it did not take place in a formally recognized school or center. Neither was it been taken as a necessary qualification for advisor duty even with conventional indigenous forces. Formalizing those and other aspects of advisor training, especially with regard to counterinsurgency advising, would improve advisor training and lend prestige both to it and to those who serve in advisor assignments.

Counterinsurgency advisors need special training because much of what they do happens in a foreign cultural environment that they must understand and work in successfully. While not commenting specifically about counterinsurgency, Frank Hoffman, Senior Research Fellow at the Institute of National Strategic Studies, National Defense University, recently wrote in the Armed Forces Journal that the military services should be preparing a generation of warfighters with the skill sets needed for working within foreign cultures while at the same time teaching them how to access specific knowledge that would allow them to understand the events and environment of specific crisis areas. He noted, "...there is great merit in calls for cultural-centric warfare in which our soldiers and sailors are prepared with an acute degree of cultural awareness (so they can fill our) need for 'global scouts' to advance our interaction with foreign societies."

Against the background of "small wars" being predicted for the foreseeable future, Hoffman emphasized that the kind of human intelligence needed "can be successfully interpreted only by a military imbued with a deep understanding of the historical and cultural context that has generated the conflict to begin with." Especially with regard to counterinsurgency conflicts, that is an important point. So is Hoffman's conclusion that despite the Pentagon's current fiscal crunch, "the American military is going to have to place education at the center of how it prepares for the future, including both history and cultural studies." This is particularly true for training in counterinsurgency, and that training will be best delivered by an organized school or center rather than by an infantry brigade detailed for the duty.

Advisors Face Uniquely Challenging Issues

Advising counterparts from any country can be difficult when that country is under the stress of defending itself in an armed conflict. Even when cultural, historical, and language differences are not great, for example the partnership between Great Britain and the United States during World War II, the effort for two nations to work together can generate

Counterinsurgency

tensions arising from differences in perception. Magnify those tensions by an order of magnitude for each difference of history, culture, or language that exists between counterinsurgency partners and one can get a sense of the difficulties facing both military and civilian advisors. While a complete listing of important problems is not possible here, three important ones are rapport (building and maintaining it), time (not enough of it), and U.S. military culture (difficulties with it).

The first and most multifaceted issue for the advisor is that of building rapport with host-country counterparts. It is a task whose difficulty increases as the differences between the two in language and culture become more profound; still, establishing that trust relationship is one of the first things an advisor must put his mind to. Clearly, an advisor's cultural adaptability and language familiarity are a part of the skill sets needed to meet this challenge.

Foreign counterparts sometimes start their side of the interaction from a position of distrust. Even though high officials of the U.S. government and the counterpart's government may have made agreements about conducting a counterinsurgency program, subordinates in that government's administration or military may be skeptical of the program's details or intent. They might fear that the Americans' assistance is merely an attempt at political hegemony; certainly, the insurgents will claim this is true. They may fear that American assistance is an attempt to grab vital natural resources. If those resources are in easy evidence, such as oil being pumped from the ground or strategic minerals being mined, the insurgents will certainly claim this is true, as well. These are fears not easily overcome and only the evidence of American national behavior can overcome them. For example, after the Second Gulf War, the Iraqi insurgents and much of the Arab world were claiming that the U.S. invaded Iraq only to get its oil. The relevant American behavior was to encourage the Iraqi government to hold a public auction for leases of its eleven oil fields. American oil companies successfully acquired only one, a result that spoke much against the original claim. A problem is that that process took years to complete, which means there was a long time between the fear and its resolution. Much damage can be done in that time, so in the interim the American advisor has to build trust and cooperation through his personal character, his actions, and the promise of hope offered by the counterinsurgency program.

Four. Those Who Do Counterinsurgency

Distrust can also arise from the American advisors. They might wonder whether an indifferent counterpart is more interested in defeating the insurgency or maneuvering to make a profit from the enterprise. An advisor might find that his counterpart has family members in the insurgency and might fear the relationship will temper the counterpart's actions and reactions. Those kinds of worries are rarely completely satisfied, so to avoid problems that can arise from them the advisor should make sure that communication between him and his counterpart is close and as continuous as reason allows. The advisor should be alert to his counterpart's performance and knowledgeable about his response to advice. The advisor's close presence should be directed in a way that builds a relationship between him and his counterpart that is as positive as possible. The two should be like a pair of travelers walking down the same road knowing where they are going but negotiating what route they should take to get there.

This is only one way in which an advisor must play the soldier as well as the diplomat. The advisor must be self-aware and must understand how even in the most congenial of relationships the fact that he is an American raises barriers between him and his colleague from the host nation. The advisor comes with an American history, an American experience, and an American way of looking at the world, but as an advisor he must realize that the military, psychological, and social context in which he now works is quite different from that background. The difference can cause culture shock, as already mentioned, but short of that extreme the differences can make it difficult to correctly perceive people and their actions. It is all too easy for the advisor to focus on his counterpart's obvious differences in language, customs, and preferences while ignoring more subtle differences such as patterns of thought, modes of action, and concepts about the world. All of these can have as profound an effect on counterpart relations as the more obvious differences that easily draw attention. Advisors have to be aware of this so they are not surprised by a subtlety while guarding against the obvious.

Many years ago General William Westmoreland pointed out to new advisors in Vietnam that counterpart relations are made difficult by the constant demands of making decisions with life or death consequences while trying to communicate through the obstacles of language and culture. He added a key observation: "The training of the U.S. military officer is characterized by conditioned traits of decisiveness and aggressiveness. (In contrast) the essence of your relationship with your counterpart is constituted by patience and restraint. As a threshold to development of a meaningful affiliation with your counterpart, you must succeed in the reconciliation of these contrasting qualities." This is a difficult challenge and one not all military personnel can overcome.

The ability to shift into another cultural mode while remaining grounded in American values is key to a military advisors being able to meet the challenge of reaching outside his usual ways of doing things to find common ground with his counterpart. This is where the advisor-soldier and the advisor-diplomat must become one. The best advisor tries to understand why his counterpart acts or fails to act in specific situations. Is it a matter of religion? Of politics? Fear? Corruption? Or is it merely a matter of language and a failure to understand?

Alternatively, a counterpart may show a lack of enthusiasm for an advisor's ideas because he has been in his job for years and has had the experience of previous fresh-faced advisors coming up with well-drilling, road-paving, or soldier-training schemes and has seen too many of them come to naught—with the advisor no longer around to share the blame. The good advisor can think through these kinds of concerns and conduct himself in a way that maximizes his chances of maintaining good counterpart relations.

Vietnam, 1969

When I arrived in my district in the Mekong delta, my district chief was a native of the region. He was also a member of the Hoa Hao sect of Buddhism, which was very strong in that part of the country. To fully understand what that meant socially and politically, I had to know several things about religion in Vietnam. The Hoa Hao sect had only been founded in the nineteen-thirties and was a somewhat separatist group within Buddhism. They rejected some of the practices of conventional Buddhism and focused on simplicity and the practice of religious ceremonies in the home rather than at shrines and temples. In large part, it was a religion of the peasant farmer and fisherman. Conventional Buddhism was the main religion of Vietnam's middle class and Catholicism was the main religion of the upper class.

Four. Those Who Do Counterinsurgency

One expression of the Hoa Hao separatist mentality was that they had rebelled against the central government in the late 1950s. They had been defeated and one of its military generals had been beheaded in public, so in their hearts the Hoa Hao were not friends of the Saigon government. Even so, by the early 1960s the Hoa Hao had become strongly anti-communist and had proven very effective in ridding their areas of communist guerrillas and infiltrators. Thus, in the Hoa Hao district chief I had a man who was from the local area, knew the local culture and politics, and was used to functioning in the delta environment. We got along well, mainly because I saw him as being effective in his job despite his limited circumstances and he was aggressive against the enemy. One day, all that changed.

Word arrived that the district chief was being replaced. Why, because a coup plot had been discovered back in Saigon, and the discovery had led to a purge. Officers not directly involved in the plot but who were family members or close associates of the plotters were, in effect, being banished from Saigon. To keep them from any other points of influence they were being shipped out to the boonies, which our district certainly was.

The new district chief was a French-educated Catholic from a prominent family in Saigon. As a young man he had received his officer training under the French and had just begun his army career when France had pulled out of Vietnam. He and his family were from Saigon, and he had spent the last fifteen years in various staff assignments around the city. He had no tactical experience, no rural experience, and no experience living without electricity and running water. He and his wife appeared to suffer more from culture shock upon their arrival than I or any of my team mates had.

The new district chief was lost, not only culturally but politically and militarily. He was a Nervous Nellie and easily flummoxed by any significant problem. He was totally out of his element and his only goal was to get back to Saigon. Any action or communication was first evaluated for that end. No controversial move could be made and no risk extended. He would rather let an enemy unit infiltrate through our district from Cambodia and let someone else worry about it rather than take the risk of running into the enemy ourselves. He feared that we might intercept a larger unit than we could handle, and did not want to accept the danger. We did not get along.

The former district chief, the Hoa Hao, had become the district's militia commander. He and I found a way to make things work. The militia com-

mander would brief the district chief about a coming operation using a tone of voice and a demeanor that assumed the chief's agreement. Neither words or body language would suggest that the briefing was actually a request for permission. We had quickly realized that the new chief did not have the self-confidence to deny our plan, if it was put to him boldly, nor the courage to accept it, if it was put to him as a request.

My relationship with the new district chief improved because I learned how to work with him on some things and to work around him on others. It was a method he tacitly agreed to, so we all got what we wanted. Were we strictly following the rules of counterpart relations? No, but knowing the background of my counterpart and knowing the local political and religious environment allowed me to work out a positive relationship with him and to get some things done despite his disinterest.

Developing rapport sometimes requires a time of adjustment for both the advisor and the counterpart; but even in persistently difficult cases a way, perhaps not exactly orthodox, can often be found to move forward. People and personalities being what they are, sometimes the unorthodox is all that one can expect, but even that will come more easily if the advisor takes seriously the challenge of knowing the local culture and people and using that information to the advantage of the relationship.

A totally separate, conceptually simple, but equally difficult problem advisors face is time: too little of it. Determined insurgencies can be long, protracted affairs. That means the counterinsurgency operation will be equally protracted and that is a problem on two fronts: the potential waning of public support in the United States and the duration of advisor assignments. The first has been previously discussed. Suffice it to say, the American public is impatient in its wars and rightly wants to see success as soon as possible. The second is a problem not only for the advisors in the field, but also for those leaders in the Pentagon who decide military personnel policy. The problem is an old one, that of meeting counterinsurgency goals with advisors who are only in their positions for a standard, one-year tour of duty or even less.

Beginning with the war in Vietnam, tours of duty for military personnel in combat zones have typically been limited to one year when at all possible. That finite period benefits the morale of the service men and

Four. Those Who Do Counterinsurgency

women involved and the morale of their loved ones at home. The problem is that a one-year assignment as an advisor does not allow for the kind of impact the counterinsurgency program needs for success. An advisor and his counterpart may initiate and complete a short-term project within one year, but more substantial projects where the consequences of success or failure are greater require more time than that one year. Serving only a year on the job, the advisor who helps initiate a major project will likely be gone before it is completed. That leaves the latter steps of the project to be completed without advisory assistance or to be assisted with new advisor who might have arrived with new ideas and new directions. The project already underway may now suffer from lack of follow-through or its potential may be diminished by the new advisor being aimed a new priorities.

A way to avoid this problem is for advisors to have longer tours of duty. At the end of America's engagement in Vietnam, the Institute of Defense Analysis in Arlington, Virginia concluded that in the future the U.S. advisor tours should not be less than three years. Instituting that recommendation would present personnel problems and political reactions that cannot be taken lightly; on the other hand, the failure to follow the recommendation has perpetuated inefficiency in U.S. advisory efforts that has undoubtedly led to the loss of time, money, and American lives. Despite the difficulties induced by extended tours of duty for advisors, ways to ameliorate the problem might include extended opportunities for advisor leave, enhanced dependent support policies, special pay and allowance policies, and better promotion opportunities, among others.

Finally, advisors face a challenge that arises from the culture of the conventional American military services. American service men and women live in a world of company, battalion, brigade, and division (to use the Army example) where officers, in particular, have been expected to be seen and evaluated performing duties in conventional command and staff roles at increasing levels of responsibility. Those evaluations are cumulative and become more and more refining as the rank aspired to is higher. This can present a challenge for military advisors because they have to spend a lot of time outside the conventional army structure acquiring and maintaining language skills, political and cultural expertise, and other special warfare competencies. This requires time away from some of those usual duties of company, battalion, brigade, division, etc. and can limit opportunities for being evaluated at those jobs that are presumed to be necessary for promotion at the higher grades.

In that military culture unconventional warfare skills can go unrewarded, which leads career-oriented officers to conclude that military advising, especially in counterinsurgency, is not a favored occupation. The attitudes of fellow soldiers can enhance that conclusion, especially if there is a widespread opinion that those serving in conventional roles are somehow a different species of officer or soldier than those focusing on counterinsurgency and irregular warfare. That difference does not necessarily carry the implication that either of the two is better than the other, just different. An example of this is illustrated by the opinions about leadership that are held by officers engaged in conventional military tasks and those doing counterinsurgency.

Leadership is what military officers do. How good they are at it is how they are rated by others and how they rate themselves. Leadership is an important career factor in the formal, professional sense as well as in the informal society of the barracks or the officers' mess. Relevant to this, a recent survey questioned two groups of young Army officers about the personal attributes important for leadership. One group was in a conventional role during a period of advanced Army training and the other was in Afghanistan doing counterinsurgency. Both groups were asked to rank sixteen different leadership attributes contributing to leadership. The attributes ranged from the very general, as in "warrior ethos" or "duty" to the specific, as in "interpersonal tact" or "physical fitness."

It is interesting and positive that of the sixteen leadership attributes considered in the survey, both groups of officers chose the same five as being the most important: judgment, interpersonal tact, confidence, duty, and respect. Still, there were interesting differences in the two groups that reflect subtle distinctions in how they view themselves and, by comparison, may reflect how they view their colleagues in their contrasting roles. Officers doing counterinsurgency thought the attributes of innovativeness, duty, resilience, ethics, and empathy were more important to leadership than their conventional colleagues and those on conventional duty thought leadership put a stronger demand on warrior ethos, integrity, selfless service, loyalty, physical fitness, and domain knowledge.

Whether any of those perceptions reflect reality is not the point; the point is that there are differences in the way the two groups of officers, viewed the attributes of leadership. Such differences in perception can lead to a subtle attitude of separation between those doing counterinsurgency and those doing conventional duties. This is bad for two reasons: first, where any separation exists within a military service, the enemy may see a weakness to be exploited; second, it is not good for the development of a counterinsurgency expertise in the military because where there is a difference of opinion, style, or motivation, the dominant consideration will almost always come from the conventional side. The conventional forces are, after all, the dominant feature in the American military structure. This is not unusual, but it begs the questions, what are consequences for a military career largely devoted to counterinsurgency, should any unintended negative consequences be ameliorated, and, if so, what are there ways of achieving that?

These personnel issues are a challenge for the individual counterinsurgency advisor, but they are also a threat to the counterinsurgency requirements of American foreign policy. The military advisor assets required to execute foreign policy in a projected century of "small wars" will only develop adequately when advisors are seen as professionals whose accomplishments are recognized and rewarded in a manner equivalent with other aspects of military service. As long as the issue remains a problem, the challenge of maintaining a committed corps of counterinsurgency advisors or, for that matter, military advisors of any kind, will remain a problem.

It is a problem difficult to resolve because having an outstanding conventional military force also remains important to American national security. The country's military must still be able to counter threats from other nations that retain large, conventional armies; and for that role, the American army in particular must maintain its ability to shoot, move, and communicate across large theaters of operations. The importance of this is shown by the resurgence of Russian belligerence in Western Europe and a growing Chinese possessiveness in East Asia, both of which are backed by large, conventional military formations. To maintain an appropriate counterforce to these threats the American military requires experienced leaders who have done well within the conventional military structure. Nevertheless, to the degree it is believed that the twenty-first century will be an era of asymmetrical warfare, of "small wars," it remains strategically important

Counterinsurgency

to retain and promote officers and senior NCOs with relevant expertise in counterinsurgency wherein military advisors must play the soldier and the diplomat at the same time. In some cases those advisors become the farthest extension of American foreign policy recognizable in the flesh, and to all who see them or feel their influence, they are *the* Americans. While they and their training are the primary concern of the Department of Defense, they become key actors on the stage of foreign affairs when the American government turns to supporting a friendly government facing an insurgency. In that way, those advisors deserve the attention of their colleagues in both the military service and in the diplomatic corps.

Relevant Readings

Brown, Donald M. *Vietnam and CORDS: Interagency Lessons for Iraq*. Fort Leavenworth, KS: School for Advanced Military Studies, 2008, 14–35.

Collins, James L. *Vietnam Studies: The Development and Training of the South Vietnamese Army, 1950–1972*. Washington, D.C.: Department of the Army, 1991, 68–122.

Counterinsurgency Advisory and Assistance Team Special Report. "Partnering: a Counterinsurgency Imperative." *Small Wars Journal*, 22 November (2010): 4–8.

Fox, J. and Dana Stowell. "Professional Army Advisors: a Way Ahead." *Infantry Bugler*, Winter (2007): 8–13.

Grdovic, Mark. "The Advisory Challenge." *Special Warfare* 21 (2008): 22–28.

Heatherington, Richard H. "Foreign Military Advisor Proficiency: The Need for Screening, Selection, and Qualification." Master Thesis, U.S. Army Command and General Staff College, 2009: 62–73.

Hoffman, Frank A. "New Principle of War: Understanding Must Take its Rightful Place. *Armed Forces Journal*, February (2012): www.armedforcesjournal.com/2012/02/8893629.

Helmer, Daniel. "Twelve Urgent Steps for the Advisor Mission in Afghanistan." *Military Review*, July-August (2008): 73–81.

Metrinko, Michael J. *The American Military Advisor: Dealing With Senior Foreign Officials in the Islamic World*. Carlisle, PA: Strategic Studies Institute, 2008.

Nagl, John A. "Institutionalizing Adaptation: It's Time for an Army Advisor Command." *Military Review* September-October (2008): 21–26.

Kilner, Peter. "The Five Most Relevant Leader Attributes." *ARMY* January (2012): 57–60.

Nelson, Carl. *The Advisors*. Chula Vista, CA: New Century Press, 1999.

Ramsey, Robert D. *Advising Indigenous Forces: American Advisors in Korea, Vietnam, and El Salvador*. Fort Leavenworth, KS: Combat Studies Institute Press, 2006.

Silinsky, Mark. "An Irony of War: Human Development as Warfare in Afghanistan." *Colloquium* 3 (2010): 1–16.

Five

Donovan's Dozens

Rules for Counterinsurgency

Lists of rules for advising foreign forces are not rare. T.E. Lawrence, the famous Lawrence of Arabia, had his "Twenty-seven Articles" published in the *Arab Bulletin* in 1917. Over the years others have posted their own lists of rules in a variety military book, journals, and other publications. The "rules" are not literally rules as in a set of explicit regulations; they are short statements of advice the writers have found useful in their own experience. Those experiences include counterinsurgency, but counterinsurgency is such a complex mix of diplomatic and military endeavors that any one list of rules to cover all the major issues involved becomes too cumbersome to be useful.

What follows are four separate lists of twelve "rules" for counterinsurgency. The first is a list of rules relevant to the design and manning of counterinsurgency programs, the second is a list of rules directed at the advisors who carry out the program, the third is a list specifically addressing advisor relationships with counterparts, and the fourth is a list of twelve cultural factors that can affect counterinsurgency programs. The lists come from my own experiences, many of which agree with the experiences and comments of others who have operated in a variety of countries from Latin America, Southeast Asia, Central Asia, and the Middle East. The references for helpful writings by others are included at the end of this chapter.

The following lists contain rules or warnings that generally apply to counterinsurgency programs and counterinsurgency advisors no matter where their location or what their environment. Some of the rules may seem a rehash of points covered in previous chapters, but it is those points that make the rule. The lists are constructed to be useful to those planning counterinsurgency programs, whether military or civilian, and to advisors actually doing counterinsurgency in the field. Importantly, they are also for the general reader who wants to be informed about the complex business of counterinsurgency.

Twelve Rules for Counterinsurgency Programs

Establishing standard procedures for counterinsurgency is difficult because no two counterinsurgency situations are exactly alike. Insurgencies occur under different political circumstances, in different cultures, and across different terrains. Those characteristics can dictate specific approaches to achieve success, but as stated earlier success has not been a hallmark of American counterinsurgency programs. That gives a hint of the difficulties that underlie those programs and suggests that they should not be entered into without sober appraisal. To that end, foreign policy guidelines of the United States should include a statement of the conditions under which the U.S. will commit to a counterinsurgency partnership. Absent emergency circumstances, only after those conditions have been met should a counterinsurgency endeavor be agreed to. The details of each program will have to be designed for the specific counterinsurgency environment involved; nevertheless, the following twelve rules for counterinsurgency programs are important. No one of them being absent will guarantee program failure, but all of them being present will maximize the chances of success.

Program Rule 1. Counterinsurgency programs should be joint military-civilian efforts under central management. They should conduct a coordinated program aimed at expanding security, improving development, and inducing government reform. This includes having development programs and civic action projects available all the way down to the small military advisory teams that may be assigned to specific villages. Monitoring program activities and follow-through on activities initiated are important lest corruption, laxity, or over-reaching (too much too soon) undermine the operation. The joint activity of military and civilian agencies can be complex and have many moving, often competing parts. The unified command is necessary to maximize efficiency. Both military and civilian arms of the effort can benefit from training, perhaps together, on how to achieve it.

Program Rule 2. The security, development, and reform aspects of the program should engage the population in actual activity, not just inert acquiescence. The program should not be seeking to only "pacify" the people, i.e. keep them quiet, but to win their loyalty by convincing them that they have a true and lasting stake in the preservation of their government.

Program Rule 3. The U.S. should harbor no illusions about the host nation or the adaptability of its security forces. An unbiased reporting of that country's strengths and weaknesses should be given a hearing that is equally unbiased. Likewise, the insurgent forces and their motivation should be given an objective evaluation. Absent extreme national security concerns a counterinsurgency program should not be entered into unless a proposed program has a reasonable chance of success given the costs the U.S. is willing to pay. Connected to that, no counterinsurgency partner should be allowed to believe that an alliance with the Unites States will present it with an open, bottomless cashbox. That impression has too commonly taken root in the past. Further, the U.S. cannot condone conduct by the host-nation forces (let alone its own forces) that ignores the international rules of war regarding combatants, non-combatants, and prisoners. This can be a difficult issue for isolated advisors to deal with, so when violations are reported, it is important that they be investigated and castigated by high authorities in the host nation chain of command.

Lesson Learned: You Can't Assume the Indigenous Troops or Their Officers Will Follow Western Military Ethics or Change Their Behavior When You Protest

First Lieutenant Richard M. Stanley, team leader, MAT I-11; Que Son District, Quang Nam Province (MACV Advisory Team 15), I Corps Tactical Zone; 1969.

Sometime in August 1969 it became obvious to me that the soldiers in our local units (nationally organized, regulated militias) were executing enemy guerrillas and soldiers taken prisoner. Previously, the executions had taken place away from my team's immediate vicinity, so it was hard to tell

Counterinsurgency

Lieutenant Stanley resting during an operation in Quang Nam Province, 1969.

what was going on. Had the enemy been killed resisting capture, trying to escape, or had they simply been executed?

Aside from the fact that the enemy deaths were happening away from us, our understanding of what was going on was hampered by language differences. Neither my teammates nor I were able to speak more than a little Vietnamese and our counterparts spoke very little English. Our interpreter was of little help. We had him only a short time because he deserted, but even while we had him he was reluctant to interpret directly for us when we tried to address the execution issue with the militia officers. In fact, he argued that it was not his place to discuss such matters and I'm not sure he ever interpreted accurately on the issue.

In any case, in August I was on an operation with my unit when a guerrilla fighter was taken prisoner. Being nearby, I saw him brought into the headquarters section of our battle column. After some sort of discussion with the unit commander, a soldier simply executed him. I saw it and knew the execution had to be with the officer's agreement, if not his instruction. The prisoner was not resisting in any way. I ran over to protest, but the militia

Five. Donovan's Dozens

officer acted as if I were making a fuss over nothing. To him, executing prisoners was clearly no big deal.

I reported the situation in writing to my District Senior Advisor, who was far enough away through hostile territory that we seldom saw him. The communications between the district team and my MAT were limited to coded radio reports or land mail exchanged through team intermediaries at some midway point. Especially to a written report of this nature, I expected a response. None came.

Concern about the executions ran throughout my team. We discussed my going over the DSA's head to province headquarters, but with the difficulties of distance, time, communication, and the absence of standard reporting protocols I never took the step. If I reported it, I wondered, would anybody listen; if anyone listened, would they believe me; if they believed me, would any meaningful action be taken; if action was taken would it remedy the problem, and so on. Having all those questions convinced me that I should put my attention to problems I had a better handle on. Unfortunately, despite our objections locally, the executions continued.

That is not a pretty recollection. When I was able to stand away from the strains of war and all the problems we faced at any given moment, I could look back and think I should have gone over my DSA's head. I should have made a report to province headquarters and if that didn't work, take it on up to MACV headquarters. Maybe nothing would have been done, but at least I would have felt that my hands were cleaner.

My team and I never found a solution to our counterparts' insistence on executing prisoners. It seemed to happen once or twice a month, usually within minutes of their capture and before any American advisor could intervene. We would protest that this was unethical, it was against the Geneva Rules, it was counterproductive, but the protests did no good. Finally, I realized that the real problem was that my team and I were coming at the issue from an ethical tradition not deeply shared by our counterparts. Their cultural background was different from ours, and to the degree that background instilled a respect for the rights of prisoners, that respect had been worn away by years of war.

American advisors of today can show up in any counterinsurgency conflict around the world and find themselves in similar situations. Certain values that are strongly held in the western, largely European based culture *of the U.S. may not be so strongly held in another culture. Once the hot action begins a counterpart may act more in accordance with his own historical traditions rather than with any ethical values he supposedly shares with his counterpart. I would say now, do not be surprised at bad events; but on the other hand, do not be silent about them.*

Richard Stanley is a retried newspaper reporter and editor now living in Austin, Texas.

Program Rule 4. Once committed to, the program must avoid the "Saigon Syndrome," that condition where the strong allow themselves to be dragged down by the weak. Especially when U.S. human and economic resources are put at significant risk the counterinsurgency program should insure that the host government adheres to its promises of performance. It should be made clear from the beginning that the U.S. has a credible exit strategy and will use it if the partner consistently fails to perform. Absent this understanding, the host nation can come to see the United States' entering into a partnership as an open-ended commitment to sustain it. That idea deemphasizes the host nation's need to work hard, to improve, and to stand alone. It can blur their understanding that from the American perspective there is an end to their deserving further assistance.

U. S. policy makers should keep an eye out for the signs of that end approaching. Further, an American public educated about the requirements and limits of counterinsurgency should be supportive of termination when the signs of that end remain persistently clear. It will be all too easy to characterize that ending as abandonment. Yes, should that end come people, ideas, and hopes will have to be left behind; but at the level of a national policy it is not abandonment, it is cessation of an effort in which the U.S. has found itself with a friend unwilling to institute reforms and unable to fulfill its responsibilities in a way that allows continuation.

Program Rule 5. Counterinsurgency program personnel should be qualified for the job by special training that goes beyond that given for advising conventional forces. The U.S. Special Forces have always had this type of training and have had a specific role in selected counterinsurgency operations as well as other special warfare situations; however, given the current "small war" environment it needs to be recognized that counterinsurgency is a form of special warfare requiring a broader approach than can be met by Special Forces, alone. Specific counterinsurgency advisor training should transmit a vision of general counterinsurgency methods and objectives, the goals of any specific counterinsurgency program, the how-to-dos and what-not-to-dos to achieve those goals, language and cultural development, and refreshers on a variety of combat skills and field expedient techniques necessary to the task. That training should be required for advisory assignments in counterinsurgency and should be sufficiently rigorous to lend prestige to its graduates.

Program Rule 6. Advisors in the counterinsurgency program should be selected, not simply assigned. They should be professionally competent in a needed field of expertise, temperamentally fit to handle the stresses involved, and physically fit to handle sustained operations under difficult circumstances. The key personal characteristics needed in an advisor are tact, patience, emotional stability, self-sufficiency and self-discipline. Civilian contract personnel should not be used for military purposes in counterinsurgency. They are mercenaries, and since counterinsurgency advisors stand as representatives of the American government, mercenaries are inappropriate.

Program Rule 7. Counterinsurgency program advisors should be language qualified, at least at the level of being able to engage in the simple formalities of polite conversation, to give and take simple directions, and to understand and use the vocabulary relevant to a military or civilian specialty. There is no skill more helpful for winning a people's acceptance than being able to speak their language, even at a basic level.

Program Rule 8. Counterinsurgency program personnel in isolated geographic locations are also isolated culturally and emotionally. This induces more stress on advisors than is often appreciated and should be alleviated by increased opportunities for either in-country or out-of-country periods of rest and recuperation.

Program Rule 9. Military advisors in a counterinsurgency program should live, work, and fight with the indigenous units they advise. For that reason, advisors should function primarily with their assigned unit and not have responsibilities with multiple units at the same time or with multiple echelons of the same unit.

Program Rule 10. Given the nature of their assignment, counterinsurgency advisors are also intelligence collectors. This should be the clear duty of all advisors and any conventional U.S. forces in theater should know that role. The counterinsurgency program should include a formalized method of collecting relevant, current information from advisors and for disseminating it to others inside the counterinsurgency operation and to relevant conventional U.S. or allied forces. Intelligence collection can be in the form of questionnaires designed for data quantification and statistical analysis, but such methods can miss the "smell" of the place, the things that are going on but not being remarked upon. Avenues for reporting qualitative information outside of designed questionnaires should always be open.

Program Rule 11. Counterinsurgency advisors should be assigned to teams and deployed as teams rather than as individual replacements rotating on and off teams already in country. This approach provides a greater consistency of effort over longer periods of time and maximizes the chances of program progress. Careful attention should be paid to times of team rotations so new teams have an opportunity to overlap with those ending their tours. Naturally, individual losses of various kinds within teams, those due to death, injury, disease, etc., have to be replaced individually.

Program Rule 12. A tour of duty in a counterinsurgency program must be seen as a professional experience that is valued in the military service. Military advising is a form of special warfare, and it has often been seen as a hazard to careers in a service historically focused on conventional ground warfare. This must change.

Twelve Rules for Counterinsurgency Advisors

Advisors are the foot soldiers of counterinsurgency. In doing their job they are often the deepest penetrating representatives of American foreign policy. They can be posted far from the help or influence of other Americans, and to the local people they may become the only representatives of American ideals and power. In that role, advisors often have to function as a combination diplomat, soldier, and aid representative. It is imperative they be suited for the task.

Advisors live with their assigned units or in their assigned villages, they observe their counterparts closely, and they advise them in all circumstances including combat. Individuals involved in military assistance but who live in American cantonments apart from their advised units and who do not accompany their units in combat are not advisors in the full sense of the word, they are trainers. The following twelve rules addressed to advisors may also be useful to trainers, but some may not be relevant.

Advisor Rule 1. Even if you have received training in counterinsurgency you have much to learn. Be humble and to the degree possible use the first weeks on the job for observation and for making a good impression on your counterpart and his subordinates.

Advisor Rule 2. Be prepared for problems and responsibilities typically encountered by officers two ranks above your own. While it may not be the standard according to program planners, lieutenants may find themselves advising a village chief or a battalion commander or captains may advise a district chief or a brigade commander. In such situations youth is not a virtue, so personal bearing and a professional attitude become doubly important. Do not let youthful enthusiasm be interpreted as American arrogance.

Advisor Rule 3. Maintain an appropriate bearing and attitude. If there is any place where surface impressions are important, this is it. Neither uncertainty nor arrogance are rewarded characteristics in an advisor. Neither is frivolity. Wear your uniform or other clothing appropriately. Just as American military insignia, badges, and ribbons have their histories and important ways of wearing, a counterpart's uniform and his native clothing have their histories and ways of wearing. If you adopt some element of your counterpart's uniform or wear elements of indigenous clothing, wear them with appropriate respect and style.

Advisor Rule 4. Know your interpreter and learn from him. Learn about his background and his education. Discover his strengths and weaknesses. Eat with him. Talk with him. Tell him what you want from him. He will not want to appear ignorant or foolish to either you or your counterpart, so encourage him to ask for clarification if he does not understand what you say or what you intend. Remind him that accuracy in translation is important to you and that accuracy must rise above his worry about your potential anger or hurt feelings should you hear something from him you do not like. The interpreter cannot always be present, so work hard at learning the language, use it when possible, and use the interpreter to learn more, especially of the local idioms and manners of speaking.

Advisor Rule 5. Establish and maintain good rapport with your counterpart. This is a complex task requiring constant study. The counterpart's nature, culture, social position, and aspirations for the future all matter in how he conducts himself and, therefore, how you conduct yourself. Building rapport is a key objective, and the process starts on day one.

Lesson Learned: Trust Between Advisors and Counterparts Has to Be Earned—In Both Directions

Captain John B. Haseman, deputy district senior advisor; Mo Cay District, Kien Hoa Province (MACV Advisory Team 88), IV Corps Tactical Zone 1972–1973.

In late 1972 I was the Deputy District Senior Advisor in Mo Cay District, Kien Hoa Province in the Mekong Delta. The district chief had recently been killed in action and my boss, the District Senior Advisor (DSA), had been badly wounded. That left me as Acting DSA at the same time a new district chief was assigned. He was a young Vietnamese army major, and although we met and talked over a period of several days, I still did not feel I had established a personal relationship with him and I had yet to go on any kind of operation with him.

One morning I got word that an ambush had occurred on the main highway between our village and the province capital. There had been casualties. Then I discovered my new district chief had rushed to the scene with a small force. Obviously, he had left me behind, so I grabbed my interpreter and we went after them.

When we arrived at the ambush site the major was surprised to see me. He explained, "I didn't tell you about this because I didn't think you'd want to come out where it would be dangerous." I was astonished at the remark, which made it clear that my district chief did not have much respect for American advisors.

"Sir," I said, "I know I'm only the deputy DSA, but when my boss is away I act in his stead. When you go to the field, I go to the field, danger or not."

The major nodded, but I wanted to make sure he understood me. "Sir, I don't think there's much actual advice I can give you, but I am an extra set

Opposite: Captain Haseman on an operation with his counterpart in Kien Hoa Province, 1972.

Five. Donovan's Dozens

of eyes and ears and hands for you. There are lots of ways I can try to be of assistance." From that time on the district chief and I understood each other on that point and he never left me behind again.

Not too many days later the district chief briefed me on an operation in a dangerous village where contact was expected. My interpreter and I went with him, and in this case I decided to carry my own backpack radio, a PRC-25 that weighed approximately twenty-five pounds. We were well into the operation when suddenly we heard the bam! of a small explosion. One of our soldiers had stepped on a booby-trap, a small mine that had blown his foot off. Minutes later the man was laid out in our tactical command post where anyone could see there was only a bleeding stump where his foot once had been. He had suffered some head wounds, as well. That soldier was in bad shape.

At this time in the war the standard operating procedure for U.S. medical evacuations was that U.S. medivac helicopters would transport American casualties and the Vietnamese military would be responsible for medivac of Vietnamese casualties. The problem on this day was that there were no Vietnamese medivac choppers available. Clearly, if our soldier was not evacuated soon, he would die.

The district chief turned to me. "Can you help?" he asked simply.

My thought was, "Of course," but I wasn't actually so sure.

Using the PRC-25 I was carrying, I called the U.S. tactical operations center in the province capital and requested a U.S. medivac for a Vietnamese casualty. The answer was no, not available. But I knew that a U.S. helicopter had just arrived in an adjacent district transporting a visiting VIP inspection team from Saigon. Getting angry, I demanded the chopper be sent over for our casualty. Response: No can do. My temper raised another notch. I persisted and after a lot of back and forth on the radio, the pilot of the VIP chopper agreed to come over and fly the medivac. With that help we got the wounded soldier to the province hospital in time for him to survive. I was glad for him, but it was hard to feel too good because I knew I was in for an ass chewing the next time I showed up at province headquarters. Making intemperate demands by radio is not an art smiled upon by those who receive the demands.

Then a surprising thing happened. Several days later I had to accompany the district chief to the province capital for a monthly meeting of district *chiefs and DSAs. My chief, knowing I was probably in trouble for the episode with the radio, had without my knowledge already explained the situation to the province chief. When the meeting began the province chief took things in hand and publicly thanked me for my help. That public praise headed off the ass chewing from my province senior advisor and got me a pat on the back instead.*

More importantly, I got a boost in the trust I received from my counterpart. That boost became the basis for a great rapport that developed between us and it was a demonstration to me that trust between counterparts is essential for an effective relationship. I had gained my district chief's trust and respect by showing him that I was willing to go into combat with him and that I was willing to stand up for him when he needed me. In turn, the district chief gained my trust by his actions in the field and by his day-to-day conduct as the district's headman. Our shared feeling of trust and loyalty came as the result of an effort on both our parts; you do not get to trust and loyalty on a one-way street. For advisors to do their jobs well, it is critical that they make the effort to find that solid ground. Once there, the entire advisory experience changes for the better.

John Haseman retried as a colonel from the U.S. Army in 1995. He now writes and speaks on Southeast Asian political-military affairs and resides in Grand Junction, Colorado.

Advisor Rule 6. Take every reasonable opportunity to enhance your counterpart's image before his subordinates. If he is the leader of a military unit, support him as being key to the unit's success; if he is a village or regional leader, support him as being important to the village's or region's future.

Advisor Rule 7. Remember the potentially negative impact of your simply being an American. Despite what may be friendly evidences to the contrary, your acceptance among indigenous people can be on shaky ground and may remain there no matter what you do. Still, your best chance of winning acceptance is to treat your counterpart, his subordinates, and the local people with respect. Your views and attitudes are likely not theirs and they may even be in conflict with some opinions or values they hold dear. Still, respect the people and remember that you have been inserted into their lives, not the other way around.

Advisor Rule 8. Be careful about accepting gifts and favors. Without being rude, try to turn aside offers of them. Accepting a gift or a favor may imply a willingness to give something in return. That might not be a problem if you were living in a context you fully understood; but in a foreign culture the extent of the obligation entailed can be very unclear. It is best to avoid the complication.

Advisor Rule 9. Keep a sense of humor. That does not mean to display levity or a lack of seriousness. Counterparts of virtually any culture appreciate humor, but humor must be applied in culturally appropriate ways, which can sometimes be difficult to judge. Until experience informs you otherwise, it is best to keep display of your humor occasional and directed at yourself or your situation, not at other people.

Advisor Rule 10. Respect indigenous religions. In many environments, religion will be a topic of much comment. If asked, say what you believe but do it without being disrespectful of other views or criticizing other religions. Remember that people can be religious without religiosity. Their faith can be woven through their personality like a thread through a cloth, and in many parts of the world offending that faith can be a grievous error. Be careful.

Advisor Rule 11. Eat the local foods. Food is a part of any culture. To eat it and eat it properly is a powerful signal of your acceptance of the people and their culture; therefore, gird up thy loins. Learn to eat what the indigenous people eat and eat it their way. Learn their manners and be at ease with them. More can be gained over a shared meal than a shared conference table.

Vietnam, 1969

The village my team and I lived in had a single street with houses made of wood planks and bamboo thatch lining each side. Much of the days activities took place in that street. Children played there, men and women chopped their wood for cooking fires there, carpenters hammered and nailed there, and people used it as a public place to mingle with their neighbors. One day a team mate and I were walking from a meeting back to our fort at the end of the street when I saw several children with partial stalks of what I was pretty sure was sugar cane. Sugar cane? I hadn't seen it or even thought about it in Vietnam, but I had grown up in southern Georgia

Five. Donovan's Dozens

where many farmers still grew small patches of it for family use and for making sugar cane syrup.

As a boy I had learned to eat stalks of cane and use a pocket knife to cut a stalk into lengths of several segments then strip off the cane's outer bark to get to the sweet, fibrous pulp inside. You would use your knife to cut the stalk of sweet pulp into small chunks then chew the chunks to release the sweet, tasty cane juice. I remembered it mostly as a children's treat available in the fall of the year because that was when the cane was ready for cutting. I was not aware that the Vietnamese even grew sugar cane, and I when went to Vietnam I hadn't seen a stalk of in years. Certainly, I hadn't noticed it locally.

When I saw the children with the cane segments I stopped to take a closer look. It was sugar cane all right, but instead of using a knife to strip the bark and cut off pieces of pulp, the kids were stripping the bark with their teeth and chewing the pulp without cutting it into small chunks. I was amazed the children could do that, and when they saw my interest, they gathered around to show me how they did it.

One of the children gave me a length of cane and the others along with some adults gathered to see what I would do with it. They all seemed surprised when I took out my knife, cut off a couple of segments from the stalk then quickly stripped the outer bark, cut myself a piece of the pulp, and happily chewed away. I cut off small chunks of cane pulp and handed them out for the children to chew. Both the children and the adults seemed amazed that I knew to do anything like this, not to speak of my teammate who was from Minnesota. He had never seen a stalk of sugar cane in his life!

One of the women in the crowd expressed her surprise and explained that no one had ever seen an Americans chew sugar cane and they didn't think I would know what to do with it. I explained to the adults and kids, all of them now smiling at the American who could chew sugar cane, how I had learned to cut, strip, and chew cane from my mother and father who had done it for my brother and me when we were small. The children all seemed impressed and the adults around nodded approvingly.

The woman said they, too, taught their children how to eat the cane, and from the expressions around the crowd I sensed I had made a connection through that stalk of sugar cane. It had provided an opportunity for each side to share something we had not previously known about each other: We all liked sugar cane. What a simple thing, but the incident was my first *intimation that what you eat and how you eat it can be a big help in making an important personal connection with people who see you as very different from themselves.*

Of course, not all food habits are as easy to adjust to as chewing sugar cane. My teammates and I had already gotten used to the pungent fish sauce, nuoc mam, used at every meal in Vietnam (actually, I had learned to like it) and we had learned that rats, snakes, and turtles were as common a source of meat in the delta as fish, ducks, and chickens. I was doing pretty well with all that, but my gastronomic explorations almost came to a halt one day when my assistant team leader, Lieutenant Rogers, and I were invited to a meal celebrating a local event. One of the main dishes served was shrimp, large Mekong shrimp that had probably been netted just that morning. The shrimp had been boiled or steamed intact and I saw that people were picking them up with their hands to shell them. Well, down on the American Gulf coast, we do that, too, so I picked up a big shrimp, broke the tail from the abdominal carapace with the head and antennae on it, shelled the tail, dipped it in the fish sauce, and ate it. I thought I had done well, but, apparently, not quite.

My host grinned and picked up the shrimp's carapace, which included the head, legs, and abdominal contents enclosed in the carapace shell. The host said I was missing the best part, and to demonstrate what to do he put the carapace to his mouth and sucked out the shrimp guts with a big slurp. He nodded in gustatory approval, smiled, and politely placed another shrimp atop my rice bowl. I looked up and saw another guy do the big slurp with a shrimp head and I realized others were watching to see if I would do likewise. I had never heard of sucking shrimp guts before, would never have thought of it, and wouldn't have tried it if I had thought of it. Still, it looked like I was going to have to give it a go even if sucking the innards out of a shrimp did not strike me as a great idea. Was the taste going to be awful? Was I going to be able to do it without embarrassing my host ... or me?

I broke the tail off the shrimp, shelled it like before and ate it. Then I picked up the head end of the shrimp and hoping for the best, made a big, noisy suck against the hard carapace. Whatever came into my mouth, and I chose not to think about that, was a pulse of very shrimpy flavor. To my surprise, it was actually quite good. I said so to our host and all around the table men nodded and smiled. Then they turned to watch as it came Lieu-

tenant Rogers' turn. He did as I had and passed the test. I could tell that both of us had made a step forward in being accepted by showing evidence of being accepting ourselves. We had eaten their food their way while some might have thought we would refuse.

We had not. Instead, I had learned a way to get more enjoyment from a single shrimp than I had before and I soon had the necessary shrimp-eating skills down pat. Eating those men's food with them and eating it their way gave us a sense of having something in common, a sense that we were a little less separated than we had thought ourselves before. That episode further convinced me that eating another people's food their way is one of the best routes to be accepted into their lives.

Advisor Rule 12. Know from whence you come. Just as it is important for you to know the history of the country, tribes, and religion(s) where you serve, it is important that you know the history of your own country, family, and religion. You are unlikely be drilled on the details of the U.S. Constitution, but you may be asked where you and your family come from and how you got where you are today. Knowing that history in broad strokes and the basic features of American history and American cultural development can prove helpful in rapport building. You may be asked about George Washington or, more likely, Lady Gaga. You might be asked if you have seen the Grand Canyon or a NASA spaceship, or you might be asked to explain the American policy on Israel or something as arcane as the Falkland Islands. Be aware, and whatever the case, engage people through their curiosities. You are the representative of America; what you know of it may be all some stranger ever learns.

Lesson Learned: It Is Important to Capitalize on American Technological Advantages.

First Lieutenant Daniel P. Reimer, team leader, MAT II-35; Dahm Rahn District, Tuyen Duc Province (MACV Advisory Team 26), II Corps Tactical Zone; 1971.

Within the world of military missions, being an advisor is a varsity assignment. Aside from the rigors and tensions of combat you work extremely hard to develop a mutually trusting relationship with your coun-

Counterinsurgency

Lieutenant Reimer next to a dug-in bunker in Tuyen Duc Province, 1971.

terpart. First, there is the issue of language, of being certain that you are being understood, and that your intent is not being clouded by some nuance missed in translation. Then there are the cultural differences that can make even simple social exchanges exhausting because you must constantly be on guard against the inadvertent offense.

Advisors have all the standard responsibilities that come with command. For example, you must develop the mission and communicate it to the troops in your unit. In the best of all worlds that is done in collaboration with the unit's leaders, but the fact is that you can find that responsibility dumped on your shoulders. You must be sure the mission is completely understood up and down your chain of command and that all logistical matters and support components are in place. You must insure that you and your team are all giving the same message and that your counterpart and his soldiers are all hearing it correctly. Your communication with them must be clear while avoiding the degree of bluntness that will cause offense, especially to your counterpart. This is not simple, which is why the fog of war can gather pretty thickly around a combat advisor.

Five. Donovan's Dozens

To use a sports analogy, imagine yourself the quarterback of your favorite football team. You know where you are on the field and you can see how your opponents have lined up against you. You want to call a sweep left. The ball is going to be carried by your star halfback; but then, suddenly, that halfback and all your offensive linemen turn into smaller, lighter players who play with the inspiration their now poverty-level wages give them. Not only that, but most of them do not speak your language, do not know the play signals, and have not read your playbook. And over on the sidelines is Vince Lombardi (in the advisor's world, that's the American senior advisor at one or two organizational levels above you). He's yelling at you to make this work, goddamn it!

Now what? Let's just say, it can get complicated. With all of that working against him, there is one thing the American advisor can pull from his rucksack that the insurgents typically cannot; he has an impressive array of technology that gets more and more unbelievable as the years go by. True, the enemy may have access to technology, too, but nothing like the variety or amount the U.S. can muster. And I don't mean just lethal technology like smart bombs or drones that fire missiles. It can be something helpful like a smaller, more useful field radio or a large earthmover that can do the day's work of a dozen men in a few minutes.

Another kind of advantage technology can bring to counterinsurgency was made clear to me when I was advising a Montagnard unit in the Central Highlands of Vietnam. My counterpart was the unit's commander. He was a captain in the local forces and, having fought alongside the French in the First Indochina War, had been in combat most of his adult life. He was experienced and had long ago learned how to work with foreign "advisors."

He was a member of the Coho tribe, one of several tribes of indigenous natives or Montagnards who had settled in the Central Highlands centuries ago. Like most Montagnards, he was dark skinned and not at all Asian in appearance. Not only did the Montagnards look different from the main Vietnamese ethnic types, they spoke a different language and had a completely different culture. The men still wore traditional loincloths and hunted with cross bows. The women were often bare breasted and carried their infants in baskets on their backs. The Vietnamese regarded them as unsophisticated savages and discriminated against them aggressively. To an on-looking G.I. they could appear similar in some ways to the American Indians as represented in the seventeen and eighteen hundreds.

One of the ways in which the Vietnamese and Montagnards were similar to each other, however, was the common adoption of a few English or French words to express an idea to an American. Americans, in turn, picked up those words or phrases and used them, as well. "Ti-ti" meant a little; "beaucoup," a lot; "fini," it's over. "Numbah-one" meant the very best; "numbah-ten," the very worst. In a war where there was supposed to be a unified effort against the enemy, this manner of expression was one of the few things the Vietnamese and Montangnards had in common.

One evening my counterpart and I were sitting outside his thatched hut in his village. The village was located about ten kilometers outside Dalat, the capital of Tuyen Duc Province, but for a number of reasons the village was having to be relocated. I had managed to get two Chinook helicopters from the Americans in Dalat to help with the job. Chinooks are the large, twin-rotored helicopters still in use in today. Every person, bag of rice, basket of belongings, jug of rice wine, duck, pig, and goat was going to be loaded into one of the big choppers and airlifted to a more secure location a few clicks away. That transport operation was going to begin at dawn the next day and I was there to help manage it.

My counterpart had been working with Americans all the years they had been in country, starting in the early sixties with the Special Forces. Because of that exposure he had an appreciation for the American's technological capabilities. In combat situations, he had seen many times the power of American air support. He had seen our engineers use backhoes to dig trench-lines within hours that would have taken his soldiers weeks to dig by hand. He had seen so many examples of American technology that it no longer amazed him, but on this clear, moonlit night in the middle of the Annamite Mountains of Vietnam, that was about to change.

As it turned out, our mission to relocate the Montagnard village had coincided with the timing of NASA's second manned moon landing. I knew this from seeing an issue of Stars and Stripes, *the American GI newspaper, so I pointed up to the bright, shining moon and told the captain that at this very minute Americans were up there walking around on the moon. The captain looked up at the moon then back to me. He didn't seem to understand or at least was highly skeptical of what I was saying.*

I had saved the Stars and Stripes *issue; in fact, I had brought it with me, so I pulled it from my pocket, unfolded it, and turned on my flashlight to show* the captain the front-page photo. He looked at the picture of the astronaut in his space suit standing there on the moon's surface. From there he looked up at the moon. Then, his eyes widening in realization, he looked back at the picture then, finally, at me. In a voice laced with amazement he said softly, "America numbah-one."

The captain comprehended in his way. To him the idea that we could put a man on the moon meant that Americans could do just about anything. It cemented his belief in us. My point is, then as now, counterinsurgency may appear to be war with the basic tools only, but that is wrong. We must fully capitalize on the technological advantages we can bring to the effort not only as weaponry but as other forms of technological advancement, as well. They can inspire respect or even awe in our counterparts. Technology demonstrates the American spirit of innovation, our will to explore, and our determination to develop new frontiers. Properly applied, it can not only help us deal with the threats of the insurgency, they can encourage that feeling in our counterparts, America numbah-one.

Dan Reimer is the retired chief financial officer of a large manufacturing firm and currently lives in Rock Hill, South Carolina.

Twelve Rules for Counterpart Relations

Many of the rules advisors should follow touch on establishing and maintaining good counterpart relations. The overarching rule in that sphere is that the advisor should be in continual study of his counterpart's language, culture, religion, and politics. The counterpart will sense the advisor's increasing ability to relate and will see that the advisor is as willing to absorb information as he is willing to provide it. Further, and perhaps more importantly, the advisor's improving his knowledge will help him discern what lies beneath his counterpart's actions, what bothers him in the night and what pleases him in the day. The advisor's success will come as much from his using that sort of information as it will from using the practical knowledge of a military or civilian specialty. The following rules are only tributaries to that main, overarching rule of being in continual study, but they are effect amplifiers and should be put to use.

Relations Rule 1. Practice proper military courtesy to all ranks and observe proper protocol with all civilian officials.

Relations Rule 2. Maintain a close but unobtrusive association with your counterpart. You will need to observe him dealing with all relevant matters and be available to give advice. Even if he needs your advice the most at the most inconvenient time for you, submit it in good spirits. If the counterpart speaks English, remember to speak clearly using basic English in simple sentences. Avoid idiomatic expressions (drunk as a skunk, once in a blue moon, etc.), as they only confuse. Your remembering to make communication as easy as possible will make your presence less of a burden.

Relations Rule 3. When at all possible give your advice in private. In urgent tactical situations this may not be possible, but keeping a cool head when others are excited or uncertain will stand you in good stead.

Relations Rule 4. If your counterpart repeatedly refuses your advice, do not try to force compliance. At its root, the conflict belongs to him. It is his to win or lose and it is he who will live most closely to the consequences. In some cases, your counterpart's way of doing things, while it may be frustrating to you, may work in the local context because it is culturally appropriate and will be useful in the end. Working out the best "best" way of doing things is why being an advisor also requires you to be a diplomat. If problems persist in getting advice accepted, rather than forcing the issue with your counterpart bring pressure to bear from within his chain of command. This means you will have to inform your own superiors and be able to provide evidence of the counterpart's recalcitrance. Let your bosses deal with his bosses.

Lesson Learned: Counterinsurgency Can't Be Forced

First Lieutenant Richard W. Webster, team leader, MAT III-87; Xuan Loc District, Long Khanh Province (MACV Advisor Team 49), III Corps Tactical Zone; 1968–69.

Changing people's way of doing things can require a nuanced approach in many settings, but nuance can take more time than the imaginers of counterinsurgency want to allow. Time is especially important when the people being worked with have managed to survive for years by doing things their way, even if it isn't what the counterinsurgency program wants them to do. The peasant in a warring countryside considers his first goal to be survival for him and his family. Outside observers of an insurgency often do not understand this and do not understand the intensity of fear unprotected villagers

Five. Donovan's Dozens

Lieutenant Webster outside his team house in Long Khan Province, 1968.

sometimes have to live under. Even village militia members, men who have been vetted to some degree, are sometimes afraid to cross the line from being passively involved in a counterinsurgency effort to being actively, aggressively involved. This can especially be true for a villager who wants to cooperate with the Americans but fears being known to do so.

Why is that? First, the peasant will have to ask himself why he should listen to an American who has just arrived on the scene when he, perhaps as a village militiaman, has been fighting the insurgents for years. Second, the peasants may know that once they cross the line to stand with the Americans the line cannot be recrossed. They will be marked by an insurgent enemy about

Counterinsurgency

whom it is likely said, they do not forget. The insurgents' threat will bide its time saying that the insurgency is here to stay while the Americans are here to leave. The peasant in his heart may fear that when the Americans do leave the government will not stand and that a day of reckoning will come for him and his whole family. The victorious enemy will exact revenge. That is the fear the unprotected villager must deal with every night and day.

In the rural areas of a country where for centuries the government has had little influence that kind of threat can be very powerful. It takes time to counteract and counteracting requires proof to the villager that there is something positive he is risking his and his family's lives for. In other words, a counterinsurgency program can come with all sorts of fanfare and promises, but it can only advance if those who feel threatened have time to absorb what the program really means to them, what the risks are, and what its chances of success. Remember, most people are not active in the insurgency and most don't want to be active in counterinsurgency, either. Most just want to be left alone and are going to align themselves with the side that offers them the best chance of survival.

I learned that lesson from one of my first counterparts, a Vietnamese officer commanding a militia company. His aim was to avoid the local enemy forces during the day and to give them free rein in the village at night. I wanted him to find the enemy and fight, but he had adopted a course that seemed best to him and I couldn't budge him from it. I eventually discovered that from his perspective I was being a naïve American.

I suppose I was. What I didn't realize at the time was that my counterpart knew there was a large enemy force, a battalion or maybe a regiment, out there in the jungle waiting to strike. If he provoked them into an attack by being too aggressive, his one company of militia would be overwhelmed, at least that's what he was afraid of. Unfortunately, neither his district chief or province chief would help, so that left the two of us in a tough spot, me urging him to be more aggressive and him getting tired of hearing it.

My team and I were eventually removed from the district because my counterpart started threatening to have me killed. Talk about a failure of rapport! He was avoiding contact and I was pushing him hard to be more aggressive. On my side of the equation my superiors were threatening me with a bad officer evaluation if I didn't get my counterpart to fight. I tried to tell my bosses that I needed time to work with this guy. True, he was no Napoleon, but he needed resources before he could take on the enemy with some hope of success. My superiors were unimpressed and persisted in their demand that I convince my counterpart to be more aggressive. I tried, but that's when he got angry and threatened to have me killed if I didn't back off. Not a good relationship.

My counterpart was afraid of failure. Could he and others like him have changed things for Vietnam if they had been more brave and aggressive? Perhaps. At the time, I was thinking I could help him improve, but the timeline my bosses were dedicated to didn't fit with the reality on the ground, which included, among other things, the fact that our last four village chiefs had been assassinated. It included the fact that the local enemy forces outnumbered the local friendly forces, and it included the fact that every villager had to keep in mind what would likely happen once the Americans were gone. In that kind of environment, things were going to move slowly, if at all.

The planners and prognosticators of counterinsurgency often do their work from nine-to-five in air-conditioned offices, and my experiences had me doubting that those types ever comprehend the pressures the front line advisor has to work under. I doubted they comprehended the fact that down in the villages where we did our work the men we were asking to fight for their government were men who lived with their families. Those men knew that the consequences of war were going to fall on everyone in the village, men, women, and children, if the enemy could make it so.

That had to affect how the village men viewed the war they were being asked to fight. Primarily it made them circumspect about any decision made by their leaders or any action that was to be taken by their unit. Sure, people might speak of target dates and deadlines for various operations or programs, but from the villagers' perspective the war can just seem to go on and on despite anyone's deadlines. Why, he would ask himself, should I be in a hurry for trouble?

That was difficult to deal with, but what I learned was that even if a counterinsurgency program has elements offering hope and encouragement, the people are going to accept them at their own pace. Beyond a certain point, counterinsurgency cannot be pushed. It's like a toy train with its heavy engine up front doing the work. If it gets pushed too hard from the rear, the boxcars will accordion together and the train goes off the tracks. By pushing too hard, the rear-echelon planners can be as deadly to a counterinsurgency program as the enemy; and if they insist that the advisor in the field push his counterpart *too hard to meet target deadlines or objectives, they can expose that advisor to danger not only from the enemy, but from those who are supposed to be his friends. The bottom line is, counterinsurgency cannot be pushed.*

Richard Webster retired from the U.S. Army Reserve as a Major in 1993. After a second career as a Low Vision Specialist he recently retired a second time and now lives in Jacksonville, Illinois.

Relations Rule 5. When your counterpart shows improvement or takes positive action give him praise for it, especially before others. If he has used an idea of yours to good advantage, let the limelight be his. T. E. Lawrence was correct when he said your ideal position is to be present but not noticed. Let your counterpart know that you will share in his failures, but the successes will be his alone.

Relations Rule 6. If you observe your counterpart's orders being disobeyed or ignored by his subordinates, support your counterpart and hold those subordinates accountable before him.

Relations Rule 7. Use your knowledge of your counterpart's political, social, and military systems to put yourself in his shoes and understand his realities. This will help you to properly gauge his actions and his responses to your advice. It may also show you where or when you should modify that advice.

Lesson Learned: Living Close to One's Counterparts and Sharing Their Hardships and Dangers Gives an Advisor Insight into Their Problems and Enhances His Credibility

Lieutenant Kenneth C. Jacobsen, U.S. Navy advisor, River Assault Group (RAG) 32, An Giang Province and River Assault Group (RAG) 31, Vinh Long Province. IV Corps Tactical Zone; 1967–1968.

I was an advisor to Vietnamese Navy units operating along the 5,000 miles of rivers and canals that were the main lines of communications in the Mekong Delta. Our units, so-called River Assault Groups (RAGs), operated with the Vietnamese army in conducting waterborne assault operations. RAGs also conducted naval patrol and interdiction missions, other types of naval

Five. Donovan's Dozens

Lieutenant Jacobsen (right) and another American advisor plan an operation in the Mekong delta, 1967.

operations, and a variety of logistic and humanitarian tasks. The patrol and interdiction missions could last for more than a week at a time, and while no combat vessel is rigged for comfort, living conditions aboard our RAG boats were especially primitive.

Sleeping accommodations were limited on the RAGs' large command boats, and were virtually non-existent on smaller boats. Officers and crewmembers, including the U.S. advisors, usually slept on deck or under jury-rigged awnings. The river was used for toilet functions as well as bathing, and cooking was limited to what could be produced on one or two burner kerosene stoves. The patrol unit was issued an allowance of rice at the beginning of the patrol, and any additions to the meals were bargained for in the local village and paid for out of pocket. In some poorer or more hostile areas the only provisions available consisted of a few wilted vegetables, a piece of fatty pork, and perhaps a fish. Although we RAG advisors were technically required to go on combat operations in pairs, I and other advisors often went on the long patrol operations alone to avoid making the crowded living conditions even worse for the Vietnamese sailors.

The spartan conditions of those patrols contributed to their uneven performance, as did the RAG commander's reluctance to accompany the patrols despite the strong advice that he do so. In the absence of a RAG's commander, the effectiveness of the patrol depended on the energy level of the more junior Vietnamese officer assigned to the patrol, usually a Lieutenant Junior Grade. In those cases, the presence of a U.S. advisor willing to urge more and better patrolling could often make a considerable difference, but the advisor had to be prepared to be persistent and repeat the same message day after day.

Living in the Vietnamese sailor's environment and operating with them in conjunction with Vietnamese army units and their U.S. advisors on the ground, allowed us Navy advisors to communicate with Army advisors, even if only by radio, and show our counterparts by example how the two services can work together more closely than the Vietnamese were prone to do.

My counterpart, a Vietnamese Navy Lieutenant, was particularly skillful at using my contact with other U.S. advisors to channel his requests into the confusing and often politically charged Vietnamese chain of command. It was not unimportant that by going through me he could get his request acted on without losing face or getting himself into trouble. The Advisor's role as a "channel" can sometimes be one of the most useful contributions he can make.

During one period of time other RAG advisors and I lived in an old French villa that had been converted into accommodations for the U.S. Army's Province Advisory Team. The house was about two kilometers from the RAG base on the river, so unless an operation was in progress we essentially went to work in the morning and returned to the house in the evening. That situation limited our contact with our Vietnamese counterparts, took us out of their living situation, and in my opinion prevented us from developing the close working relationship that an advisor in the field needs with his counterparts. Living and working closely with the Vietnamese Navy officers and men while on long patrols helped to establish a relationship, but the considerable difference in our lifestyles once we returned to the RAG base created a barrier that we never quite overcame.

At the base of a second RAG unit I worked with things were considerably *different. All the advisors lived on the Vietnamese base in the same grim style as our counterparts. In the months after the Tet offensive of February '68, which caused considerable damage to the base, many of the sailors, including my counterpart, moved their families from the local town into the limited base housing. The good side of this was that the advisors' living quarters were next to his and on a quiet evening we could share a glass of brandy, play with his children, and talk about our lives outside of work. We lived together, worked together, and when necessary defended the base together. This created a close sense of shared experience and camaraderie and it gave the U.S. Advisors a much better appreciation of the world our Vietnamese counterparts had to live in. It also enhanced our credibility with our counterparts and was a great help in earning their loyalty and respect.*

Kenneth Jacobsen retired from the U.S. Navy with the rank of captain in 1986. He has since worked as a freelance writer, editor, and defense analyst. He currently lives in Charleston, South Carolina.

Relations Rule 8. Do not give verbal advice only. When possible, give your counterpart a draft of your idea or plan on paper. Invite his response. This gives the counterpart early input and your modifying the plan to incorporate his ideas will make the final result "his," not yours. Putting the idea or plan on paper also has the advantage of making a record that can later be called upon as evidence, should it be needed, of a counterpart's inaction or inadequate responses to advice.

Relations Rule 9. When possible, give your counterpart advice in a way that allows him to select options for how to achieve the desired task. Providing only a straight-line, do-it-this-way suggestion may be rejected only because it sounds too much like a dictate. Even when options are presented, you should use interpersonal skills (courtesy, respect, sensitivity to "face," etc.) to make it clear which of the options is preferred.

Relations Rule 10. Learn the art of negotiation in a way that fits your counterpart's culture. In many areas of the world, negotiation is a respected method of finding a way forward whether it be in a market buying fish or in a headquarters planning an operation. In those regions, negotiation is just another way of defining interpersonal relations and each bargain is made or each operation is structured through that process rather than the same goods-same price approach the typical American is used to. Do not think of negotiation as a sign of your weak influence (thinking, why can't this s.o.b. just accept my advice?); rather, think of it as a way to maximize your influence.

Relations Rule 11. Maintain your integrity. The military advisor can be presented with a host of moral and ethical issues requiring difficult decisions, some of them with life or death consequences. Know your ethical standards and hold to them without being preachy about it. In this way, too, you communicate who you are and what you stand for.

Relations Rule 12. Persevere. More can be accomplished with persistence than with flowery speeches or floods of instructions on how to do a task the "right" way. Patience and tact are high value traits in an advisor.

All the above being said, having a good relationship with a counterpart is a mechanism to achieve a goal, not the goal itself. Program success is the goal. Building rapport cannot become a permanent excuse for an advisor's accepting substandard performance from his counterpart. Counterparts are supposed to be leaders, and it has been an unfortunate, consistent feature of American counterinsurgency endeavors that poor outcomes have ultimately been due to indigenous leaders never having learned the meaning of consistent, noncorrupt, positive leadership. This reflects a failure not only of advisor relations to make a meaningful, lasting difference in the quality of indigenous leadership, but a failure of Challenge Three (Understand the host country's manpower needs and resources) in Chapter Three and of Program Rule Four (Avoid the Saigon Syndrome), above.

Twelve Cultural Factors That Affect Counterinsurgency Advising

The objectives of a counterinsurgency program may not be difficult to describe, but attaining those objectives involves cultural factors that are. Those factors, even if an attempt is made to describe them, are often not easy to understand and certainly are not easy to quantify. Still, cultural and social factors, so-called "cross-cultural incongruities," can be stumbling blocks to an otherwise well planned counterinsurgency program. The forewarned are forearmed.

Cultural Factor 1. The indigenous people's dislike for foreigners. In countries with a significant number of foreign soldiers on their soil, especially in a war setting, most of the indigenous population wants the outlanders gone. Remember this: they do not want you here! The people's politeness may have them hide this feeling most of the time, but it is true, nevertheless. In some countries, this is due to an ingrained xenophobia or hostility towards any kind of foreigner even if they come bearing gifts and promises of a better life. The long histories of Britain and France, let alone the United States, in dozens of places around the world over the last two centuries have shown that in almost any country people prefer to bear the vices of their own rulers than have the virtues of foreigners imposed upon them. The former are at least their own, the latter are intrusions. From the elevated, self-confident view of functioning democracies with their material benefits evident, this attitude may seem a rather rude response to beneficence, but it is true, nonetheless. The virtues of foreigners are usually accompanied by the foreigners' vices, which will be as evident to the native as the native's are to the foreigner. In that way, choosing whose vices are worse becomes a matter of perspective.

Evidence of this kind of ingrained hostility to foreign authority, even when that authority is by its own lights trying to be constructive, has been prevalent formerly in Iraq and presently in Afghanistan. Xenophobic zealots have found it easy to inflame the people and foment violent demonstrations against the Americans or other foreigners at the hearing of some wrong done, real or imagined. To those crowds in those moments of released rage, the foreigners' sacrifices for them are unimportant. The highways laid, the schools built, the clinics opened don't matter. The lives lost in fighting their oppressors don't matter. Deep inside themselves, the native people don't like the foreigners being among them, especially in large numbers. They want them gone; thus, their animosity is always alert, lurking in the shadows awaiting the prick that will turn animosity into rage.

Vietnam, 1969.

I had injured my foot, so I had been brought back to province headquarters for a couple of weeks to run the American side of the province's Tactical Operating Center (TOC) while the usual TOC officer was on leave. I was given a bunk in the province team's compound, a nice place relative to my usual lodgings out with my team. The province team's compound housed between two-and three hundred Americans, had electricity, billets, a mess hall, a volleyball court, green grass always in trim, a large covered patio where movies were shown at night, and a small club where enlisted and officer personnel alike could get a drink after duty. The greatest thing about the club was that it was air conditioned. It was an island of cool in a sea of muggy heat, so in the evenings, if you weren't on duty, it was a place you wanted to be. You could chat with friends, join in a song, or play a game of cards, anything to be distracted from the daily pressures of a war zone.

A Vietnamese contingent also lived in the province team's large, walled compound. They were a Vietnamese Special Forces company garrisoned there to help provide security. They had their own barracks on one side of the enclosure, and they had their own officers and NCOs who interacted with those of ours in charge of running and maintaining the compound. They were not our advisees, not formally our counterparts; from what I could see they were more a part of "the help," those Vietnamese from maids to gate guards who were necessary in keeping the compound safe and in good repair. The difference was that the maids, kitchen staff, and other workers all went home at the end of the day. The soldiers went nowhere. Their barracks were inside the compound with us and that brought a real problem to the fore.

The problem was that the Vietnamese were not allowed in the province team's club. With all advisor activities there was the legitimate concern that infiltrators might have gotten into our units and even be among the government authorities we were working with (see Col. Mullen's Lesson Learned in Cultural Factor 12, below). That was one reason we had a rule out on my MAT that at least one team member had to be awake and on site twenty-four hours a day. It was also why here in the province team's compound similar rules applied despite the heavier security provided by paid civilian guards and the Vietnamese Special Forces. The caution about the danger from possible infiltrators plus the fact that the Americans wanted a place to relax without having to worry about counterpart relations and counterpart interpretations of what was commented on or joked about meant that a rule had been set some time in the past: No Vietnamese allowed in the province team's club.

To be fair, not many Vietnamese had any reason to know about the rule because not many had any reason to be inside the province team compound after the usual workday hours, which was when the club was open. If any

Five. Donovan's Dozens

counterparts knew about the rule, the sophisticated ones might have understood the reason for it, but even for them it must have been some level of irritant. For the unsophisticated who knew of it, it was doubtless an offense, and to the Vietnamese soldiers living in the compound with us, those helping provide our security, it was the kind of ever-present affront that could intensify any underlying animosity. Built up over time, that animosity could turn to loathing and cause a reaction that we Americans would see as being all out of proportion to the problem.

One evening after finishing a day at the TOC I had gone to the club after dinner at the mess hall. I had a couple of beers with some friends, but after an hour or so I said good night intending to go on back to my room. One good thing about being in the province team's compound was that you could usually get a good night's sleep, and I planned to take advantage of it while I could. I walked toward the club's entrance and was reaching for the front door handle when the door suddenly burst open. A fiery-eyed Vietnamese man charged through yelling angrily and wielding an M16 assault rifle. He slammed into me, the M16 raised to his chest. Shocked, I grabbed at him more by reflex than thought. One hand grabbed at the man's back, the other gripped his M16 as I pulled him backward going with his momentum. We crashed to the floor, he on top of me and my left hand desperately grabbing for his right trigger hand. Suddenly, someone grabbed the rifle's barrel and jerked it away. Others quickly grabbed the man, pulled him off me, and pinned him to the floor with him still yelling angrily in Vietnamese.

It turned out he was one of the Vietnamese Special Forces soldiers in the compound, so his company commander was called. The commander came and listened to what had happened. He was clearly embarrassed and soon had the man hauled away under armed guard. He gave his apologies to the senior American officer present then he, too, went away; but the episode was not over. Within the hour the commander had his entire company standing in formation under the compound's lights where everyone could see. I had heard the barking of orders from my room, so I went out to see what was going on.

The company commander had been humiliated by his soldier's act and in his perception had suffered a loss of face. Now he had the offending soldier standing at attention in front of his company. The commander berated the man loudly in front of the ranks. He even slapped the man a time or two *and made a great exhibition of questioning him and condemning him for what he had done. Clearly, the commander's loss of face was being passed on to the offending soldier. In the process, the commander was making the point to his unit and to any watching Americans that his soldier's breech of discipline was not something he was going to tolerate. The public display of correction was the commander's way of gaining face, and even though I never learned what happened to the soldier, I suspect the commander meant what he said.*

The next day I heard from the American officer in charge of compound security what the story was. The soldier had apparently resented Americans for a long time and had felt especially offended that there was an air conditioned club in the compound where the Americans could go but he could not simply because he was Vietnamese. This was his country. The Americans were supposed to be his allies. Yet, here he was excluded from their club because he was Vietnamese.

This is not right, the man felt, and while he was an anti-communist, he had grown to despise the Americans for the offense of exclusion and a hundred other offenses he had either seen, heard of, or had experienced himself. Finally, with his resentments built up over many years, something had set him off. Indignation had flooded out from a deep well where it had pooled in his heated mind and fueled a rage. He had grabbed his rifle and set out for the offending club with the intention of asserting his right to be there. That included shooting up the place to make the point and if that meant killing some Americans, so be it.

If the soldier hadn't bumped into me as he had come through the door, he might have accomplished his mission; but whoever had grabbed the rifle away had been the savior of the moment and had prevented what could have been a real tragedy. Not a tragedy caused by enemy action, but a tragedy caused by Americans being despised by one of their allies. Already, I knew he was not alone.

The kind of hostility evident in that anecdote, the kind that can underlie an indigenous people's friendly relations with foreigners, is too often amplified by the truly bad behavior of foreign soldiers (see the formerly described incident with the bicycle; worse, think of Abu Ghraib). When that happens a situation already difficult can rapidly become dangerous. American advisors have to be aware of the problem and realize that relatively few of their counterparts have truly positive feelings toward them. Politeness, either as a façade or as the result of some depth of true appreciation, can hide the underlying fact that, really, they want you gone, and that feeling is likely amplified in the general population. This is a truth that can be uncomfortable to acknowledge on either side. Americans are brought up to think of that Sesame Street world where all cultures are equal, tolerant, and inclusive. A villager in an underdeveloped country, friendly or not, is unlikely to believe that for one minute; and any experienced American soon knows it isn't true, either. Inequality, intolerance, and exclusivity put a dissonance between the helper and the helped that can rise to a resentment embarrassing to acknowledge. In fact, it rarely is in plain English. Still, that underlying emotion of I-wish-you-gone, held by "friendlies," whether official counterparts or native villagers, is a problem that each advisor has to face every moment of every day. It is why an advisor's persistence in duty, discipline, and decorum are so important.

Cultural Factor 2. An inattentiveness to time and the related attitude of fatalism. To Americans and most other westerners time is viewed as a linear, one-way experience. An opportunity lost will not come again. Further, to take advantage of opportunity, personal action is required. It is the individual's responsibility to act. Those are not the habits engrained by all cultures. In some, time is thought of as cyclical rather than linear; an opportunity passed will come by again sooner or later, and if it doesn't there is nothing the individual can do about it. Fate is more important than personal initiative. Whatever God or the stars ordain will happen; the individual's actions are not important. This influence can embed the *mañana* (tomorrow), *insha'allah* (if God wills it), or *lat nua* (by and by) attitudes deep within a culture where they reside with an influence much more complex than simple laziness, irresponsibility or indifference to the future. Rather, they are a force responding to deep cultural concerns shaped by centuries of experience in a particular place and a particular environment. It may be true that those concerns are inconsistent with modernity or societal advancement, but that may be irrelevant to the people an advisor has to deal with.

Cultural Factor 3. The importance of taboos and rituals. Even though taboo and ritual form some part of virtually every religion and culture, most Americans view strict adherence to them as superstition or cultural backwardness. Nevertheless, in some cultures those taboos and rituals are deeply embedded and respected. The beliefs and practices reflect ancient traditions, and to ignore them will put stumbling blocks in the advisor's way. To actually disparage them can not only be foolish, it can be dangerous. Certainly, it can interfere with the advisory mission.

Cultural Factor 4. The relationship of the leader to the led. In the American system, especially in the military, leadership is idealized as being about the leader's sense of obligation to his or her subordinates and the leader's personal responsibility for the task at hand. In other cultures, the leader may be in his position because of familial, political, or religious ties. The practice in that system may be that the leader's subordinates, whether they are in a military unit, a religious group, or a political department, are there to serve the leader rather than the other way around. That concept of leadership can make a counterpart relatively indifferent to an American's advice about what his unit ought to be doing or how the counterpart ought to be going out of his way to improve his unit. The belief that the leader is he-who-must-be-served can be a difficult practice to turn around, but patient advice and the example of positive leadership given by the advisor have the best chance of making changes.

Cultural Factor 5. The concept of "face" or "saving face." "Face" is the social posture of never causing a person embarrassment in front of others. It is a social courtesy that exists to some degree virtually everywhere, but only outside European-based cultures does it become so intense as to receive a name. Saving face, avoiding embarrassment, may be simple to describe, but it can be difficult to manage in the stress situations advisors often operate under. It is important to remember that face is about more than embarrassment; it is about power, position, and the perception of who has them and who does not.

In many developing countries, people who turn up in leadership positions get there, as mentioned previously, because of political, tribal, or family connections, not because of merit. Still others believe that their religious background gives them the mandate of heaven. In any of those cases, a loss of face, especially when caused by a total outsider, can be felt as an insult not just to the individual, but to the cultural, religious, or political system that put them there. An American advisor who sees multiple issues he believes need addressing quickly will need face-saving techniques that allow him to offer advice in a way that stimulates action without causing his counterpart embarrassment.

Lesson Learned: Always Be Learning

First Lieutenant Tucker Smallwood, team leader, MAT IV-36; Binh Chanh District, Gia Dinh Province (MACV Advisor Team 44), IV Corps Tactical Zone; 1969.

The ability to communicate in the local language is an important tool in an advisor's skill set. I was fortunate because after advisor training at the Special Warfare School and a Vietnamese language course provided by Uncle Sam, I'd become relatively fluent in Vietnamese. I was able to communicate easily with the Vietnamese people I encountered in local villages and with the militia units I advised. My language ability was critical to the rapport I was able to establish with my counterpart and fundamental to the relationship my teammates and I enjoyed with the soldiers we advised. We not only spoke with those soldiers, we lived with them, drank with them, trained them, and operated with them. All of that is to say that language proficiency provided me a way to reach people and to appreciate their culture and traditions. Communication is fundamental to being an effective advisor.

I had a very close working relationship and friendship with my counterpart, the commander of our local militia unit. Late one afternoon, he accompanied me on a trip to a distant U.S. signals installation where we intended to scrounge for supplies. Our home base was in a "VC-contested area," meaning the enemy and their sympathizers were always around us. My base could only be reached by boat or helicopter. To get to the signals station, we first had to travel by boat to a bridge several kilometers away then take a jeep the rest of the way. At the signals station, we scrounged what supplies we could then started driving back to the bridge.

At a certain point, we came to a stretch of heavy civilian traffic going in both directions: Foot traffic, mopeds, cars, busses, trucks, and animals. One moped in particular seemed bent on engaging us, driving ahead, falling behind, cutting in and out of traffic, and generally being annoying. At some point, the moped driver (there was also a passenger) cut in front of us from the right, braked hard, then went down in front of us. It seemed deliberate

Lieutenant Smallwood with his counterpart on an operation in Gia Dinh Province in 1969.

to me, but there had been a light bump of contact, so we stopped to assess the damage.

My counterpart and I got out of the jeep, both of us armed and ready in case this was an ambush. I listened intently as the driver began wailing to my counterpart about his loss. Neither he nor his rider had been injured

Five. Donovan's Dozens

and the damage to his bike was a broken taillight and a dented fender. As small crowd began to gather around us the man's wailings increased and I became convinced he was trying to shake us down. I was an American and I knew we are handy targets for that kind of thing. It was a hot day like most days in the Mekong Delta and I was impatient to get on our way, not only for safety's sake, but I had work to do back home and a night patrol to prepare for. It didn't take long for me to lose patience with this man's attempt at extortion.

Because I spoke Vietnamese, I understood all that was being said. Clearly, our "victim" didn't know that. Finally, I spoke up and when I did I spoke pointedly and as clearly as I could. I told him that his conduct was not honorable, that he had caused the accident and was refusing to take responsibility for his own actions.

My speaking to him at all shocked him, but more that than, what I had said embarrassed him. Venting my frustrations, I told the man that I would treat him like I would someone not really a man, someone who had to be cared for, like a child or a woman. Then I offered him a few hundred piasters (perhaps five dollars or less in value) and bluntly advised him to take it.

The man went silent, but so did the small crowd around us. I heard my counterpart switch off the safety on his M-16. I did likewise, realizing this might be a set up for an ambush, rather than just this guy trying to rip us off. Clearly the atmosphere had suddenly changed in a negative way.

The man grudgingly accepted the money and my counterpart and I drove away, both of us still alert for something else to happen. Nothing did. We reached the bridge without incident and returned the rest of the way to our base by boat. On the way, my counterpart and I talked about what had happened. Basically, we talked about "face."

I knew already that face is an Asian concept involving respect, either having it or losing it. Face is an important consideration in all social interactions and must not be forgotten out of carelessness. For a westerner, such an unfamiliar concept must be consciously thought about and constantly referred to. I had not done that.

I had been convinced that the moped driver had tried to rip us off. Yes, he'd gotten his few piasters, but I had become angry; I had belittled him in front of others. I had caused him to "lose face," something that was deeply offensive to him, no doubt, but was embarrassing to the villagers looking on, as well. From the standpoint of "winning the hearts and minds," I had not done things the right way. My anger had made it all too easy for onlookers to conclude that I, the big American, was a pushy, ham-handed clod abusing one of their own, even if he might have brought his problems on himself.

Culturally speaking I had been a bull in a china shop. I knew that issues like saving face needed to be handled correctly, even in difficult circumstances, but I had let my anger and impatience push aside my intention to live within the local customs. At the time, I had considered myself culturally adept; I had had been exposed to foreign languages and cultures from an early age and had even lived in Europe for five years. I truly respected the Vietnamese culture, but none of that prevented me from doing damage that day; damage to that man, to be sure, but in the eyes of the villagers, damage to myself and the American advisory effort.

My counterpart, a good guy, talked me through it all and I learned from the experience. It took some reflection, but I had learned in a personal way that a westerner's impatience played out before an audience of rural villagers in a foreign country, particularly those in the Mideast and Asia, can undermine a lot of good work. They say classrooms explain, but experience teaches. An advisor has to be able to learn from his experiences. He needs to have an open mind that can absorb new information and process it in a way that informs his behavior. His reactions cannot always be those he might employ in his own culture. An advisor's success, even his life, depends on the ability to learn and adapt. A salesman's mantra is said to be ABC–Always Be Closing. An advisors mantra should be ABL—Always Be Learning.

Tucker Smallwood is now an actor and author. He is presently engaged in veteran advocacy and lives in Los Angeles, California.

Cultural Factor 6. The relative indifference to the suffering of others. The requirements of daily life in poor societies, especially in those with subsistence economies, can develop a culture where attention has to be focused on the survival of the individual and his family. An extended layer of concern may cover his village, but beyond that, the suffering of others becomes too ephemeral to have much impact. The actors are too far away, their stage too unknown, and their story too irrelevant to that local person's focus on simple survival. Religious, cultural, and historical factors also play a role, but the sum effect is a dulled sense of concern for the suffering of people not in one's immediate frame of reference. To a western advisor this can make the indigenous people seem callous or insensitive to the plight of others, but the impression needs to be kept in context.

Cultural Factor 7. The weak sense of nationhood. This is closely connected to Cultural Factor 6, above. The need to keep such a focus on local needs diminishes a people's sense of bonding and shared responsibility with other people hundreds of miles away, let alone thousands of miles away, even if they and those distant people are citizens of the same country. In many cases, most villagers might be illiterate and never have been more than ten miles from their home. In other places they might have never left the valley of their birth. What do such people know of nationhood? Further, in some countries rural people feel the bond of nationhood very lightly because their national governments have never had significant contact with them. In those situations, the idea of "nation" is not the compelling social force found in most western countries. Advisors will usually be disappointed if they expect flag-waving and calls for the defense of the nation to have much effect.

Cultural Factor 8. The importance of family and tribal relationships. In the United States and most of the western world nepotism is seen as improper or even illegal, especially in government office. In other parts of the world this aversion to family ties in the workplace is not so strong and an advisor would be wise to know who in his circle of contacts relates to whom and in what way. Cabinet ministers, regional governors, village chiefs and a variety of officials in between may have close relatives working in their offices, but absent discrete inquiry, learning who they are may be difficult. The quiet clerk at the district chief's elbow or the attendant discretely pouring tea in the governor's office may be a son, son-in-law, or other relative who is not just a factotum but someone being trained to be a future chief or governor himself. That man knows where his allegiance lies, and the advisor should be aware of who he is and should expect that whatever is said within his hearing will likely reach his superior's ear.

Cultural Factor 9. Discussions with or about women. This can be a difficult sea to navigate because the social currents vary among cultures. It is safe to say that in almost all traditional societies, the position of women is different from that in most western countries. How those women are treated ethically, religiously, socially, and politically can be very different, usually in ways that reduce the impact of women on public life. One simple example of differences is that in the U.S. and other European-based cultures, it is common for men and women to shake hands upon meeting and, in some circumstances, to even exchange a light kiss on the cheek. In most traditional societies women are treated with much more distance even if they are included in government offices, business meetings, or social settings. A woman in those societies might not expect even to shake hands with a man and let alone receive a kiss on the cheek!

In other situations, the separation of women may be more extreme, but still there are wide variations in practice. There may be cases where a professional woman is present but it would be a social error to speak to her unless formally introduced. In other cases, women may be present in an official's home or at an official event, but not acknowledged. Paying attention to them will likely cause discomfort for everyone. In the most restrictive societies, speaking with women is not a problem because they will not even be allowed to be in the same room when male visitors are present.

Certainly, there are non-western societies in which women are not so closeted. They may be present and friendly, even engaging, but the western male must be careful to curb his enthusiasm and to follow his counterpart's traditions with regard to the women in his household or those under his protection. While the rules of male-female relationships vary widely between cultures, a general statement is, the advisor must follow the local rules whether he is comfortable with them or not.

Even talking with men *about* women can be fraught with danger. An advisor speaking of his wife and daughter as a part of telling about himself can be thought to be poor taste in some conservative countries and actually showing a photograph of a wife or an adult daughter can be even more inappropriate. On the other hand, no culture, Christian, Muslim, or otherwise, has completely prevented sexual adventures between men and women. Once friendships with other men are established a western man may hear sexual comments or jokes, but the wise advisor avoids such banter. Sexual commentary, even in jest, can be a minefield where missteps are dangerous. The mines are hidden within layers of culture and language that can be very difficult to navigate, and the foreigner who makes an error can find himself in considerable difficulty. Counterinsurgency advisors should

Five. Donovan's Dozens

maintain their probity in such matters and will likely find it to be an image enhancer in the end.

Cultural Factor 10. Concepts of personal space. Personal space is that zone around any individual that is psychologically "theirs," the space that cannot be intruded upon without making the person feel uncomfortable. For an American that comfort zone may be wider than for those from a different cultural background. An American accustomed to being at arm's length from others in a conversation might feel uncomfortable when someone persistently leans in and speaks to him very closely. An American man may be equally discomfited if a man speaking to him about a serious matter takes his hand and holds it, but in some cultures that handholding can be meant to imply friendship between the conversants. In other places it may only be a common method of emphasis or of keeping a listener's attention.

In some Arabic and Asian countries, men may also hold hands or clasp arms as they walk together. To the average American male this would be a violation of personal space, but to the Arab or Asian it is only an affirmation of friendship sometimes clearly intended to be seen by others as an imprimatur of acceptance. In group meetings where men sit without chairs, a man might lean against his neighbor as if relaxing. An American could sense this as an invasion of personal space, but to an Arab it can imply trust and acceptance. The well-schooled advisor will recognize these habits for what they are and weigh his reactions accordingly.

Cultural Factor 11. The importance of religion in daily life. In Buddhist countries, the religion can be very understated in the lives of the people yet at the same time be very penetrating in their lives. In Islamic countries the religion can be very pronounced, very evident. Calls to prayer regulate daily activities and clerics strive to affect the public mood. They involve themselves in political affairs much as Christian clerics did in Europe a thousand years ago or, in some countries, even a hundred. While religion can be a positive influence in a culture, it can also lead to disunity and distrust between groups within a common religion and between one religion and another. Advisors should be aware of the issues important to the locally predominant religion(s) and seek not to disturb them absent the violation of law and threat to his mission.

Cultural Factor 12. The preference for indirect communication. Americans, especially American soldiers, tend to be direct and frank in their communication. They make a statement or ask a question and expect a direct response; anything else and the American sees an "Oriental" or "Arab" mentality engaged in deviousness or some sort of sly chicanery that makes a person unworthy of trust.

Asian and Arabic cultures differ widely, but they are both famous for their hospitality and politeness. That politeness leads them to distaste for personal disagreement or confrontation, especially in front of others. In some cultures the aversion to disagreement is so strong that a no may actually come out as yes because it is so impolite to say no directly. To understand what is really being meant by his respondent, the advisor must be aware of the cultural environment he is working in. He must be alert not only to what is being said, but be attentive to how it is being said. An excellent example of this kind of thing is that in the Vietnamese culture the frank answer, no, is considered impolite; thus, a no should be preceded by a yes. Yes-no. Understandably, the unwary might be confused. Was that a yes or a no? Yes.

The aversion to direct disagreement or to public disharmony is a cultural habit that can appear as false direction to a westerner. A counterpart's refusal to clearly say yes or no to an idea, his failure to act on a plan the advisor thinks has been agreed to, or even his hiding discord behind an inert facial expression may all be his ways of muting direct disagreement; but to an American they can contribute to his being characterized as one of those "inscrutable" people from between Suez and the China Seas.

What may appear to an American as habitual disingenuity may actually be due to specific things the advisor may be able to discern and move beyond if he uses his training and his personal skills. What is at the root of the problem? Is the counterpart's apparent duplicity or failure to act due only to a failure to understand? Is it due to his having a relaxed sense of urgency about the issue at hand, or is it due to a true disagreement with his advisor and his being too polite to say so? The good advisor has to sort this out and find a way to move his mission forward.

Lesson Learned: If You Get 15 Percent Done, You're Not Doing Bad.

Lieutenant Colonel Ray Mullen, Fifth Special Forces, Team B-43; province senior advisor, Cao Lanh, Kien Phong Province (MACV Advisor Team 84), IV Corps Tactical Zone; 1967–1968.

Colonel Mullen (left) with a teammate in the B-43 compound in Kien Phong Province, 1968.

An advisor doesn't literally command anyone but the Americans on his team. You recommend, you cajole, sometimes you even plead. If that doesn't work you threaten to stop helping your counterpart get something he wants but can't get himself, especially at the prices you can get it. Does he need parts for repairing equipment or vehicles? Electricity from your generator? Does he like getting booze or American cigarettes from your supply chain? Is he used to having influence at higher headquarters, but through your contacts? The counterpart always wants something—just like you do—and if you know him as you should, you'll know what it is he wants. That knowledge may not be an attractive card, but it is often a trump card.

A counterpart who doesn't want to take your advice is sometimes being held back by that old issue of "face." He doesn't want to appear to need your help with ideas or ways of doing things. His superiors or even his colleagues might think he should have come up with those ideas himself! I found that patience paid off. I would present an idea to my counterpart and he would hear me out, but he would often take no action. Two or three weeks would go by then he would come back to me and, virtually using my same words, he would present the idea as if it was his own. I never let that ruffle my feathers. It got the job done.

That was just one way in which an indirect approach worked better than a direct approach. No way of getting things done works in all situations, and if things are really going downhill fast, say, in combat or some other tight fix, you sometimes just have to make some demands, not to say, give orders, which, of course, you technically cannot do. Absent that kind of situation, the coy, indirect suggestion or hint often worked best for me. One of my most successful methods was the "Gee, I wonder if I could do that" method, which was, in effect, issuing a challenge to my counterpart. Implicit in the comment was the idea that if my counterpart would not or could not do it, I would give it a try. Not wanting to be made to appear more lazy or less competent than I was, he would usually do what needed to be done. Sometimes I would offer an asset I had or could get with the idea for their use implied, but not stated. I wouldn't say, "I can get shovels and sandbags, but you guys need to make a bunker." It would be more like, "If I can get shovels and sandbags, you think it would be a good idea to make a bunker over there?" Sugar draws more flies than vinegar, as Mama used to say.

Another impediment to getting things done was corruption. It was every-

Five. Donovan's Dozens

where. If you had money, you could buy anything and no one would ask where the money came from. An ambitious man with money was golden. If there was a position open somewhere up the ladder of success, that position's immediate superior would open the slot for bidding. The highest bidder would win the competition, move up the ladder then get most of his money back by putting his old slot up for bids. The highest bidder would pay him and so on it would go. My province chief got his job that way. It was a method that went back centuries and no amount of "newby" American ethics was going to change it.

That kind of thing affected the U.S. effort, as well. Let's say you're an American USAID administrator. You need warehouse space. You cannot deal with all the potential contractors yourself, so you contact the official indigenous guy who deals with taking contractor bids. Guess what? The high bid wins, not the low, especially if part of that high bid is money that goes in the pocket of the indigenous contracts guy. As Mr. USAID you're screwed, but there's little you can do about it. After all, there are rules to this game and, unfortunately, those rules have you playing checkers while the other guy is playing chess.

Getting things done in a hostile environment is always difficult, but insurgencies carry more than the usual weight of spies and infiltrators, which only makes it worse. The whole deal about guerrilla warfare is that the enemy is part of the indigenous population. How do you tell who is on who's side? Geneva rules about wearing uniforms and identification tags don't apply, so you never know who in your counterpart's system might be working to obstruct progress or ruin an operation. When I was senior advisor in Kien Phong province, it didn't take me long to notice that the operations conducted by our Vietnamese army units weren't making many contacts with the enemy. There were plenty of enemy around, so I suspected that someone on the province chief's staff was warning the local guerrilla units when our operations would be coming their way. I began a process of elimination by advising the province chief to restrict his planning staff to certain individuals on a rotating basis. It turned out that every time the province chief's chief of staff was not at the planning meeting the operation we had planned made contacts. If he was present, no contact. I told the province chief my conclusion, but he didn't say anything. I could tell he didn't believe me.

Two days later, the province chief asked me to go with him and a truckload of troops to inspect a bridge that had been blow up. It was out in the countryside, so we took along a couple of armored cars, as well, just for safety's

Counterinsurgency

sake. All went well, but on the return trip the truck full of soldiers, which was immediately behind my jeep, was blown up by a mine. It turned out to have been a mine set off by someone using an electrical switch with a connecting wire to the mine.

To make a long story short, the province chief had told his chief of staff about my suspicions and, as the man later confessed, he and a couple of his Viet Cong cronies had followed us on the way out to the bridge. They had stopped at a quiet stretch of road, set the mine, run the wire, and hid in the roadside thickets. On our return, the chief of staff had hit the switch when my jeep went over the mine, but it didn't go off. He hit the switch again, but by then the truck was over the mine and he blew it up, instead. The last time I saw the man was when he was handcuffed to a chopper seat and being lifted off to an interrogation center in another province. How long had his activities fouled up our military operations? How many more like him were in the staffs of hundreds of other military or civilian organizations? We had no idea. Is it any wonder then that getting even 15 percent of the jobs done was a good thing?

Ray Mullen retired from the U.S. Army as a leutenant colonel in 1977. He died in Thailand in 1986 after giving the author a commentary on his time in Vietnam and Laos from which this lesson-learned was extracted.

A list of rules for counterinsurgency, whether meant as a general guide for programs or as a list of warnings specific to advisors, can never be comprehensive and useful at the same time. There are too many situations, too many personalities, and too many cultural factors to address in one list of rules. Further, enumerations that become too long are too easily ignored, which is why the lists of "Donovan's Dozens" have been divided into the applications intended: rules for counterinsurgency programs, rules for counterinsurgency advisors, rules specific for improving counterpart relations, and a listing of cultural factors that can affect counterinsurgency operations.

Such lists must be taken with an eye on the course of events like medicine is taken with an eye on the course of the disease. Experience, correctly absorbed, leads to the wisdom of knowing which rules are right for a particular situation and which may be wrong or at least require modification. Experience allows one to make his own list of rules that suits his situation better than any previous list from any previous experience. Finally, a list of rules or admonitions cannot become a border fence that hides what lies beyond. While the basics of counterinsurgency have remained much the same for at least the last half century, each new conflict opens the possibility of new insights that may help counterinsurgency become a more successful aspect of American foreign policy and a military application with higher efficiency than in the past.

Relevant Readings

Galula, David. *Counterinsurgency: Theory and Practice.* New York: Frank A. Praeger. 1964.
Jones, Robert A. "The Nationbuilder: Soldier of the Sixties." *Military Review* January (1965): 63–67.
Kilcullen, David. *Counterinsurgency.* New York: Oxford University Press, 2010.
Lawrence, Thomas E. "Twenty-Seven Articles." *The Arab Bulletin* 20 August (1917).
Metrinko, Michael J. *The American Military Advisor: Dealing With Senior Foreign Officials in the Islamic World.* Carlisle, PA: Strategic Studies Institute, 2008.
Ramsey, Robert D. *Advice for Advisors: Suggestions and Observations from Lawrence to the Present.* Fort Leavenworth, KS: Combat Studies Institute Press, 2006.
_____. *Advising Indigenous Forces: American Advisors in Korea, Vietnam, and El Salvador.* Fort Leavenworth, KS: Combat Studies Institute Press, 2006.
Ricklefs, Norman. "Fourteen Rules for Advisors in Iraq." *Small Wars Journal* August (2008): http://smallwarsjournalcom/jrnl/art/fourteeen-rules-for-advisors-in-Iraq.
Silinsky, Mark. "An Irony of War: Human Development as Warfare in Afghanistan." *Colloquium* 3 (2010): 1–16.

Six

Counterinsurgency Failure
A Dozen Ways to Do It

In Leo Tolstoy's *War and Peace,* General Mikhail Kutuzov, speaking of his campaign against Napoleon, tells a young acquaintance, "Believe me, my boy, there is nothing stronger than these: *patience and time*" (italics Tolstoy's). That is an especially apt statement for wars of insurgency/counterinsurgency. Insurgents often feel they have plenty of both and counterinsurgents often feel they have little of either, especially if the counterinsurgency program being run with them is one inspired by Americans. Time and patience are not strengths typical of Americans, a fact that most present-day insurgents are aware of and a fact most assisted governments become sharply aware of.

The American's sense of urgency is more complex than a simple get-it-done-now mentality. The Americans or the personnel of any helper nation, for that matter, are aware that time spent in a military conflict is costly in money and lives. The money comes from taxes that have to be justified before an electorate back home and the lives are another kind of tax, a national expenditure that has to be defended before a public that knows it is giving what never can be returned. It is inevitable then that not long after a conflict begins, especially a conflict as murky as a counterinsurgency operation, the feeling arises that time is short. Let's the job done and begone.

Being short of time means that being short of patience is not far behind. In any conflict requiring the loss of American lives and money,

Six. Counterinsurgency Failure

public watchdogs and elected officials soon begin examining the cost/benefit ratio of continued involvement. Too often in the past that ratio for counterinsurgency has not been good, which means that after the experiences of the past American patience begins wearing thin very quickly. Pressures will mount for ending the mission and time will grow shorter still. At some point the only real question remaining will be, can the host government learn to prosper before time runs out?

A study by Seth Jones in 2008 (see references) counted nearly one hundred insurgencies that have occurred worldwide since the end of World War II. The U.S. or European powers have mounted counterinsurgency operations in only a minority of those conflicts, but to the citizens of the U.S. or the pertinent countries in Europe that minority are the most remembered, e.g. Indochina, Malaya, Algeria, Vietnam, etc. The points commonly remembered are that, first, the financial and human costs of counterinsurgency are high and, second, the effort often fails. The latter makes the former even more distasteful and highlights the need to evaluate the causes of past failures in hopes of avoiding them in the future.

A decent regard for humanity demands the frank evaluation of those past failures. The headstones of the dead, the pains of wounded, and the sacrifices of hundreds of thousands of others plead that the errors of the past not be repeated, whether those errors were in the original commitment to a specific counterinsurgency program, that program's design independent of how the design was applied in the field, or the program's application in the field independent of its design.

Counterinsurgency is a complex task and going forward with a program is like moving a truck down a road filled with potholes. Progress is made only with twists, turns, and occasional halts to make repairs. Counterinsurgency may be thought of as "small war," but that does not mean it is an easier or simpler kind of war than another. There are many ways to fail in the effort. What follows is a short list of twelve factors that contribute to such failures. Each factor should be considered by policy makers before agreeing to undertake a counterinsurgency campaign and by counterinsurgency leaders once a campaign is engaged. As with the preceding lists, this one arises from reflections on a personal counterinsurgency experience long ago but is informed by the thoughts of others made at different times and different places. The list is not in order of importance; that ranking will depend on individual situations. References to the thoughts of others are included at the end of this chapter.

Factor 1: Failure to get demographic control of the population. In most societies, the people are settled. They live in the villages, towns, or cities where they work and have their homes and families; in short, people are where they are and they tend to stay there. Insurgents are also embedded in their home communities and some of them may also stay put while others of their colleagues move about. Guerrilla fighters, insurgent officials, and insurgent "mules," those primarily involved in transporting supplies, can be frequent travelers who come and go from specific locations, so an important question for the counterinsurgency operation is, who is where and when are they normally there?

Learning who is where and when is a difficult task. It requires either a large, coherent census be taken all at one time, or a more low-key, house-by house inquiry be taken that takes more time but is less disruptive. The best way to address this is for every citizen to have an identification card with a picture and a thumbprint. Importantly, a central authority should have a copy on record and local authorities should have one, as well. Accurate maintenance of the records is critical because they allow counterinsurgency or police officials to know who lives within their area of responsibility and it gives those authorities the ability to cross-check individual identifications. If strangers appear or if people seem to come and go under suspicious circumstances, the question should be asked, who are they and what are they doing?

Information on the comings and goings of suspicious individuals does not need to be learned by breaking down doors and thundering into private homes. It can be gathered partly from knowing the population and observing them, partly from polite conversations in the streets, and partly from the use of intelligence cells that are a part of most counterinsurgency operations.

Building the basic information base takes time and is best done by trained indigenous officials, not by big-booted Americans. One of the reasons the information building process fails is that the recruiting and training of indigenous officials is never accomplished and the local intelligence nets are never established. Another reason the demographic database is never built is that the activity is subject to abuse if not properly monitored.

Six. Counterinsurgency Failure

Citizens may fear that ethnic or religious information kept on them will be used to their disadvantage, and given the history of some countries that can be understandable. It is another factor that makes knowing who is where when a difficult undertaking.

To the American citizen sitting safely at home this kind of information gathering may seem intrusive and too open to abuse to be allowed. The only appropriate response is, this is war. It is war in the village where insurgents wants to extend their fingers into whatever space they can find. First, they want a finger-hold then a grip then a sanctuary. It is the way insurgency works, and one important tool in defeating it is to know the local population and to know when its pattern of life is being disturbed.

Factor 2. Failure to achieve civil justice. This is a broad brush that includes failing to establish a civil administration that treats its people with a reasonable standard of fairness. A functioning civil administration is foundational to a government. It can mean something as simple as a citizen being able to obtain a marriage license or as complex as being able to properly assess and collect taxes. A properly functioning civil administration also means that all citizens should be able to expect fair treatment by an honest police force and an honest court system.

In the long run, those attributes are more important to the success of counterinsurgency than military victories and are why it has been said previously (Chapter Two) that the constabulary, whether organized as a national force or a local one, must be fair-minded, not corrupt, and trained to be concerned about the communities they serve. To have and hold to these characteristics, the police must be as selective as possible and appropriately paid for their level of responsibility. It is a common fact that the police are neither highly selected nor well paid; therefore, they are corrupt, they do not serve their communities, and civil justice is an orphan with no chance to develop. A government that does not change its police and court procedures to improve civil justice is a government injured by its own hand and it produces a political wound easily infected by the germ of insurgency.

Factor 3. Failure to sustain a program of development (expand commercial activity, enhance agricultural development, improve physical infrastructure, etc.). As noted in Chapter Three, one of the requirements for successful counterinsurgency operations is the expansion of development. It is a difficult task, especially in a war environment, but it must be pursued. A man with a job and a paycheck is less likely to be joining an insurgents' ambush or planting terrorist bombs in the middle of the night. A man's family that sees hope in the future because a local factory starts hiring workers or because farmers have been helped to achieve higher yields from their crops is a family that is less likely to sympathize with the insurgency. It is not so much the mire of poverty that feeds an insurgency, it is the lack of hope that things will ever change. Insurgents prey on that kind of despair, but government programs that offer hope are protections against it.

Development programs improve opportunities for small businesses, expand industrial development, stimulate agriculture, and improve the country's infrastructure (roads, bridges, ports, etc.). Development activities can be complex with many competing parts, and unless they are properly managed they can lead to little improvement in conditions but to much stirring around of resources. That stirring of resources is sometimes permitted because it leads to the enrichment of those doing the stirring. When that happens, the government *cognoscenti* may grin over their gains, but the insurgents will eventually grin over theirs.

Factor 4. Failure to establish an open political process. Even with all the above being true, history has shown that people in tribal societies still care about having a political process, and they will go out of their way to participate in it if they know what it is and believe it will be fairly administered. That participation is important because it is evidence of the people's hope that political change can be effected without resort to arms. Since insurgencies thrive where people feel powerless to effect political change in any other way but the force of arms, a clearly understood, fairly administered political process is a move against the insurgency. To be blunt, a counterinsurgency program that leaves a people with no effective redress of grievances and no functional process for political change is a program that has failed. An insurgency may be temporarily tamped down, but when the people continue to lack a way of addressing their government through an open process, the insurgency is left with a fertile field it will plant, plough, and eventually harvest.

Factor 5. Failure to effectively use propaganda. It has been a common observation that the population caught in an insurgency can be divided into three groups: a small group actively involved in the insurgency, a large group who are neutral and want to be left alone, and another small group actively working against the insurgency. All of those groups are proper targets for information about the government, information about the insurgents, and information about the government's program to counter the insurgents' claims and activities. All of that is fairly termed propaganda.

Elements within each of the three groups, anti-insurgent, neutral, and insurgent, may respond best to a particular kind of information. Some of the insurgent group might respond best to news highlighting government successes on the battlefield. The large neutral group might respond best to reminders of improved security, reminders of development activities in their area, or clarification of government reforms. The active anti-insurgents need information offering hope, news of government victories, and promises for a better future. Bombast and drama in any of these presentations make what most people think of as propaganda, but in truth propaganda is any information produced to support a desired goal.

For maximum effect, the propaganda effort within a counterinsurgency campaign should speak to all three groups, which means there needs to be considerable overlap in the information being directed at each group. This is a complicated task that takes place through several media including tangible products like newspapers, magazines, brochures, posters, etc.; the airwaves (television and radio), and the internet. Done well, a propaganda campaign requires more people and resources than are sometimes allowed either because its importance is not fully understood or because memory holds examples of propaganda gone to foolishness.

The insurgents will not allow American or host-nation propaganda to stand unchallenged. In many cases, their own propaganda machine will have been spreading messages long before any Americans arrive on the scene and it will continue to promote a cause the insurgents passionately believe in among a people with whom they share a common language, culture, and, often, religion. Those things held in common give the insurgents a powerful psychological advantage over any late-arriving, pro-government messages, especially those delivered by foreign forces. That advantage is a significant one and has to be overcome both by government action and by propaganda supporting that action.

Factor 6: Failure to block the insurgents' access to the population. It is a truism in counterinsurgency that the general population will side with the force that best protects it. When insurgents have easy access to the population they are able to commit banditry, threaten those who are opposed to them, and spread their propaganda. This is why establishing security is one of the five central requirements of an effective counterinsurgency program (Chapter Two). Insurgent fighters are typically guerrillas, and Mao Tse Tung famously said that a guerrilla fighter must be able to move through the population like a fish through the sea. He was correct, but that means the fish must have access to the sea. A counterinsurgency program has to push the fish up on the sand and kill it or let it die for lack of oxygen.

The first step in denying insurgents access to the population is knowing they are present in the first place and determining where are they and when are they there (see Factor 1 above). The practical work of rooting the insurgents out of the population and preventing their return has to be done by the government's security forces. An aggressive program of patrol, ambush, and attack will put the insurgents back on their heels and reduce their ability to terrorize the population (see Chapter Two, Requirement Two). That program can best be provided by a four-pronged organization of forces: a motivated, well-trained conventional army to deal with enemy formations and sanctuaries, a nationally regulated militia to keep the enemy from returning to the villages, a police intelligence organization that can identify resident insurgents and other criminal gangs, and a uniformed police force to deal with ordinary crime and other conventional police matters.

A counterinsurgency program can train those security forces and provide material resources to them, but it cannot provide the lasting motivation required for an effective force. That can only come from each individual fighter's deeply held hopes and beliefs; a rule that applies to loyalists and insurgents, alike. Both the government and the insurgents must be able to gain adherents, train them to be aggressive fighters, and put them in the field where they are ready to die for their cause. If the insurgents can accomplish those steps more efficiently or faster than the government, the eventual outcome is obvious. This means that for each side the key questions are: how many adherents are there to the cause, how many of those adherents are fighters, and how many of those fighters are ready to die? A few insurgents fully prepared to die can overcome a much larger government force that is unprepared to make that same sacrifice, and for the host nations in several of the United States' counterinsurgency efforts this kind of difference in zeal has been a problem. It was sometimes true in Vietnam and has repeatedly been seen as an issue in Iraq and Afghanistan. In those latter two, even after years of operations by host-government security forces, the insurgents still have access to too much of the population whom they can intimidate and propagandize almost at will. The insurgents have not been denied access to the population, yet any successful counterinsurgency program must achieve that difficult, multifactoral task.

Factor 7. Failure to provide basic public services (electricity, potable water, garbage removal, waste treatment, public health, etc.). This is arguably a subset of the failure to sustain development (Factor 7), but it is more specific and deals with frustrations that both the urban elites and the rural poor can have with their government. Development will fail if factories, hospitals, schools, and the like cannot reliably receive electricity or water, but residential areas will face difficulties, too. People blame their government when a failure of services strikes at the home and each failure gives the insurgents another example of government incompetence, corruption, or misfeasance.

Over the last decade Americans have heard multiple stories from Iraq and Afghanistan about public utilities (electricity, water, gas, oil pipelines, waste treatment plants, etc.) that have failed due to the damages of war and the incapacity of governments to get them working again. Basic health care fails as well. Diseases spread, traumas are left untreated, pains are left unabated, and death sometimes comes even from the lack of sanitation.

Vietnam, 1969

As was true throughout most, if not all of the Mekong delta, there were no public sanitation facilities in our village; no sewer system, no running water, no waste treatment plant. The vast network of delta canals, rivers, and streams were the sewer system. In many areas the population was so dispersed and the waterways so numerous, it seemed to those used to it that a small square of privacy thatch supported over the nearest waterway by bamboo poles was toilet enough. Other garbage and solid wastes produced by daily life either went to feed the free-roaming pigs and chickens or was tossed into a nearby canal to be swept away with the tidal shift. Naturally, the wastes from each upstream village quickly made its way to each downstream village, and that included the agents of human disease: Bacteria, parasites, viruses, you name it. That was troublesome enough on the face of it, but having little recourse to piped, running water from clean sources, villagers used the canals not only as toilets, but for bathing and as a source of water for cooking or other cleaning needs. This caused a constant stress on public health throughout the delta. That was no secret. Any sentient biped knew it, but I was never aware of anything significant being done to address the basic problem or the health challenges that sprang from it.

One morning a woman came to our headquarters asking to see me. It turned out the woman had come from a distant village with her infant, who was sick, she said. She had come to ask for our help. Could we cure her sick son?

The infant was wrapped in a light cloth and was being held in its mother's arms. Gently, she unwrapped the child and I suspect I curled my lips in dismay and distaste. The child appeared to be about a year old or less and was covered in what appeared to be ringworm lesions. They must have been there for some time because many showed scabs and the swelling and redness of secondary infection. The boy's face was edematous, his eyes dull, his reactions lethargic.

I called for Sergeant Mau, our team medic, but while he was coming I asked questions and heard the woman's story. It was a common one. She came from a hamlet far up one of our canals. There was no soap to be had in her village, she said, at least not a price she could afford, so while she knew she should use soap and water to clean her child, she had been using water only. There was no soap. Was she using boiled water, I asked. That, too, she knew she should do, but firewood was also expensive and she did not have a husband to help her gather it or to earn money to buy it. He had been a soldier in the army and had been killed a few months before. So, no, she had not been boiling the water because she could not afford the firewood needed.

She had tried the remedies of traditional or "Chinese" medicine, but they had failed and now she had spent almost all of her money to come by water taxi to ask for the Americans' help. Sergeant Mau arrived and looked the infant over. He said he could give the child a shot of penicillin for the secondary infections, but he had no drugs to treat the ringworm. I told him to do that and to give the woman a bar of soap, as well. We explained to the woman again what she probably already knew about the importance of clean water and soap for bathing the baby. She said she understood and

Six. Counterinsurgency Failure

thanked us for the soap and the injection; still, as she left the fort to make her way back home I could see the worry in her face and eyes.

Several days later Sergeant Mau came where I was working and told me the woman with the baby was back and asking to see us. We went to the fort wall where she had been stopped by a guard and she began a pleading that was even more distressed than before. She had been using the soap, she said, but her child was getting worse. Now she was completely out of both money and firewood and didn't know what to do to save her child. She had left her home early that morning and had walked the many kilometers to our fort with her child because she could no longer pay for a water taxi. Her son was very sick, she said almost weeping, surely we Americans could help; and with that she handed the bundled child to me.

I took the child and turned to hand him to Sergeant Mau, but as I did I pulled the cloth away from his head. This time I'm sure my reaction was noticeable. I was shocked at the look of the infected face, pallid and slack-jawed. The infant's eyes were closed and his head lolled loosely on its shoulders. To me that was death right there in my face and I'm sure my head jerked back before dropping to the child's chest to listen for a heart beat. I heard nothing. Mau took the child and unwrapped him showing the body to be still covered with ringworm sores and puffy from edema. Using his stethoscope he listened for a heart beat then looked at me and shook his head. The child was dead.

We didn't have to say anything to the woman, she read it on our faces and in the shaking of Mau's head. Still, we said the bad news and she squatted there by the wall wailing in protest and crying. She had lost her husband in the army and now her only child to disease. What was she to do? How was she to live? What was the point? As with so many things, we had no answer.

As for me, I disconnected from the scene emotionally. It was the only way. Otherwise, one could dissolve in rage at the ridiculousness of it. A child was dead essentially because of ringworm. Why did he have ringworm? Because he had no soap! A simple bar of soap. What would it have meant for that child to have had soap all the months of his life? A little soap could have saved that child's life and likely the lives of thousands of others. The U.S. was giving the Vietnamese government all they could handle of guns, bombs, and bullets, but, oh, what we could have done with some soap.

To be honest though, I've often wondered what Americans would have *made of a plea for a steady supply of soap. Would Americans even take seriously the fact that somewhere in the world there is a desperate need for such a cheap, basic thing? Americans have soap all over the place. We probably throw more soap away in our motels and hotels than even exists in some countries. We have no cultural memory of what it means to be without soap and have children dying of ringworm infestation, so articulating the problem would hardly make real the magnitude of it when it occurs in a fetid environment like the moist heat of the Mekong delta. We find it too easy to believe some underdeveloped country needs our cash, our military assistance, and maybe even our advanced technology, but soap? Who in the world could need soap?*

If a host government will not or cannot provide some level of elemental health care or at least assistance, its insurgents will likely be making what efforts they can, even if they are rudimentary. Medical care, even the basic kind, is just one inroad to the people's idea of who is their friend and who is not. If there is no electricity, no potable water, no medical care, or no whatever is basic and possible, the people will see that as a failure of their government. It is a failure the enemy will exploit where at all possible. In some cases those failures of government have persisted for many years and people living in the western democracies where life is relatively ordered sometimes fail to appreciate what it means when nothing a modern society depends upon actually works. We lose the idea of what it means to persistently have unreliable electricity, no running water, no garbage collection, no health care, and the like. Not so in other countries where frustrations and resentments build as governments prove themselves incapable of providing even the most basic services. Those government inadequacies add grist to the insurgents' mill and produces a flour many people will eventually buy.

Factor 8. Failure to blunt sectarian and tribal rivalries. Ethnic and religious groups throughout the world have histories of competition that have led to armed violence. Within Europe armed factions claiming to represent the Irish in Northern Ireland or the Basques in the southern Pyrenees have only recently called off their fights against the British and Spanish, respectively, but the Walloons, the Bretons, the Scots, and others all have a history of competition by war. In Africa the internecine wars within Somalia, Sudan, Rwanda, Congo, and others all break down along tribal lines. Tribal animosities exist throughout Asia, as well, including Iraq, Afghanistan, Pakistan, India, China, Laos, Vietnam, and Burma, among others. In

Six. Counterinsurgency Failure

Iraq there is a strong competition between Kurds and Arabs, and within the Arabs a variety of tribes elbow each other for a place at the government's table and at its benefits dispensary. In Afghanistan the major tribal division is between Pashtuns and Tajiks, and that division affects everything from who is selected for government appointments to how the army is recruited and how aid is dispensed. Overlying this tribal competition are the religious divisions of Shiite Islamists vs. Sunni Islamists, Islamist vs. Christians, Islamists vs. Hindus, and so on through all possible permutations.

Most Americans view this kind of tribalism and sectarian violence as medieval, even uncivilized, the emotion-driven work of barbarians. It seems bizarre and does not fit with the modern world most westerners know. It is another factor that contributes to counterinsurgency failure; programs that come from the western mind too often fail to give credence to the lasting power of tribal and religious divisions.

A well known example of such division is in Iraq where under the government of Sadaam Hussein a Sunni minority lorded it over the Shiite majority for decades. When the Americans removed Hussein in the Second Gulf War they also destroyed the largely Sunni government that had run the country. Now the Shiites wanted their turn at the helm, and after so many years of abuse they were far less concerned about being "fair" to the minority Sunnis than were the Americans who wanted to develop a democratic society that would survive. In Iraq, as of this writing, one of the primary methods both Shiites and Sunnis use to try to influence the public is still the bomb blast. That is not the stuff of a lasting democratic society.

In country after country, group animosities like those in Iraq repeat themselves. Groups held down or discriminated against by others want their day in the sun—with knives. Counterinsurgency programs must confront this through social programs, education, and development schemes that take care to reduce tensions; but tribal conflicts often go back for centuries and a few years of enforced egalitarianism is rarely a cure. The experiences of the Croats, Serbs, and Bosnians after the dissolution of Yugoslavia speak to that.

There is another reason that strong tribalist or religionist traditions are dangerous to the success of counterinsurgency programs. An important underlying principle of those programs, at least from the American perspective, has been that the U.S. should support democracy where it can; but the European and American concepts of democracy are based on the idea that individuals matter, that individuals are empowered to form an opinion, and that individuals may express political opinions in the form of a vote. Thus, western democracies at their best are about the competition of ideas among individuals. That is not the case in tribalist societies. In those societies, democracy is not about the competition of ideas; it is about the competition of groups. There the group, the tribe, is expected to largely vote *en bloc.* The only thing that matters is the headcount of tribesmen, not the values of alternative political ideas, and in that way the transplanted democracy becomes only the faintest facsimile of what the planters meant it to be.

A counterinsurgency program may quell insurgent violence and preach equanimity between tribes or sects, but without reducing tribal animosities and discriminations in a significant, enduring way, that violence will likely rise again and change what once appeared to be a counterinsurgency success into yet another counterinsurgency failure.

Factor 9. Failure to establish national a executive that has nationally-reaching authority. South Vietnam, Somalia, Iraq, and Afghanistan are examples of countries that once had or still have long-lasting insurgencies. In each case, the country's national executive has had difficulty establishing its authority throughout the country, and, in some cases, even outside the capital city. War lords with strong ties to specific regions or tribes, recalcitrant province chiefs pursuing their own programs, or politically ambitious generals sharpening their bayonets have too often been able to obey or not obey the national authority as they wish, and too often the national executive has not had the power to do anything about it or has not been willing to exercise the power for fear of the consequences.

Sometimes the warlords or regional authorities ignore the central authority because that authority failed to consult with them on important issues or to coordinate with them for the delivery of its programs. When those kinds of things happen the local authorities feel put upon, disrespected, and resentful. Further, the absence of consultation and coordination can reinforce the belief that the higher authority is out of touch with local realities. These problems appear in both the civilian and military sides of government.

The problem often arises as one where a national executive is unable to rein in a willful subordinate. That subordinate may be either military or

Six. Counterinsurgency Failure

civilian, but to do the reining in the national executive may need the support of the rest of his government, which can be lacking for at least two reasons. First, the remainder of the government may be expending itself in the fight against the insurgents and not want to get involved in a struggle within its own ranks. Alternatively, that remainder is thinking of how it, too, practices selective obedience and knows that it will not be able to continue the practice unless it allows the same foible to others. This presents a dilemma to counterinsurgency programs because without an effective central authority, a nationally approved program will not be carried out in a consistent manner. Practices will differ region-by-region or even village-by-village. Success will vary in like manner and the countryside will be scattered with strong points and weak points. The wise insurgent will bypass the former to attack the latter.

A supposedly subordinate leader acting independently raises serious questions for a national executive. Does the executive spend his political capital to reel in the free-wheeling warlord or province chief? What if the attempt fails? Will a failure strengthen the insurgency? Typically, the outcome of such struggles are uncertain; uncertainty leads to irresolution, and irresolution leads to no effort being made to deal with problem. That result leads to the national executive being national in name only. His failure to exert authority across all the arms and agencies of government is a weakness in the national armor and is a common contributor to the eventual failure of counterinsurgency programs.

This problem can be seen in microcosm within a military where at each level of authority, national, regional, and local, the command centers assume all authority unto themselves. In such situations, each level of command pays little attention to the one above it because it was not consulted with on some important decision or because historical animosities blunt the will to obey the decision. Sooner or later, it can become the norm that national or regional headquarters issue orders but do little to exert control over those receiving the orders. The relative independence of subordinate commands can become a national military disease that the advisor in the field can do little about. On both the military and civilian sides of counterinsurgency, this is a problem that has to be addressed high in the government administration and by the American advisors with counterparts at that level.

Counterinsurgency

Lesson Learned: Many Problems Facing a U.S. Advisory Effort Cannot Be Solved by the Relatively Junior Advisors in the Field
Lieutenant Kenneth C. Jacobsen, U.S. Navy, advisor, River Assault Group 32, An Giang Province and River Assault Group 31, Vinh Long Province, IV Corps Tactical Zone; 1967–1968.

I was an advisor to two different River Assault Groups (RAGs), each of which consisted of heavily armed command boats, gunboats, patrol/scout boats, and minesweeping boats. Some of the boats, such as the 60' Command Boat, or Commandament (still referred to in the French) had been built for the French riverine forces back in the 1950s; others were converted U.S. landing craft. We were part of the "brown water navy" that operated on the 5,000 miles of rivers and canals that were the main lines of communications in the Mekong Delta.

Vietnamese Navy riverine forces had their antecedents in special combat groups developed by the French in the First Indochina war. Some of our Vietnamese officers and senior Petty Officers were veterans of those groups and were fiercely proud of their fighting heritage. The RAG's had a primary mission of conducting assault operations with embarked Vietnamese troops and providing fire support for the those troops once they were ashore. Secondary missions were patrol and interdiction, minesweeping, fire support of outposts on the waterways, and various logistic and humanitarian tasks, such as medical team visits to isolated or Viet Cong controlled villages and hamlets.

Although the French combat groups had operated independently with their own troops, aircraft and command structure, the Vietnamese military, at the recommendation of their U.S. Advisors, had stripped the RAGs of their integral troops and air support and essentially placed them under the command of Vietnamese Army division commanders. This decision had the effect of ending any capability of the RAG to plan and conduct independent assault operations. In one of my RAG areas, routine patrol operations became the primary mission, a situation that RAG personnel, from commanders to boat crews, generally resented. Patrols ranged from seven to eleven days in duration, and were generally composed of one Commandament or "Monitor" gunboat and several patrol/scout boats or converted landing craft.

Six. Counterinsurgency Failure

In general, the patrolling was desultory. The border patrols were considered to be dull, unimportant tasks assigned to the assault groups by Corps headquarters, which was far away and out of touch. Part of that being "out of touch" was because the Vietnamese army controlled Corps headquarters, which had allocated the RAGs as an army division asset, similar to artillery or aircraft. The Vietnamese Army also had a history of ignoring the Navy's river-based assets and capabilities and excluding Navy commanders from operational planning and frequently failed to coordinate with them on the kinds of amphibious operations the assault groups were designed to do.

Unfortunately, most senior U.S. Army staff advisors at Division and Corps level had little understanding of waterborne operations and sometimes exacerbated the problem by urging their counterparts to use ground or air-based assets rather than the RAGs. In contrast, U.S. Army advisors in

Lieutenant Jacobsen with his counterpart on a *commandamant* boat in 1968.

Counterinsurgency

the field who worked with Vietnamese Army or militia troops had learned of the importance of waterborne forces. They had a keen appreciation of the RAG's capabilities, and were usually enthusiastic about joint operations. That did not stop the RAG I was assigned to at the time from being reduced to patrol duty which was not only usually dull, but along the Cambodia-Vietnam border was complicated by the delicate international situation and the extensive smuggling that went on across the border.

No effort made by me or any other RAG advisor I knew of succeeded in changing the Vietnamese officers' less-than-intense approach to patrol operations in the border area. Boats usually patrolled for several hours each day and remained beached for the remainder of the time. Occasionally the boat crews would check the sampans that came within hailing distance, but others simply went by unchecked.

Despite any lethargy on patrol, once engaged, the Vietnamese officers and men I served with never showed hesitation in a fight. My counterpart for example, would make it a point to remain on the open deck of the command boat during an ambush or firefight so he could direct the operation of his boats. He and most of the senior petty officers in the RAG were tactically experienced in riverine warfare, so in firefights and ambushes, my most valuable work as an advisor was to call in U.S. air support and to coordinate with any U.S. Army advisors who's units were in the fight on land.

Most Vietnamese Navy line officers gave non-combat tasks like training and maintenance a low priority. There seemed to be few navy-wide "ship level" training programs, standardized training records, or lesson plans. Often, supervision and inspection of equipment and weapons maintenance was delegated to enlisted petty officers because the commissioned officers considered it beneath their dignity to get involved in that grimy part of the business. Others had a maintenance philosophy of "leave-it-alone-till-it-breaks" or, long ago frustrated with their own superiors' lack of support, began depending on the resources of U.S. advisors to solve their problems.

The advisors in the field already had problems aplenty, many of them having originated in the decisions, policies, or actions of authorities at higher headquarters. Those problems could only be solved at those higher levels, but getting counterpart cooperation in reporting problems upward was difficult. Traditional Vietnamese culture did not permit junior officers the appearance of criticizing their seniors, so Vietnamese officers in the field

Six. Counterinsurgency Failure

were reluctant to share problems with a higher command. A Vietnamese officer also knew from experience that his enthusiastic, well-meaning, but largely ignorant American advisor would be gone in a year or less only to be replaced by another of the same kind while he, the Vietnamese officer, would still be there facing the daily demands of war.

The habit of the Vietnamese army headquarters to not include our Vietnamese navy counterparts in pre-operation planning caused problems that often beleaguered the advisors in the field and their counterparts. Troops would end up being landed on high river banks at low tide, boats would often be overloaded, and on occasion they would return to base empty at the end of an operation because the Vietnamese army commander preferred a quicker ride home by road in a truck convoy to a slow trip in a boat.

On at least one occasion this practice had tragic results; the truck convoy returning troops to base was ambushed and a number of Vietnamese soldiers and U.S. advisors were killed. My counterpart and I had strongly recommended to the senior U.S. Army advisor that day that the troops be re-embarked in our boats rather than travel by convoy on a road known to be dangerous. The senior advisor's counterpart, however, had insisted his troops be returned by road. As a result, my navy counterpart and I had ended up on the troopless RAG boats headed for home and were less than a mile from the convoy when the ambush happened. Unfortunately, there was nothing we could do to help. Properly planned, that operation would have ended with those troops and their field advisors on our boats, not on that dangerous road for the ride home.

When problems like those above, whether the absence of a standardize training program or the improper planning of operations, are caused at higher headquarters, correction of those problem has to originate at those headquarters, not down in the field where the junior advisor is faced with a historically embedded problem he cannot control. Relatively junior officers serving as advisors in the field can sometimes get the blame for those kinds of problems when the failure lies far upstream. In those cases, the American authorities at higher headquarters are the responsible parties. It is only their advice, perhaps even their insistence that will be corrective.

When the junior advisor is faced with a problem that originates at the senior advisor's level, the junior advisor's only option is to submit specific recommendations to his superiors in the advisor chain of command. Once the advisors at higher headquarters are informed of the problem, the responsibility for improvement lies with them; but, unfortunately, reports from advisors in the field can be ignored, disregarded, or not carried through to correction. It is very frustrating for an advisor to have complained about a long-standing, ingrained problem at the beginning of his tour and see that problem still unaltered at the end of his tour.

The perception, at least in the time I was in Vietnam, was that the unofficial MACV policy was that it was more important to "get along" with counterparts than to correct problems. This sometimes left the junior advisor in the field with significant problems he could do nothing about even if he wanted to do more than just get along.

Kenneth Jacobsen retired from the U.S. Navy with the rank of captain in 1986. He has since worked as a freelance writer, editor and defense analyst. He currently lives in Charleston, South Carolina.

Factor 10. Failure to adjust conventional military forces for their role in counterinsurgency. This applies to the conventional American forces acting in a counterinsurgency role and the conventional forces of the host-nation. When counterinsurgency was first formalized as a performance area for the American military, the primary concept was that small teams of American soldiers, the Special Forces, would carry out the military part of the counterinsurgency mission. The effort in Vietnam began that way, but it eventually grew beyond the Special Forces to include a larger group of trained advisors within the CORDS organization. A complicating factor was that conventional U.S. Army divisions also conducted counterinsurgency operations, most of which were *ad hoc* and carried out by units with no counterinsurgency training. In fact, for those conventional units counterinsurgency was largely an afterthought, an ancillary activity that came after the main point of killing or capturing the enemy. This has still seemed to be an issue in Iraq and Afghanistan.

In those cases, U.S. Army and Marine units were first employed in their conventional roles, but after swift victories they were forced into a counterinsurgency role for which they were not designed on paper nor organized in fact. Advisor training continued for a long time to be decentralized and varied in duration and intensity. Some advisors trained con-

Six. Counterinsurgency Failure

ventional troops of the host nation's national army while others trained and advised in various aspects of counterinsurgency. Varied training and varied roles led to varied results, which might be expected when the organization of the large American units remained that of the land army they were and their role alternated between being a well-trained force for conventional warfare and an advisor unit for the training of indigenous forces.

The kind of training and advising American units can offer could be improved by an American unit structure made for the conduct of counterinsurgency operations and by having those units constituted by personnel specifically trained for counterinsurgency. Such units should be able to conduct counterinsurgency as a form of special warfare but fill a need beyond that of the Special Forces as presently organized.

Counterinsurgency units can be tasked and organized in a number of ways, and large efforts like the former one in Iraq and present ones in Afghanistan could profit from specifically designed and trained counterinsurgency units in addition to the Special Forces. Their training would be similar in many aspects because counterinsurgency is special warfare. While it recognizes the primary importance of security for the people, it also recognizes that the ultimate goal of a counterinsurgency operation is not just to kill insurgents, it is to win the loyalty of the people. The former happens better with improvements of the latter, not the other way around, and if the twenty-first century is going to be the century of small wars, that is insurgent wars, the sooner the American military adapts to the task the better.

Factor 11. Failure to control strategic terrain. Controlling strategic terrain can mean securing the critical high ground and key communication points (bridges, river and road intersections, etc.) in the countryside. It can also mean controlling the sparsely inhabited regions that otherwise serve as the travel and communication corridors for the insurgents. Typically, that is the job of the conventional army; but in counterinsurgency, a village center is also strategic ground, and it must be secured against threats from the insurgents. That is best done with organized, regulated militias that have been motivated to protect their own homes through the belief that their government offers them a better life than whatever the insurgents have to offer. If that offer for a better life is delayed or inconsequential, the motivation to protect it will be similar.

The work of securing a village requires a motivated force because the task is not easy. It is a full time job both night and day. Daylight patrols should be aimed at finding the local enemy, harassing him, and keeping him disorganized. Night patrols and ambushes should disrupt patterns of enemy activity and help prevent terror attacks. Two important things: (1) the night cannot be yielded to the insurgents, and (2) a body-count mentality, one that focuses on the number of enemy killed rather than the underlying sense of security in the village, is wrong minded. Yes, it is true that providing security is the first active step in a counterinsurgency campaign, but it is an error to let that primary goal cause either the military or civilian leaders to lose contact with the idea that the main point of the program is to convince the people that their loyalty belongs with the government. That is a more complex task than killing the enemy.

Factor 12. Failure to control the country's borders. It is not particularly insightful to say that when faced with an insurgency a country must secure its borders. It is true, nevertheless, and getting the job done can be difficult. It is generally true that the only clearly marked, easily accessible borders are those formed by bodies of water like rivers, lakes, and oceans. Elsewhere, borders run over mountain tops, through dense jungles, and across empty deserts. Borders in those regions often lack the attributes of either clarity or accessibility, which makes them useful to guerrillas needing sanctuary areas.

Vietnam had its Viet Cong sanctuaries in Laos and Cambodia, Iraq its al-Qaida and Sadarist sanctuaries in Iran and Syria, and Afghanistan its Taliban sanctuaries in Pakistan. All of them give witness to the importance of cross-border sanctuaries and to the difficulties implicit in making those sanctuaries unavailable through border control. Connected to this problem of a government needing to control its own borders is the attendant one of a neighboring country needing to control its borders. A neighboring country can sometimes be complicit with foreign insurgents by allowing them sanctuaries in its territory, yet claiming inability to do otherwise.

Wrong. It is a recognized obligation of sovereignty that a country must control its territory in a way that prevents attacks on a neighboring country unless the two countries are at war. A country not carrying out that international obligation has no legitimate right of complaint if a neighboring country, the one being attacked from cross-border sanctuaries, responds

Six. Counterinsurgency Failure

by crossing that border itself to destroy those sanctuaries. This, too, is a part of border control and a part that must be used when necessary.

No one list can encompass all the reasons that counterinsurgency programs fail, especially one intentionally limited for brevity. In fact, counterinsurgency programs rarely fail because of one or two reasons only. The programs are multifaceted and so are the reasons for their failure, and each case is likely somewhat different from the next. It needs to be recognized that counterinsurgency is a complex business difficult to complete with success, and to be fooled by its "small war" disguise is a major error.

The list of twelve factors associated with counterinsurgency failure are consistent with my training of long ago, my experience in Vietnam, and the experiences of others reporting from a variety of theaters across a span of decades. Only the latter three factors refer to direct military tasks, which reinforces the idea that it is an error in counterinsurgency to focus on conventional military tasks while undervaluing the importance of involving the people and improving their lives.

That idea is far from being uniquely mine. It has been advocated by others, but the problem has been in making the concept work in an army whose conventional job is to confront and destroy the enemy. In guerrilla war, the favorite war of insurgencies, that is difficult to do because the enemy finds it all too easy to avoid the confrontation until he chooses the time and place. French Sergeant Guy de Chaumont-Guitry wrote from Vietnam in 1948 (quoted by Gloria Emerson in her book, *Winners and Losers*) to say that a conventional military operation against a guerrilla insurgency is like making a sword thrust into water. The blade goes in, the water gives way, the blade comes out, and the water returns; but because the process can be repeated with little damage to the blade, each thrust cycle comes to be called a success. It is not. Some understand that from the beginning, some never do; and those carrying out the conventional efforts of stabbing at water eventually extinguish themselves from an exhaustion of will.

That contrast in perception is illustrated by Louis Sorley in his book, *Honorable Warrior*. He shows that during the Vietnam War, General Howard Johnson, Army Chief of Staff from 1964 to 1968, often argued that the war against North Vietnam and the Viet Cong being directed in South Vietnam could not be won by the type of main-force, ground and air war General Westmoreland was conducting. General Johnson was convinced that the main effort should shift from that kind of war, basically one of attrition, to counterinsurgency operations out in the villages and hamlets of the countryside.

It may seem strange to an outsider that as Army Chief of Staff General Johnson could not simply give orders to change the way things were being done. In actuality, military life is not that simple and Johnson found that politics, both the civilian and military kind, made it very difficult to change the mode of ongoing operations. Only at the end of his tenure was the warfighting mode changed to one more focused on counterinsurgency; but by then billions of dollars and tens of thousands of American lives had been spent on a war that had now lost the favor of American public opinion. In the end, the war in Vietnam would prove to be a largely wasted military enterprise, but that fact alone means it is a war from which much should have been learned and once learned not forgotten.

Relevant Readings

Cooper, Chester L., Judith E. Corson, Laurence J. Legere, David E. Lockwood, and Donald M. Weller. *The American Experience with Pacification in Vietnam.* Vol. 1. *An Overview of Pacification.* Arlington, VA: RAND Corporation, 1972,1–61.

Emerson, Gloria. *Winners and Losers: Battles, Retreats, Gains, Losses and Ruins from a Long War.* New York: Random House, 1978, 274–77.

Fitzgerald, David. *Learning to Forget: U.S. Army Counterinsurgency Doctrine and Practice.* San Francisco: Stanford University Press, 2013.

Galula, David. *Pacification in Algeria 1956–1958.* Arlington, VA: RAND Corporation, 1963.

Gardner, Lloyd C. and Marilyn B. Young, eds. *Iraq and the Lessons of Vietnam or How not to Learn From the Past.* New York: The New Press, 2007.

Gentile, Gian. *Wrong Turn: America's Deadly Embrace of Counterinsurgency.* New York: The New Press, 2013.

Hoffman, Bruce. "Insurgency and Counterinsurgency in Iraq" (an "Occasional Paper"). Santa Monica, CA: RAND Corporation, 2004.

Jones, Seth G. *Counterinsurgency in Afghanistan.* Santa Monica, CA: RAND Corporation, 2008, 135–36.

Kilcullen, David. *Counterinsurgency.* New York: Oxford University Press, 2010.

Porch, Douglas. *Counterinsurgency: Exposing the Myths of the New Way of War.* New York: Cambridge University Press, 2013.

Sepp, Kalev I. "Best Practices in Counterinsurgency." *Military Review* May-June (2005): 8–12.

Sorley, Lewis. *Honorable Warrior: General Harold K. Johnson and the Ethics of Command.* Lawrence: University Press of Kansas, 1998, 227–58.

Seven

Counterinsurgency Program Organization

It Can Work in Its Specifics but Still Be Overwhelmed

In January of 1969, General Creighton Abrams, Commanding General, Military Assistance Command, Vietnam (MACV) was speaking at a staff meeting at MACV headquarters in Saigon in response to a query about adding more Mobile Advisory Teams (MATs) to the MACV counterinsurgency program. According to Lewis Sorley (*The Vietnam Chronicles: The Abrams Tapes, 1968–1970*) General Abrams responded, "These (Mobile Advisory) teams have been eminently successful. They've done a *hell* of a lot for the RF and PF…. They live with them, *fight* with them, *patrol* with them, *ambush* with them, and so on. *Then* you get communication, *then* you get reaction (italics Sorley's)." MATs were the Vietnam version of small advisory teams sent out into the villages as a part of the overall counterinsurgency effort, CORDS, introduced in Chapter Two. Apologies to the reader, but here and below the need to deal with some acronyms of the Vietnam era becomes inescapable.

Abrams, like General Westmoreland before him, was in command not only of the military advisors within MACV but of all the in-country USARV (United States Army, Vietnam) units, as well. USARV was made up of conventional Army units like the 1st Cavalry Division, 1st Infantry Division, and 101st Airborne, among many others. It was in this context of Abrams' competing responsibilities, i.e. MACV advisor units versus USARV conventional units, that the question of more MATs arose: would it be better to have more advisory teams working in counterinsurgency with the Vietnamese allies or to assign that same number of officers and men to needy USARV units who were taking the fight directly to the enemy? Abrams' response was that the MATs had proven themselves effective in their task of improving the Vietnamese Regional Forces (RF) and Popular Forces (PF).

The RF and PF, often referred to as "territorial forces," were essentially militia units responsible for the defense of their home districts (RFs) or villages and hamlets (PFs). They were different from the Army of the Republic of Vietnam (ARVN), which was South Vietnam's conventional army responsible for the more general defense of the country. The RF were better paid and equipped than the PF because of their wider responsibility, but neither had the pay and equipment of the ARVN.

Military assistance advisors from the U.S. Army had been assigned to the ARVN in increasing numbers since the late 1950s, and by the mid-1960s advisors were represented at every major ARVN unit level down to the battalion. Through those same years the territorial forces had never had advisors assigned to them. The RF and PF were as poorly equipped and led as they were poorly paid, that much was known; but MACV's lack of direct contact with those units down in the villages had left it with little specific information about their troop strengths, true condition, or methods of improvement. That situation improved greatly in 1968 when MACV activated the new CORDS counterinsurgency strategy that included the formation of MATs to be posted in selected villages and hamlets in every province in the country.

At the time of his comments in 1969, General Abrams was making the point that MATs were living with local militias in their villages and hamlets, training them, and fighting along side them. As a result, their RF and PF units were experiencing more combat success and communicating better with ARVN and U.S. Army units. Consequently, those regular armies were getting better information on enemy activity and achieving better reaction times to it. In Abrams' view, the MATs had been "eminently successful" in the U.S. effort to help South Vietnam stave off an insurgency being organized and assisted by its neighbor to the north.

Seven. Counterinsurgency Program Organization

MATs remained important to the combat effectiveness of the RF and PF units, thus to the overall CORDS program, throughout the period of the American drawdown in Vietnam (1969–1972). In that draw-down environment, the U.S. conventional forces remained committed to finding and taking on the enemy in direct combat or working with conventional ARVN forces in doing likewise. With those requirements ongoing, the U.S. advisory corps for counterinsurgency remained relatively small and was never able to provide advisors to most territorial forces units. As a consequence, the overall performance of those units remained highly variable and often seriously deficient. Further, local militias, no matter how well performing, could not overcome the inadequacies of a national government that was commonly characterized as corrupt, inept, or both. A persistently underperforming government cannot inspire confidence in its people or courage in its soldiers, which is why government reform (Program Requirement 4, Chapter Two) is so important to counterinsurgency campaigns. U.S. counterinsurgency planners, U.S. counterinsurgency advisors, and all elements of the host government must realize that counterinsurgency is not just a program for soldiers in the field; it is for the policemen on their beats, the bureaucrats in their offices, and the politicians in the halls of power. It is a difficult task that requires the commitment of everyone, not of just the grunt out on the battlefield.

Despite the MATs' successes in helping push back the Viet Cong insurgency they have remained little remarked upon in an era when counterinsurgency has once again come to the fore in military and international affairs. This is perhaps because American advisory teams, MATs and otherwise, had such a low profile in Vietnam in the first place. Unlike what would happen for the Special Forces or for the permanent Army divisions, for example, no centralized record of them would be made. MATs operated with relative independence and often in isolated posts. In many ways, they took over a role Special Forces teams had had earlier in the war. Their insertion was necessary because by 1968 the Special Forces had become more oriented toward reconnaissance, raiding, and interdiction deep in enemy sanctuary areas.

MATs were not a part of the Special Forces and were not a part of the larger USARV picture; thus, they were easy to overlook, especially when U.S. counterinsurgency efforts in general lost cachet after the collapse of

South Vietnam. In the present times, however, their experience rises to relevance given that counterinsurgency has once more gained profile in American foreign policy and in American military doctrine. Given that, it may be useful to think back to the concept of advisory teams in counterinsurgency operations, MATs being an example of one kind of team within one kind of organization that was arguably successful at its assigned task. Such reflection might be helpful in considering how counterinsurgency organizations might be structured today. Finally, it is important to be aware that counterinsurgency success can be overcome by events not directly related to counterinsurgency. That, too, will be addressed below.

Relatively Independent, Small Advisory Teams: Where They Fit in a Counterinsurgency Program

The U.S. effort in counterinsurgency in Vietnam started with several civilian agencies doing their work and the U.S. Army, Navy, and Marines doing theirs. The most prominent Army unit involved was the Special Forces who had their twelve-man "A-teams" working in selected outposts around the country. They were especially important in remote regions where they led armed units against the enemy. CORDS was MACV's later counterinsurgency effort initiated in late 1967 under then MACV commander, General Westmoreland. Westmoreland's agreement to focus more on counterinsurgency—the popular term at the time was pacification—came only after persistent pressure from the Pentagon assisted by a fresh advocacy for counterinsurgency from the White House. Otherwise, Westmoreland's inclination had been to continue going after the enemy in a battle of attrition.

CORDS was aimed at increasing village security while at the same time promoting development in the rural areas, two major requirements of any counterinsurgency program (see Chapter Two). CORDS was the brainchild of Mr. Robert Komer, in 1967 a member of the National Security Council and Special Assistant to President Lyndon Johnson.

Komer was aware that there had been previous efforts at counterinsurgency in Vietnam, but they had all failed for a variety of reasons ranging the long history of political turmoil within the South Vietnamese government to the endemic weaknesses in that government. Those weaknesses included corruption, cronyism, and a mandarinate style of administration.

Seven. Counterinsurgency Program Organization

On the American side, there had been a divided leadership between the civilian and military pacification efforts, a division that had led to a lack of coordination and sometimes to conflicting goals of the counterinsurgency efforts. With these types of problems afflicting all sides, the counterinsurgency programs previously attempted in South Vietnam had had little effect in the countryside.

Komer wanted to change that. He had suggested to President Johnson that a new effort be initiated with the American military, especially the U.S. Army, becoming more involved in the pacification program. He wanted the American military to make greater manpower and resource commitments to pacification, and to have a unified command structure for the effort—civilian and military programs combined within one system headed by one person.

Komer designed the CORDS program to address three key points, each of which he considered important to a successful counterinsurgency effort: (1) security—village populations have to feel safe from the predations of local guerrillas; (2) development—village life has to be enhanced by programs that win the people's loyalty; and (3) aggression towards the enemy—the insurgents' infrastructure has to be destroyed and his claims of legitimacy countered. Dealing with all three issues at the same time would require coordination between military, police, intelligence, and civilian aid operations. Not only that, but the civic action programs, development advances, and battlefield successes would need to be advertised by a vigorous public information program or propaganda campaign.

General Westmoreland accepted Komer's program as a combined military-civilian counterinsurgency effort with a unified command under military control. General Westmoreland would be in command given the large military commitment, but in May of 1967 Komer was appointed MACV deputy for CORDS (DEPCORDS) to serve on Westmoreland's general staff as a civilian in a position equivalent to that of General Abrams who at the time was Westmoreland's deputy for USARV forces. As DEPCORDS, Komer had authority over both the military and civilian sides of CORDS and reported directly to Westmoreland. This relationship of CORDS to the theater military commander remained the same when General Abrams became the MACV commanding general in June, 1968.

The unified civilian-military structure for CORDS was carried down

Counterinsurgency

to the province level by the advisory teams already existing in all 44 provinces of South Vietnam. These Province Teams were headed by a Province Senior Advisor (PSA), typically a U.S. Army colonel, whose counterpart was the Province Chief, in Vietnam usually an ARVN colonel. The Province Team's Deputy PSA was typically a civilian from the United States Agency for International Development (USAID) or Department of State, and the team itself was composed of both military and civilian staff, each side managing their own areas of expertise. Education, agriculture, public health, and other aspects of civil affairs were the responsibility of the Province Team's civilian advisors while security, including the militia-like RF and PF, were the responsibility of the military advisors. Intelligence and counterintelligence were a joint responsibility of the military and the Central Intelligence Agency (CIA). All these programs were coordinated under the CORDS umbrella and were represented at the district level by much smaller District Teams advising district officials at their headquarters.

The District Teams were usually all U.S. Army, though civilian members were sometimes included. The teams were originally to consist of 5–8 advisors headed by an Army major as District Senior Advisor (DSA). In reality, the DSA was often of lower rank and the District Teams were often significantly smaller than originally conceived. The District Teams advised and assisted the Vietnamese District Chief and district-level staff in carrying out development programs and security operations as directed from province headquarters. District Teams also gathered information on the status and activities of the RF and PF units in their districts and on the economic and security status of each hamlet in their district. This information, compiled by the HES and TFES reports (see Chapter Two) fed into large CORDS and CIA databases used to evaluate the overall counterinsurgency effort.

At the bottom of the CORDS organization, typically serving under the District Teams, were the Mobile Advisory Teams. The MATs lived out in the villages and hamlets of Vietnam and were the basic military operating units of the entire CORDS system. By early 1968, 354 MATs had been authorized to advise and assist the Vietnamese territorial forces across all four military regions of the country (I Corps in the north, II Corps along the central coast and highlands, III Corps around and above Saigon, and IV Corps in the Mekong Delta). These small teams operated with relative

Seven. Counterinsurgency Program Organization

independence and were often out of sight of everyone save for their villagers and the enemy around them.

In Iraq and Afghanistan the CORDS model has been suggested but never fully applied. In both Iraq and Afghanistan, a new type of organization, the Province Reconstruction Team (PRT), was devised to be in charge of the development, civic affairs, and propaganda missions in a province while the responsibility of active combat advising was placed elsewhere. The PRTs are relatively large being manned by a mix of 60–100 soldiers and civilians, but there are differences between the PRTs formerly in Iraq and those still in Afghanistan at the time of this writing.

One example of those differences is that in Iraq, the PRTs were generally led by a State Department official and the teams were staffed with a substantial number of civilians. In Afghanistan the teams are led by senior military officers and are manned mostly by military personnel. Those differences have been chosen largely because of differences in the conditions within each country that range from ability to provide security to tasks that are particular to each country.

Importantly, the central management of counterinsurgency that was advocated in Chapter Two has largely been missing in both Iraq and Afghanistan. PRTs have been more loosely managed and in Afghanistan the problem is compounded by there being PRTs run by other NATO forces. There have been PRTs run by the American, German, and British forces, perhaps even others, and those different forces run their PRTs according to the interests and risk-averseness dictated by their home governments. That does not contribute to uniformity of programs or centralized management.

It was realized early on in Afghanistan that there was a need to move the counterinsurgency mission outside of the large towns and into the villages of the countryside. To achieve this goal, so-called Team Village units were organized. These units were made up of a varying mix of U.S. medical, civil affairs, psychological operations, and public affairs personnel along with accompanying Afghan security forces and interpreters. Team Village missions go into the villages, but they do not live there and do not partner with the local tribal or village authorities to maintain a permanent counterinsurgency presence in the village and to provide security for it. An organization somewhat like an expanded MAT could do that.

Structure and Mission of Small Advisory Teams: The MAT Experience

As mentioned previously, counterinsurgency has long been a focus of the U.S. Army's Special Forces, but the present threat environment requires a broader approach to the problem than Special Forces alone. Specially trained counterinsurgency teams similar in mission to the MATs of Vietnam working in programs similar in principle to CORDS could be useful in a wide variety of circumstances. Advisory teams like the MATs in Vietnam could serve as a model to adapt for similar efforts in other parts of the world.

In the following retrospective, the terms, usually, commonly, or typically will often appear. The caution is necessary because MATs varied not only in their location and provision, but in the security environment in which they operated, the types and ethnicity of units they advised (RF or PF, Vietnamese or Montagnard, etc.), and their experiences on the ground. What follows is an attempt to describe a broad average that relates to most teams wherever and whomever they served. They are discussed in this detail because advisor teams are the final operating point of a counterinsurgency program and the MAT experience is relevant as a comparison for other possibilities.

MATs consisted of two officers, three enlisted men, and an interpreter. The Team Leader and Assistant Team Leader were authorized to be a captain and a first lieutenant, respectively, though in practice, team leaders were commonly first lieutenants. Both of the team's officers were to be from a combat arms branch (Infantry, Armor, or Artillery). The enlisted men were originally to be non-commissioned officers (NCOs) at the rank of sergeants first class or master sergeants and were to serve as the team's light weapons specialist, heavy weapons specialist, and medic. In reality, as with their officers, the MATs' NCOs were often of a less senior rank than authorized.

In other environments it is easy to conceive of MAT-like teams that could be twice as large, still with two officers and perhaps two interpreters, but with more NCOs trained for counterinsurgency and focusing on light weapons training, heavy weapons training, basic medical care and public health, basic civil engineering, civil government development, and public

Seven. Counterinsurgency Program Organization

information. Not only would the increase in numbers of men on a team increase group's safety, but the expanded capabilities in development activities and public information would be a benefit, no matter what the environment. These kinds of teams would deliver counterinsurgency with their counterparts at the village level. A CORDS-like structure above them could be the source of province and district level programs and projects to provide security, development, and reform.

When the first levy of soldiers was made to establish the MATs in Vietnam, the levy was applied to officers and NCOs already serving in USARV units but who had at least six months remaining on their tour of duty. Those advisors were sent to a two-week, in-country advisor school before being assigned to their teams. While that schooling helped prepare those soldiers for their advisory roles, it was acknowledged that the limited amount of training possible at the in-country school was inadequate to the need. Subsequently, after early 1969 many of the officers and some of the NCOs assigned to MACVCORDS had completed a six-week military advisor course at the Special Warfare School, Fort Bragg, NC. That course, previously mentioned in Chapter Four, took much from Special Forces training and focused on weapons and explosives training, counterinsurgency techniques, intelligence operations, field-expedient engineering, the CORDS program, and Vietnamese language and culture. Some of the future advisors additionally completed either an 8-week or 12-week Vietnamese language course run by the Defense Language Institute headquartered in Monterey, California.

MACVCORDS also soon recognized that MAT advisors needed to be in their role for the entire 12 months of their tour; thus, beginning in 1969 most MAT personnel arrived in-country directly assigned to MACV, which would then send them to their Province teams to be assigned to their MATs depending on local needs.

Once established with their RF or PF units, MATs instructed them on such topics as individual and crew-served weapons, small unit tactics, and field first aide. The teams also accompanied their units in the field, advising and teaching on the spot to improve daylight operations, night ambushes, intelligence operations, and other aspects of village or hamlet security. The patrolling and ambush techniques employed were often unique to the terrain and people involved, which called for flexibility and ingenuity on the part of advisors as well as an ability to give credit to their counterparts as being the most experienced fighters within their native environment.

The original concept of a MAT was that it would work with their RF or PF unit for six-to-nine months then move on to another; thus, the "Mobile" in Mobile Advisory Team. In practice, many advisors performed their entire tour with a MAT that never moved, likely because of the importance of the unit it was assigned to or the needs of the immediate area in which they were working. In other environments, small advisory teams might similarly be assigned in one place for a long time or be moved to new locations, depending on need. In any case, the idea of the teams moving every six-to-nine months will be unwise in many situations and as a practical matter the teams are likely to be more STATs (Stationary Advisory Teams) than MATs.

While MAT advisors did not command the unit they were advising, the RF and PF commanders were instructed by their superiors to follow their advisors' directions. Recognizing that reality and wanting to improve recruiting for advisor positions, MACV began crediting MAT officers with combat command time while recognizing that RF and PF leaders had to be taught to be commanders, themselves. While to a civilian reader the benefit of "combat command time" may seem dubious, it is an issue to military officers wanting to progress in an Army career. That it arose as a problem in Vietnam speaks to a point raised in Chapter Four where it was discussed that advisors have commonly felt that their service is either not understood or is underappreciated in a conventional military structure.

Finding the balance between taking command to get the job done and letting the indigenous commander learn the ropes by having to do it himself is a difficult task that has to be adjusted from situation to situation depending on the urgency and the safety issues involved. In some situations, the advisor may feel that a point has been reached where mere advice will no longer suffice. At the same time he may recognize that taking charge of the task, perhaps helpful in the short term, might cause difficulties later on. Having to deal with these kinds of decisions is why advisor training and maturity of mind are important for advisor success, another point already discussed in Chapter Four.

As a practical matter, assignment of a MAT to a militia unit was also an assignment to the village or hamlet in which that unit lived. The advisors lived in that village and worked with its officials, and in some areas like the

Seven. Counterinsurgency Program Organization

Mekong Delta, they could be the only Americans for miles around. Depending on where it was posted, a team's living conditions could range from a bunkered, brick-and-mortar house to a one-room team-house designed for easy assembly and disassembly consistent with the original mobility concept. Most often, the team's billet was a village's or hamlet's mud-walled fort typically surrounded by a moat and barbed wire entanglements. The forts and the RF or PF troops assigned to them were the advisory team's protection from the local insurgents though it was often easy to question whether that protection was going to be sufficient.

Advisors sometimes got the word that there was a price on their heads. That kind of news tends to make one feel exceptionally exposed, and on combat operations that feeling could be heightened by the fact that the advisor often stood out in size relative to the smaller Vietnamese. In such cases, size is not a positive attribute. Insurgents also often attacked advisor's compounds, usually small forts or cantonments, which made security even at a team's home base a dubious proposition. The sum effect of those unrelenting threats made life not only dangerous but mentally wearing.

The mental stress of working in small teams was difficult to escape. With only five members on a MAT, for example, there were no spare hands available once even the minimal requirements for daily operations were met. One member of the team always had to be awake and present in or around the team house to guard against intrusion and to keep radio watch. That left two two-man teams to rotate in going out on night ambushes and daylight operations while still doing the other advisory duties. Too small a team means there is never enough time or enough people to do what needs to be done, so if the concept of MATs should be thought useful, then increasing their size to ten or twelve men for improved security and function would be a good idea. In that regard, at the time of this writing the Marine Corps has a Special Operations Regiment that ultimately breaks down to fifteen man teams. All team members are selected, not randomly assigned, and all have special warfare training including language training and some teams have had advisory responsibilities. The Army, too, could have units of this type trained as advisors for both the civil and military responses to insurgency at the village level. History suggests this kind of unit would be very useful in U.S. efforts to help a host nation.

Clearly, specific conflicts will dictate the kind of organization that

Counterinsurgency

will work best in specific environments, but one example similar to that of the Marine Corps' Special Operations Regiment above would be to have specially trained U.S. Army special warfare teams organized into counterinsurgency brigades, battalions, and companies. The companies could be organized into platoons and individual teams with each team being in place of the squad in a conventional formation. In round numbers, four ten-man teams could make up a forty-man advisor platoon with those teams being posted in different villages within a general area. At the various levels of team, platoon, and company, the counterinsurgency resources of small-unit tactics, weapons, medics, civil affairs, engineering, intelligence, and psychological operations could be covered. With the increased numbers of trained team members available in even the smallest units (ten-men as opposed to, for example, the five-man MATs of Vietnam) the various tasks of counterinsurgency could be more adequately completed. While this may sound like a facsimile of a Special Forces A-team, there are significant differences. For example, the units need not be airborne designated and team members need not be airborne qualified, language training could be conflict specific rather than more broadly covered as in the case of A-teams, and individual teams could be led by senior NCOs with appropriate training rather than commissioned officers as was the case with MATs and is the case with A-teams. The first level "senior advisor" role in that case would be held by the counterinsurgency platoon leader. Rank structure in such units would likely vary from conventional formations in needing more senior ranks leading at the company level and under, i. e. platoon leaders may need to be captains and team leaders (in place of squads) may need to be Sergeants First Class or Master Sergeants.

The U.S. Army has tried Security Forces Advise and Assist Teams (SFAATs) in Afghanistan as a way to use small units of soldiers from conventional American units as advisors. Typically, SFAATs consist of from ten to twenty men pulled from a conventional Army division or Brigade Combat Team. The SFAAT mission has been to advise and assist Afghan army battalions or *kandaks*. Properly trained (see Chapter Four) they could advise and assist in the broader counterinsurgency mission out in the villages; however, the problems with SFAATs are several. First, in one method of constituting SFAATs, men are "borrowed" from their conventional companies or platoons for the SFAAT job, not replaced. That means they are

Seven. Counterinsurgency Program Organization

still needed in their home unit for that unit to achieve its conventional mission. A company commander, for example, can be pulled for an SFAAT and have to leave his company to function without him. He will still be that company's commander, but he will not be there to command. He will be expected to do the job through electronic communication with his executive officer while he advises in Afghanistan. Thus, the process pulls the SFAAT member two ways, home unit vs. SFAAT, and makes the advisory job doubly stressful. Secondly, SFAAT personnel are designated, not selected in any rigorous way. Many factors in the home unit can affect who is chosen for an SFAAT deployment. Whether the abilities and personality traits of the chosen are the most compatible with being a good advisor might or might not be high among them. Thirdly, while SFAAT training varied over time, it has generally been minimal. In one iteration, the designees received approximately three weeks of advisor training (language skills, cultural sensitivity, relationship building, field exercises, etc.) at Fort Polk, Louisiana. The language instruction, for example, consisted of between ten and twenty hours, which is not sufficient for teaching anything substantive.

In another method of staffing SFAATs, entire brigades (currently designated brigade combat teams), have been assigned to the task. That appears to only heighten the selection and training issues already raised, but it does resolve the pulled-two-ways problem caused by detailing individuals from stay-at-home units.

Despite their limitations, SFAATs were useful in their role of working only with Afghan army units. Similar but appropriately trained advisory and assistant teams working at the village level with both military and civil authorities could also prove useful in a counterinsurgency role, but the practice of extracting the teams' personnel from conventional units without replacement will remain a problem. For that reason, establishment of dedicated advisory units or even an Advisor Corps has been previously advocated.

Counterinsurgency SFAATs, like the MATs in Vietnam, could train their militia or army units and fight beside them, but also support other aspects of a counterinsurgency program like CORDS. A counterinsurgency advisor might assist a local village official in developing a school, a clinic, or some other help for making an improved life in the villages. In Vietnam, it was not an uncommon sentiment that being on MAT was like being in the Peace Corp with guns. That's what makes the civil affairs, public health, and field engineering advisors so important for a counterinsurgency operation. They are a necessary accompaniment to an aggressive campaign to root out the enemy. That was an important part of the CORDS strategy and should be the strategy in any similar program aiming at securing the lives and property of a people and winning their resolute loyalty.

In Vietnam, as in any counterinsurgency effort, combat operations against the enemy were rarely simple. The conventional army and the militias fought the Viet Cong and their NVA allies while the Phoenix program, a joint effort by the military and the CIA, went after the silent insurgents in the villages who formed the "shadow government" or Viet Cong infrastructure (VCI) having its own district chiefs, village chiefs, finance officers, couriers, and the like. MATs worked with their assigned militia units in fighting the guerrillas and the NVA and worked with the American and Vietnamese intelligence apparatus, including the Phoenix program, to further weaken the enemy in their villages. Teams like SFAATs with the proper selection and training could do similar things in Afghanistan or in any other counterinsurgency conflict.

Advisory teams have to deal with the multiple responsibilities of combat training and operations, civil affairs, intelligence operations, and a miscellany of other concerns that defy categorization. Each responsibility makes a demand on time, attention, and energy, each of which could only be split so many ways. This is where a small, five-man unit like a MAT can really suffer. As mentioned previously, there are no extra hands on board, and if the team is a man down due to leave, hospitalization, or administrative issues, that's a twenty-percent loss in personnel. That kind of loss leaves too many things that simply don't get done. The problem is compounded when, as occurred in Vietnam, lieutenants fill the positions that are supposed to be held by majors and captains and slots that are supposed to be filled by experienced master sergeants and sergeants first class are filled instead by lesser ranks with less experience. Experienced, trained people should be used to staff an appropriately-sized team for its situation. Absent that, the advisory effort will be far less successful than its planners hoped it would be.

Despite the CORDS efforts to have its civilian and military personnel working in concert with each other, the attempt did not always work well. Each side sometimes felt stymied or undercut by the other, and because of

MAT leaders' varied level of advisor training, some arrived on the job never thinking of their teams as having any meaningful role in the development part of the CORDS mission. As a result, they fulfilled their military role of working with their RF or PF units but left the development side of counterinsurgency to someone else.

Even when small military advisory units like MATs did do some development work, their relationship with the civilian side of the rural development programs could be strained, likely because the training, experiences, perspectives and goals of the two sides could be considerably different. In a joint military-civilian counterinsurgency effort, these differences need to be ameliorated, perhaps through a period of joint training.

A Persistent Difficulty: Supply and Sustenance of Remote Advisory Teams

There is no question that advisor units have usually been the poor cousins in American military expeditions overseas. In Vietnam, for example, MACV's original plan for MAT members was for them to arrive in country and be issued a personal weapon, a basic load of ammunition, jungle fatigues, boots, a backpack, and the other basic equipment for an individual soldier. After that, the advisor was to be supplied from the Vietnamese logistics system. This was supposed to insure that advisors paid attention to the supply and sustenance of their territorial forces units and was supposed to help eliminate corruption in the Vietnamese supply system. The reality was that MAT advisors and their units were at the bottom of the supply chain for territorial forces and were in a poor position to have any significant influence on the corruption happening above them. As a result, the small advisory teams were usually forced to become proficient scroungers from whatever USARV, U.S. Air Force, U.S. Marines, or U.S. Navy units they could reach. It was common knowledge that an enemy flag, an AK-47, or even an old inventory U.S. weapon like a Thompson submachine gun could be potent trading tools back at the U.S. bases. Rather than help build a proper logistical system, the advisors commonly developed a barter system that substituted for proper logistics. Whether the need was sandbags, ammunition, or construction materials, self-authorized supply expeditions directed at conventional American units were often as important to a MATs' survival as its combat operations directed at the enemy. This aspect of the CORDS operation did not help the counterpart's logistics system and should not be repeated. The advisor in the field is unlikely to be a significant contributor to improving a host nation's logistics system because it is often broken far up the pipeline from him and his unit.

Small advisory teams were often posted to remote locations difficult to reach by any route but air. This meant that food, laundry, or any other billeting services had to be obtained locally and often paid for from a team member's own pockets. MATs could purchase food supplies from a "country store" maintained in most Province Team compounds. The store had a supply of American-style canned goods, flour, sugar, frozen meat, and condiments, but since the supplies varied over time, the remote MATs rarely knew what was available. That had the effect of limiting their access to those supplies, so most MAT members learned to eat on the local economy using the local foods and adopting the local manners at table. If one could not learn to learn to do that, he likely ended up being shipped to the rear because of malnutrition, culture shock, or both.

Lesson Learned: Not All Supply Channels Are Equal—Do What Works to Complete the Mission

First Lieutenant William. M. Treadway, team leader, MAT II-36 and District Senior Advisor; Van Ninh District, Kanh Hoa Province (MACV Advisor Team 35), II Corp Tactical Zone; 1969.

My Mobile Advisory Team (MAT) rode a circuit of several hamlets in my district working with the militias in those hamlets to help them do two primary things: 1) go on the offense in hunting down the enemy's local infrastructure or "shadow government" and 2) maintain a good defense in fending off enemy attacks. We were constantly moved from one hamlet to another. Our tactic of not staying in one place for long was a significant aspect of my team's defense. We were a five-man team; the idea was to not give the enemy time to mount a major attack against us at any particular location. Our key methods were to avoid patterns, travel light, and stay alert: That's how we operated and how we survived.

Opposite: **Lieutenant Treadway at the door of his MAT's team house in Kanh Hoa Province in 1969.**

Counterinsurgency

High mobility combat advising was my team's way of life until we were assigned to a more advanced militia battalion guarding a large salt production facility. That was a change of mission and it concerned me because it put us in a fixed-base situation where the team was not equipped to protect itself. We had no heavy weapons, no direct combat support, and little of the equipment needed for a fixed-base operation. Being tied to one place made the team feel we were about to be sitting ducks. The things we felt we needed were not part of a MAT's table of organization and equipment; therefore, they would not be made available, at least through conventional U.S. Army channels. Luckily, there are other channels available and we put them to use.

Being close to a large U.S. Air Force base, we knew they had all sorts of equipment that would be useful to us. We also knew that while the Air Force guys would rarely leave the safety of their base, they were hungry for "war" souvenirs they could take back home. We decided we could provide the souvenirs and would use them to bargain for the equipment we needed.

Our most effective approach was in making "guerrilla" maps on parachute cloth. The idea was to make crude maps that looked as if they had been captured from the enemy. We made the maps by first collecting parachute material from air-dropped parachute flares. We cut the canopy material into squares and had the wives of local militiamen hem the squares. Then we would draw terrain features and place names on the squares, sometimes adding attack arrows pointing at some bogus unit designation. To heighten the look of authenticity we would fold the maps neatly, shoot them a couple times, then smear them with blood from the next chicken or pig the militia killed. When doing our trades we could always concoct a story of how we had captured the map in a fight with the local guerrillas.

The Air Force guys went nuts over the maps. They had time and the equipment to trade for a good souvenir and we had the ability to put reallocated assets to good use. After all, we considered the process just a repurposing of material within the military family.

Our best trade for just one guerrilla map included a 2.5 ton truck, a complete 81mm mortar, an overhaul of our beat-up M151 jeep, which included steel-plate reinforcement in the floor to protect against land mines and a pedestal mount for our M-60 machine gun. None of that was authorized for my MAT nor was it available through Army channels, but we used it all; and given our change of mission, exposed position, and absence of other support, we were only doing what was necessary to accomplish our mission.

The point is this: Advisors, especially advisors in a counterinsurgency campaign, often have to work outside of conventional channels. Counterinsurgency warfare is unconventional warfare and unconventional warfare requires unconventional means. Counterinsurgency advisors have always had to be masters at "asset reallocation." It is an aspect of conventional and unconventional warfare that the Army and other services know exists but have a hard time formally admitting to, let alone sanctioning. So, don't expect approval and don't ask permission; do what works so long as it doesn't violate the trust you have been given to achieve your mission, protect your men, and stay on the right side of the Geneva Convention.

William Treadway is a retired banker now living in Georgetown, Texas. He and his wife of 30 years own a real estate brokerage.

The sustenance and supply system for remote advisory teams in Vietnam was an irregular one, at best, and while difficulties were understandable, it is a problem that should have been adjusted for by now. Apparently, they have not. Advisors in Iraq and Afghanistan have also complained about equipment and supply availability and have felt overlooked when contrasting themselves with their colleagues in the conventional America units. The depth of this problem is difficult to assess from here, but to the degree that logistical problems for advisors have persisted across a variety of campaigns over a span of fifty years illustrates the problem has not been solved.

Effectiveness of Small Advisory Teams in a Counterinsurgency Environment

General Abrams made it clear in 1969 that small advisory teams, in that case the MATs, were doing the job expected of them. That kind of report persisted through the remainder of the MACV advisory experience with others reporting that MAT effectiveness was demonstrated many times by the improved performance of the territorial forces units they were advising. Interestingly, former MAT advisors often report having seen a positive difference in their units' performance during the time they were with them,

Counterinsurgency

but they also often observe that their units' improvements in the field were largely because MAT's brought with them increased access to both tactical air support and artillery fire support. Those improvements were understandably important to a unit's confidence and willingness to fight; but that doesn't remove the fact that when the enemy is willing to fight without requiring artillery fires or air support, as insurgents often do, the government forces have to be willing to fight that way, too, and win.

So, what was the effectiveness of small, counterinsurgency advisory teams like MATs in Vietnam? The eventual success of North Vietnam's conventional army, the NVA, against South Vietnam's conventional army, the ARVN, might seem to make that question irrelevant, but it is not. The success or failure of the MAT idea, especially in improving the fighting ability of the territorial forces they advised, remains important because it was inseparably a part of the overall counterinsurgency effort. No aspect of that effort operated in a vacuum, and any analysis of the whole must consider the success or failure of the parts.

While MATs were in the villages primarily to advise and assist their local militia units, they were also there to help with civil affairs projects and intelligence operations; thus, MATs had connections to several important parts (security, civil affairs, intelligence) of the overall counterinsurgency strategy. That strategy, in a phrase, was to push the insurgency from the countryside. The effectiveness of the MAT approach should be judged in the context of that strategy, not the outcome of combat between two conventional land armies.

First, it should be acknowledged that counterinsurgency statistics (data like the number of hamlets in a district judged to be secure, the number of insurgents killed or captured, the progress of development programs, etc.) can be manipulated and are often complex in their meaning. In the case of Vietnam, they are additionally fogged by North Vietnam's eventual victory in conventional combat; nevertheless, the available data relevant to CORDS over its time of operation (1968–1972) indicates that the program made significant in-roads against the communist insurgency. This is a conclusion corroborated by a number of U.S. and North Vietnamese sources that have emphasized the reach and impact of the CORDS program including the anti–VCI successes of the Phoenix program, the development programs supported at the province and district level, and the MAT advisory effort in the villages. In fact, it was the success of the counterinsurgency program that forced North Vietnam to launch its major conventional-force offensive in 1972. What the North could not gain by a popular uprising, it would take by main force.

The North Vietnamese victory over South Vietnam led historian Richard Hunt to conclude in his book, *Pacification: The American Struggle for Vietnam's Hearts and Minds,* that CORDS' overall achievement was ambiguous, at best. That ambiguity is, no doubt, a lasting characteristic of the American effort in Vietnam and of what can happen when counterinsurgency is rendered irrelevant by a main-force army invasion. This points to the tension referred to earlier (Chapter Four) between the need to maintain and train an excellent conventional force within the same Army that trains and maintains a force with expertise in insurgency/counterinsurgency operations. The loss of either can have serious consequences.

While the success or failure of a host nation's conventional army to fight off an invasion from the outside is different from the success or failure of counterinsurgency, some common issues can affect either. The morale of the forces, the intensity with which they feel a sense of nationhood, and the strength of their belief in their government are examples of those issues, each of which is addressed in some way by effective counterinsurgency programs. When those programs reduce corruption, improve the quality of life in the villages, or promote civil justice they affect the morale of the conventional forces and strengthen their belief in the central government. To the degree that it did not do more, the counterinsurgency program shares in the defeat of South Vietnam, but what should not be lost is the value of an approach like CORDS with its small advisor teams driving a counterinsurgency program in the villages. Done well with properly organized and staffed teams, they improve security, aid in development, and make a path for an improved quality of life. Beginning their work early in the conflict maximizes the chances of victory.

Relevant Readings

Andrade, Dale and James H. Willbanks. "CORDS/Phoenix: Counterinsurgency Lessons from Vietnam for the Future." *Military Review* March-April (2006): 9–26.
Brown, Donald M. *Vietnam and CORDS: Interagency Lessons for Iraq.* Fort Leavenworth, KS: School of Advanced Military Studies, 2008, 41–44.

Coffey, Ross. "Revisiting CORDS: the Need for Unity of Effort to Secure Victory in Iraq. *Military Review* March-April (2006): 24–34.

Hunt, Richard A. *Pacification: The American struggle for Vietnam's Hearts and Minds.* San Francisco: Westview Press, 1995.

Jones, Seth G. *Counterinsurgency in Afghanistan.* Santa Monica, CA: RAND Corporation, 2008, 106–33.

Sorley, Lester. *The Vietnam Chronicles: The Abrams Tapes, 1968–1972.* Lubbock: Texas Tech University Press, 2004, 115.

Sorley, Lester. *Honorable Warrior: General Harold K. Johnson and the Ethics of Command.* Lawrence: University Press of Kansas, 1998, 227–41.

West, Francis J. *The Village.* New York: Harper and Row, 1972.

Eight

Counterinsurgency and the Potemkin Village

    Gregory Potemkin was a favorite of Catherine II of Russia and played a key role in the Russian annexation of Crimea in 1773. The story is told that on the occasion of Catherine's visit to the region in 1787 Potemkin wanted to give his empress the impression that all was well in the Crimea, so he had a series of villages built along the main river Catherine would be using for her travels. In truth, the villages were facades only. They were built to give an impression of well-being and calm that was not matched by the facts. Whether or not that story is literally true, the phrase, Potemkin village, has come to mean something built or put together to give a good impression where the substance of that impression does not exist.

    In that sense, it is difficult to find any civilian or military enterprise that is not to some degree a Potemkin village. Everyone wants to put the best face on things, and this includes U.S. counterinsurgency programs whether in Vietnam, El Salvador, Iraq, or Afghanistan. The difference between putting a best face on things and building a false façade can be very small, and the former can all too easily become the latter. The consequences of that mutation in Iraq are still being played out in the aftermath of the American withdrawal. Unfortunately, the situation in Afghanistan is no better and may be worse. There the threat seems very real that the American leadership in country has had a history of trying hard to present a façade of program progress where little relevant progress actually exists.

To make his villages, Potemkin intentionally had false fronts erected where no real building existed. The American counterinsurgency program in Afghanistan, to pursue the village analogy, is not necessarily one of hollow houses intentionally built to deceive. Rather, the deception can arise over houses that were actually intended to be fully built, houses where hammers, nails, and carpenters were planned with every intention of making a complete, solid building. All that can be true, but the problems come when the foremen (politicians) and building contractors (generals) choose to focus on the exterior elevations, the outward appearance of the buildings, rather than making sure that the trusses and studs of the internal structure are true or, for that matter, that they have been obtained in sufficient quantity to complete the building. When those failures come into play, the building's façade becomes the only thing that is constructed and maintained while the foremen and contractors hang around hoping that the construction delays will soon be taken care of. The difference between those foremen and contractors and Potemkin is that while Potemkin ordered an illusion, he was careful not suffer from it himself.

The Potemkin Village: Constructions in American Counterinsurgency

According to a number of Department of Defense documents including "Irregular Warfare: Countering Irregular Threats, Joint Operating Concept" dated 17 May 2010 (hereafter referred to as the Irregular Warfare document) and the Army field manual on stability operations (FM 3–07 dated October, 2008), the U.S. military participates in what is referred to as a "whole-of-government approach" to irregular warfare, which includes insurgency/counterinsurgency operations. A U.S., whole-of-government approach means that all branches and agencies of the U.S. government cooperate and participate in the struggle as called upon. No department or agency is outside the zone of responsibility.

One would think this understanding should apply to any host nation the U.S. is helping face an insurgency. In fact, the five requirements of a counterinsurgency program discussed in Chapter Two imply this whole-of-government or "all-in" approach by the host nation; yet, somehow, after

Eight. Counterinsurgency and the Potemkim Village

having been in Iraq for nearly ten years and being in Afghanistan even longer there clearly are elements in both populations and governments that have not been all-in, or, perhaps, even interested. Thus, while the U.S. government claims an all-in approach itself, it does it imperfectly and has not been able to get anything like an all-in commitment from the host nations it has helped. This is perhaps not surprising given the nature and conditions of insurgencies, but it emphasizes that the concept of a government being all-in, whether the helper or the helped, has not been and is unlikely to ever be a reality. If anything, the concept is a shell of what one would like to see but does not exist in fact. In other words, it is a Potemkin structure.

It is also clear from a number of U.S. Department of State and Department of Defense publications, including the two already mentioned, that there is widespread understanding that insurgency/counterinsurgency is not primarily a contest for terrain; it is a contest for legitimacy in the minds of a population. It should be understood then that such a contest makes the population especially important because the population is not only the objective of the battle; it is the ground over which the battle is fought. Influencing that population through providing security, development, and reform is how a counterinsurgency program works.

That this is accepted, at least in the general sense, is shown in the Irregular Warfare document mentioned above. It states: "(The American armed forces) in conjunction with civilian agencies, will conduct military, political, economic, and information-related actions as well as civic actions to defeat an insurgency. The primary focus of effort for the (military force) is to establish security, counter subversion, and disrupt the insurgency and its external support network. As it establishes security, the (military force) will also help build the host nation's ability to provide security and support development and governance to gain or maintain its legitimacy." Further, the document stipulates that the ideal model for successful counterinsurgency is an integrated civilian-military command structure as was advocated earlier in Chapter Seven. The Irregular Warfare document says that counterinsurgency requires a concerted effort to address the root causes of the insurgency and that the scale, footprint, and capabilities of a counterinsurgency operation can vary depending on circumstances.

All of those comments are in concert with what has been said in previous chapters of this very book; yet, after observing a decade of the U.S.

pursuing counterinsurgency programs in two different countries, one might be forgiven the concern that the dense language used to articulate the American government's understanding of counterinsurgency might be a case of having all the right words written on paper be like having all the right boards nailed to a façade. Potemkin at work.

Another example of dense linguistic correctitude from the Irregular Warfare document is this: "In particular, because these activities may be undertaken on a small or large scale, depending on the level of the threat and the capability of the host nation, the (military force) must be able to provide scalable, flexible force packages to support distributed operations, including logistics support for small unit operations, transportation, lift/mobility air support, human and technical intelligence, surveillance and reconnaissance, force protection, engineering, communications, medical assistance, and other enablers." That's a huge world of capabilities covered in a single sentence. One might reasonably ask what real understanding lies behind those easy-to-say-but-hard-to-do words? What ability or interest is there to follow-through with them?

The concern becomes even more amplified when one considers that that list of capabilities (scalable, flexible force package, logistics support, transportation, intelligence, engineering, communication, etc.) are said to be things that *must* be provided (italics mine), yet the need for appropriately selected and trained advisors is addressed with a less emphatic, "Advisory personnel with the requisite language and cultural skills are needed." Needed, not required. Understanding the need is one thing, insisting that the need be addressed is another. Should a counterinsurgency effort go forward without properly trained advisors it would indicate that the program planners are thinking about getting by with the least input, about having warm bodies in place to do the best they can, never mind the inefficiency and blunting of success that implies. That should never happen because it is a recipe for lost lives and treasure beyond what is absolutely necessary.

Going into a counterinsurgency environment without properly trained advisors is like trying to tame lions with bus drivers. Trained advisors are *required* (see Chapter Five) for a successful program, but that requirement will not be met until the elements of Chapter Four (The Advisors) are taken seriously by the military establishment.

There is another threat to U.S. counterinsurgency campaigns as well:

Eight. Counterinsurgency and the Potemkim Village

the presence of a large body of conventional American soldiers with all its support facilities and equipment. That presence may look impressive from a distance, but it also looks foreign. It is a reminder of intrusion to indigenous populations that don't like being intruded upon even if that intrusion is saving them from a fate they deplore. A fully armor-vested, helmeted, sunglassed, machinegun-toting American soldier looks as strange to them at first sight as a Star Wars storm trooper once did to American movie-goers, and a fully caged, mine-resistant, ambush-protected troop carrier is as out of scale to them as an eighteen-wheeler is at a pickup convention.

In many environments, all this American bulk adds to the general resentment held by many against any foreign presence among them. While there are clear military advantages to a large, impressive troop presence, there are also disadvantages, and any progress they achieve with regard to counterinsurgency may be at the surface only. An example of this is in Afghanistan where a "surge" in American troop strength in 2009 was said to be necessary to eliminate Taliban gains in the countryside. While the surge occurred and did help to suppress enemy activity, events current with this writing show a remaining widespread, religion-based animus in the population against any foreign forces on Afghan soil. That rejection of foreign presence is in part a rejection of foreign ideas, and those ideas, like the value of democracy, the importance of toleration, and the advantages of modernity, are what provided the rationale for counterinsurgency in the first place. This troublesome reality has been hidden by the veneer of well-intended activity put on by the large American and coalition forces. In that sense, those forces have become Potemkin structures; they are impressive on the outside, but have given an illusion of success where from the counterinsurgency perspective success does not exist.

The Department of Defense is not alone in having expertise in counterinsurgency and having difficulty making it work. The Department of State also has its experts, and their understanding of counterinsurgency basics is illustrated in the department's "U.S. Government Counterinsurgency Guide" dated January, 2009 (referred to hereafter as the Counterinsurgency Guide or, simply, the Guide). It correctly states that, "American counterinsurgency practice rests on a number of assumptions: that the decisive effort is rarely military (although security is the essential prerequisite for success); that our efforts must be directed to the creation of local and

Counterinsurgency

national governmental structures that will serve their populations, and, over time, replace the efforts of foreign partners: that superior knowledge, and in particular, understanding of the 'human terrain' is essential; and that we must have the patience to persevere in what will necessarily prove to be long struggles." All of those things are true (see Chapters One and Two of this book).

That same document gives full credence to the complexity of counterinsurgency and recognizes that it must be a joint civilian-military effort. To use the State Department's terminology, that effort must be population-centric (focused on securing a population and promoting its welfare) rather than enemy-centric (focused on destroying the enemy) and the Guide recognizes that counterinsurgency can be politically controversial because it involves ambiguous events that are difficult for even experts to interpret, let alone the average citizen. These and other complexities can be compounded by large attitudinal differences between the helper and the helped in areas like social standards, expectations of the future, and world views. The summation of all this is that governments doing the helping have sometimes gotten involved in counterinsurgency campaigns only to discover they have severely underestimated the financial and human costs involved and that the duration of the effort will have to be much longer than originally anticipated.

With all of that being understood within the State Department, one would think the department would be an important guard against wasteful counterinsurgency enterprises in environments where extreme difficulty and low reward are predictable. Military leaders, especially general officers, are genetically hesitant to step back from mere difficulty. We expect them to be forward leaning, can-do kinds of people who are not put off by difficulty. It is their type and their training, so it is foolish to expect military leaders to recommend not doing something simply because it will be difficult. Doing the difficult is their job. Ask the infantry: their mantra is, the difficult today, the impossible tomorrow. They are the military, private to general, and in the United States they exist to do one thing: difficult jobs at the bidding of an elected, civilian government.

The State Department is different. It is a part of that civilian government. It helps decide what the military is going to be told to do and should be a reliable proponent of rationalist views about the insurgency in a poten-

Eight. Counterinsurgency and the Potemkim Village

tial host country. It should know the American national interests at stake there, the potential cost and difficulties of a counterinsurgency campaign, and, by comparison, the potential cost and difficulties of *not* getting involved. Further, the State Department and intelligence services should be dependable for judgments not influenced by the likes or dislikes of a particular administration; a condition, one can argue, that is too often left unmet.

The State Department should be a reservoir of reason even when the public's blood is up, and absent their giving that rationalist view, the understanding of counterinsurgency noted in the Counterinsurgency Guide becomes part of a façade of competence that has no real meaning. In the United States' most recent counterinsurgency campaigns (Iraq and Afghanistan) advice from the State Department has either been to proceed or, if not to proceed, has been ignored by other parts of the political administration. In either case, those results make the department's written understandings of counterinsurgency seem another Potemkin structure nicely done on the outside but with little substance on the inside.

Decisions That Lead to the Potemkin Village

Counterinsurgency is one tool in the shop of foreign affairs. Its use must be preceded by reviewing intelligence gathered from reliable sources, and experienced minds must sort the relevant facts from the irrelevant. They must also shape those facts into knowledge, knowledge into wisdom, and wisdom into correct decisions. An important early decision is the question of whether or not to engage in a particular counterinsurgency effort in the first place. If engaged in, the next questions will be about how much effort and how soon, and once the operation is underway the decisions will be about whether to continue the operation as is, amend it in some way, or end it at a date certain. Those are all critical decisions and making them is an unrelenting challenge made difficult by the realization that each decision has consequences that can be lethal to many. So, what happens when those decisions turn out to be wrong?

One possibility is that a counterinsurgency program can be begun where the margins for error are very thin but the only tools available are very blunt. An air strike or artillery bombardment would be a very blunt tool indeed if it destroyed one hundred percent of a village to deal with the fifteen percent of the people actively supporting the insurgency. Even non-lethal measures can be harsher than sometimes appreciated. A curfew that prevents a villager's access to his fields or his fishing grounds, for example, can be a punishment to everyone. Unless carefully thought out, such curfews can keep people from their livelihoods and have broad destructive effects even though their intent was to help the local people by isolating the insurgents. Explanations about how temporary difficulties help achieve long-term progress will carry little weight in a poor village where the average family has no resources to get them over yet another obstacle to survival. In situations like those, blunt tools of any kind are a recipe for failure.

Another possible result of bad decisions is that the massive force and massive aid already expended in an operation become the necessitators of the operation's success. In other words, the goods, services, and lives already committed to the counterinsurgency effort start being a more powerful driver of decisions than does the wisdom that comes from day-to-day knowledge of the facts on the ground. For a variety of reasons including political calculation, career concerns, and personal egos, what has been committed so far now becomes the thing that demands success. To get that success, leaders can decide that the current situation must be projected as positively as possible. Briefing officers get the hint; difficulties can be acknowledge but their importance should be minimized. After all, any difficulties will be overcome. We *will* have success. No one wants to be the down draft in an up-beat, can-do world, so another façade of words is built and the Potemkin village rises.

How does this play out in the real world? In Vietnam it was seen in such things as the hamlets being given higher pacification ratings than they deserved; it was seen in inflated body counts, overstatements of ARVN capabilities, and confident assurances to the press and to Congress that things were about to turn around. There was "light at the end of the tunnel."

No middle-management commander would let one of his junior officers brief a significant superior without first hearing the briefing and making sure everything sounded as up-beat as possible. One does not actually have to lie to make a so-so report sound much more positive; it all depends on what you chose to emphasize.

Eight. Counterinsurgency and the Potemkim Village

Lesson Learned: Frank Treatment of Uncomfortable Information from the Field Rarely Survives the Filtering Process Between the Field and Washington, D.C.

First Lieutenant Terry T. Turner, team leader, MAT IV-32 and District Senior Advisor; Hoa Binh District, Kien Phong Province (Advisor Team 84), IV Corps Tactical Zone; 1969–70.

I had been assigned to be my province advisory team's pay officer for the upcoming payday, so I had been pulled from my district for a couple of days and sent back to Can Tho, the delta capital and IV Corps (delta) headquarters. There I was to draw the pay, count it, then get back to the province where I would visit all the district and MAT teams to distribute their pay. Can Tho was a city with a large U.S. presence, so there were officer and enlisted "hotels" in the downtown area where transients could stay for short visits. My visit was to be for just one night, but the benefit of it was that the four-story, concrete block hotel had hot water for its showers, one shower per floor, and an open-air bar on the roof. Believe me, I was going to use both to good advantage.

After taking my first soap and hot water scrub-down in months, I went to a local restaurant for dinner then went up to the rooftop bar just in time to watch the sunset. The bar was a simple affair, basically a table set up under a shelter with a guy behind it who could give you beer or a Shasta cola. Sometimes there would be ice for making the beer and soft drinks cold, sometimes not. There were also some tables out on an open, patio that looked out over the nearby Mekong River. From the rooftop you could look out at the river and see everything from small, five-plank sampans to ocean-going freighters moving slowly by.

There must have been at least a dozen of the hotel's other temporary residents up there on the roof having a drink and catching the evening breezes. A number of them were MACV advisors from other provinces. Like me, they were passing through Can Tho for one reason or another, and before long, four or five of us were sitting around a table watching the sunset dim to darkness.

The group was an interesting mix. There was a captain who was a DSA

Counterinsurgency

Lieutenant Turner in his team's outpost in Kien Phong Province, 1969.

from a province to the east of mine, a lieutenant who was an engineer advisor from a province advisory staff somewhere to the south, and a major from MACV headquarters in Saigon. The conversation turned to what we were doing at our locations and how things seemed to be going out where we were. Not so well, apparently.

Our views on the pacification and Vietnamization programs were pretty grim given the difficulties we were seeing, but it was obvious that was in contrast to the official pronouncements being made at the time. All of us

Eight. Counterinsurgency and the Potemkim Village

agreed that the facts at our locations were less optimistic than what was being advertised by the officials above us. The lieutenant from further south said he doubted people back in the States had any idea about the realities of life in a Vietnamese village. The cares and fears there were too different from anything that would be experienced in hometown America.

We all agreed there was a separation between perception and reality and someone suggested that the television evening news was partially to blame. Heads nodded at the observation. Television cameras were only interested in things that go Bang! which is no way to explain complexities, either for the war as a whole or for the counterinsurgency part of it.

After that, the conversation went something like this:

Captain: "The people back in the States might not be getting the right information, but it's hard to bitch about that when even Washington can't get the facts right. How can they with all the filters between us and them? Guys like me out on a district team send information to province headquarters. Province compiles a report from all the districts and sends it to IV Corps. IV Corps makes a report from all the provinces and sends it to Saigon. Saigon takes the info from all the Corps headquarters, makes that into yet another rendition, and sends that to D. C. At each step along the way the people putting the reports together filter out what they disagree with or think sounds too negative. By the time the big report gets back to D.C., you know it sounds more positive than it started out being back here on the ground. It's no wonder the people at the top of the pile can't figure out what's happening at the bottom."

Me: "You're right. Nobody wants to hear any bad news. General Weatherill (the IV Corps Commander) has been out to my team twice. Both times my PSA came out in the chopper the day before to hear what I was going to say. He wanted to make sure my briefing was going to be up to snuff and not make things look bad. If I had negative information to report, it was to be minimized and I had to say what corrective measures had been taken to remedy the problem."

Captain: "Even if it was just a gloss over."

Me: "Yeah. And when Weatherill came around the next day the colonel was with him, listening. It was hard to say much that was negative. Pissed me off, but nothing I could do about it."

Lieutenant: "You could'a told the truth."

Me: "For what good? The colonel'd probably play it down, anyway, then after the general was gone he'd come back and tear my ass off. Probably relieve me or something. The only thing I would have accomplished was to put some other joker in my job."

Lieutenant: Shrugs

Captain: "I've seen the same kind of thing. Who wants to be a martyr for nothing? I don't think generals hear much bad news on those district tours. Briefings they get up at province work the same way: Emphasize the good, don't say much about the bad. Weatherill probably thinks things are looking up all over, so he tells that to Saigon and Saigon sends the good news to D.C."

Major: Nods. "That's for sure. Been there. You wouldn't believe how people have to jump through their hats when General Abrams (MACV commander at the time) has to go back to brief the joint chiefs or the senate or whatever. Everybody tries to make a rosy scenario. You don't have to lie, it's just the way you use your facts; and if you don't play along, you're gonna look bad, like you're working against the cause or something. (Pause) A lot of people are smelling smoke, but nobody wants to yell, 'Fire!'"

After that, the conversation went off in other directions. Darkness had set in, so the barman set up a projector and showed a movie. We all leaned back to watch, but I kept thinking about what we had said. I had made my flimsy excuse for not being brutally honest in a briefing or for not putting the most grim interpretation on what was happening in my district. It was clear that I was not alone. We were all part of an information network and we were all participating in a result that was actually misinformation. Each one of us likely had an excuse for his part of the problem and each of us hoped someone else would be able to pick out the hints of truth and pass that on. It was no wonder that the government in Washington was operating in a fog of optimism; by the time the information from the field gets back there, I thought, all the bad news has been downplayed and the good news magnified. Information filters at several levels were in operation, so based on what actually got through, how could anybody expect good decisions to be made?

It was depressing, but at the time our inadequate reporting was just one more trouble in a long list of them and I was behind in taking care of almost all of them. I took a big gulp of my drink and watched the movie.

Eight. Counterinsurgency and the Potemkim Village

Vietnam was far in my past before I let the lesson learned from that rooftop experience actually come into words. The lesson learned is that information passed on to higher levels of command, especially negative information, is inevitably filtered to put the best face on reality. Sometimes that "best face" becomes unreality, and everyone doing the filtering bears part of the blame.

Terry Turner is a retired professor of urology and of cell biology at the University of Virginia. He lives in Coolidge, Georgia.

David Corn's book, *Blond Ghost,* a biography of a CIA officer deeply involved in the Indochina wars of the 1960s and '70s, makes the point about data filtering very clearly. The book tells of CIA officers' complaints during the final days of the South Vietnamese government that "creative intelligence gathering" was putting tight quality controls on reports of Vietnamese corruption and security problems. Those controls were a way of insuring few such reports made their way to Washington, the result of which was to foster a belief by some that the South Vietnamese government could be sustained even while it was collapsing like a tent with no pole. Those who did warn of imminent disaster felt they were given the cold shoulder and perhaps even negative career marks when speaking against what was politically correct within the agency.

Are those examples an oversimplification of the problem? Yes. There are many connecting factors, exceptions, and adjustments that can apply, but these paragraphs do sketch out a basic problem. They point to an attitude that says, we're going to put a good face on this operation because, by god, we're going to make it work and no one is going to be a naysayer on *my* watch! This is a problem in any organization whose driving purpose is to actually accomplish something. Being positive is rewarded, being negative is not; so when it comes to passing bad news upward, the military has difficulties that are innate to it and bred within it. Civilian agencies, the CIA obviously among them, often share the same problem, but because the consequences of failure with them are usually less direct, the problem can seem less, as well.

For any government to work well, correct information must flow from the points of action to the conference rooms where decisions are made.

That is not to say that all information must go to all people or that brutally frank information is always the most helpful. Sensitive information can be legitimately restricted to proper channels; that is what a classification system is for; but the information itself must be accurate and not manipulated to generate a desired public opinion. Doing the opposite, that is, using inaccurate, manipulated data to generate public or even in-house reports is the making of a verbal Potemkin structure, a façade meant to hide a difficult reality. That can end very badly.

Potemkin in Iraq and Afghanistan

The U.S. paid a high price for the Potemkin problem in Vietnam, and it is frustrating to see evidence that the lesson has remained unlearned. It was certainly unlearned in Iraq where official estimates of progress commonly outpaced reality. After ten years of trying to get that country on its feet, the U.S. military left an arena where security was still tenuous and development was still blunted by corruption and political conflict. To compensate for the tardiness of security and development there, the American government left behind thousands of contracted civilians doing jobs traditionally assigned to the military, jobs such as military training, institutional security, and logistics training and development. This is Parthian shot counterinsurgency that leaves the true outcome in question.

The problems dealt with in Iraq also seem rampant in Afghanistan. Lieutenant Colonel Daniel Davis, an Army officer who has served in both Iraq and Afghanistan, recently made the extent of the problem clear. In the February, 2012 issue of Armed Forces Journal, Davis wrote that he had spent a year in Afghanistan over a span of months bridging 2010 and 2011. His assignment took him all over the country as he interviewed U.S. troops and their Afghan counterparts. He spoke with over two hundred fifty conventional and Special Forces soldiers ranging in rank from private to general officer. He also interviewed Afghan security officials, civilians, and village elders. In short, Lieutenant Colonel Davis got around.

He saw the difficulties our military forces are having in pacifying the countryside and he noted that after ten years of the U.S. and its coalition partners being involved in the country, there was little evidence of what could be called a truly functional Afghan government. At the time of his writing the government there was still unable to provide for the basic needs

Eight. Counterinsurgency and the Potemkim Village

of its people and, in fact, had turned many of its citizens against it because of its incompetence and corruption. Chapter One of this book argues that reforming government is a key requirement in counterinsurgency; in the absence of those reforms it is not surprising that Davis saw progress as being less than generally advertised. In fact, Davis says, after ten years of war insurgents still controlled virtually all the terrain beyond the immediate vision of the U.S. and Coalition forces. That being the case, it completely fulfills expectations that development programs like education, health, and commerce in the villages have made little headway.

It is haunting to many of us who have been in these kinds of wars (wars of the village and countryside, wars of insurgency and counterinsurgency) that these difficulties are not being frankly discussed in the American public sphere, not at a level where their meaning is fully absorbed. Those of us with experience know what a lack of candor portends and we chafe at official pronouncements that might admit that, yes, there are some modest difficulties, but then go on to list how the difficulties can be explained away or adjusted for and why we are still expecting good things for the future. This polishing of the apple or adding scent to the rose is dangerous because it only gives credence to what is in reality a fatal illusion.

According to Davis's descriptions, to imply a manipulation only at the surface visible at press conferences might be minimizing the problem. He saw a large gulf between conditions on the ground and the official pronouncements of progress coming out of the headquarters in Kabul and the public information offices in Washington, D.C. Davis says he went to Afghanistan hoping to learn that conditions there were improving and that the Afghan government and military forces were becoming self-sufficient. Instead, he saw government corruption and Afghan military units that still refused to aggressively take on the enemy. American soldiers and officers were dismayed at the quality of their Afghan Army partners and they had little hope that that army would outlast the insurgents once the Americans were gone. The 2014 virtual collapse of the Iraqi Army seems a portent.

A number of incidents typified the bad state of affairs to Davis. A story about a Taliban kidnapping/murder that took place within view of an American base was told to relate how insecure villagers must feel even with the Americans present. Davis went on to say, "In all of the places I visited, the tactical situation was bad to abysmal. If the events I have described—and many, many more I could mention—had been in the first year of war, or even the third or fourth, one might be willing to believe that Afghanistan was just a hard fight, and we should stick it out. Yet these incidents all happened in the 10th year of war."

Davis was pointing out that his experience in multiple areas of Afghanistan clearly showed an absence of progress in helping that country move toward stability and security. After ten years of American involvement there was little that could be called success in any aspect of a counterinsurgency campaign; yet, that is not what is heard from the State Department or the Pentagon. This is dysgnosis writ large. Davis also points out that he is not the first to note the discrepancy between official statements and the facts out in the villages and countryside of Afghanistan. In early 2011 a coordinating office for non-governmental organizations in Afghanistan reported that its views were "sharply divergent from (U. S. and Coalition forces') 'strategic communication' messages suggesting improvements. We encourage (non-governmental organization personnel) to recognize that no matter how authoritative the source for such claims, messages of that nature are solely intended to influence American and European public opinion ahead of the withdrawal, and are not intended to offer an accurate portrayal of the situation for those who live and work here."

Also in 2011, Anthony Cordesman, Arleigh Burke Chair in Strategy at the Center for Strategic and International Studies, Washington, D.C. noted that the U.S. leadership in Afghanistan was failing to accurately report the realities there. He wrote in part, "Since June 2010, the unclassified reporting the U.S. does provide has steadily shrunk in content, effectively 'spinning' the road to victory by eliminating content that illustrates the full scale of the challenges ahead." Further, "The U.S. is scarcely alone in failing to provide adequate reporting on the Afghan conflict. No allied government provides credible reporting on the progress of the war, and the Afghan government provides little detail of any kind." Even when information is provided, Cordesman wrote, there are "many areas where meaningful reporting is lacking and the reporting available is deceptive and misleading. The U.S. (and its allies) may currently be repeating the same kind of overall messaging as the "follies" presented in Vietnam." For those of us who remember those "five o'clock follies," which were upbeat news conferences held for the press in Saigon, that sentence is particularly damning.

Eight. Counterinsurgency and the Potemkim Village

How does this separation from the truth happen? How does a public information office become a "spin" factory? In the enterprise of war, as in any other important undertaking, most organizations have a default mechanism for bad news: put the best face possible on it and move on. The underlying expectation is that things will be better tomorrow. It worked for the U.S. after Pearl Harbor. It worked when facing the initial news from the Battle of the Bulge or from Korea during the retreat to Inchon. In those cases putting the best possible face on bad news helped America to eventually push through to victory. It didn't work for Germany after the Allies landed at Normandy or for Iraq after U.S. and NATO forces fell on it during Operation Desert Storm and again in Operation Iraqi Freedom. Those examples show that filtering of public information and prevaricating in public forums are not only uncertain tools for success, they have within them the threat of becoming a façade that cannot be taken down with any grace. It can become a Potemkin village constructed of words and images suggesting all is well when the truth is, things are not well at all.

Dealing with this is so old school, so Vietnam! I hate to trot out that name as a proper comparison for Afghanistan, but as a former doer of counterinsurgency and a current watcher of it, the soul winces at hearing the finely parsed word choices of official reports. The mind immediately sneers at any dissembling or evasion by officials in response to straight questions and it discounts reports that are as much editorial as they are about facts on the ground.

The kind of disingenuousness implied by the "follies" label has ill consequences for counterinsurgency programs. For one thing, the American public learns to distrust the integrity of the program because they have learned to question official pronouncements about program progress. Firmly attached to that, they learn to question whether the expenditure of American treasure in lives and money is worth the supposed benefit. Cordesman commented about his experience in Vietnam, "The end result (of not dealing forthrightly about program progress) is not to control the message, but to fail to provide one. It is hardly surprising that a great deal of media coverage is questioning or negative or that public opinion polls reflect a steady drop in support for the war." After all, the public might reasonably question what is going to turn out to be true and what not true. Is what we are being shown the real thing, they might ask, or has a Gregory Potemkin been at play?

Avoiding the Potemkin Village

How is the Potemkin problem best avoided? It is tempting simply to say, tell the truth! That's elementary and declarative: tell the truth. Tell it without artful dodging and making complex word choices that are intended to be literally true but not truly revealing. This recommendation will be uncomfortable to many because there are times where national security legitimately requires withholding information or even dodging around an issue. I, for one, understand that. What I am talking about when I say, tell the truth, is a comment on those situations where military and diplomatic agencies of government adopt a practice of persistent prevarication when it comes to dealing with bad news from America's foreign adventures. Sometimes, despite the best possible effort, a program does not go as expected, a host government turns out to be an unreliable partner, or the national interests that originally stimulated American involvement diminish or completely vanish. In those cases, whatever the reason for the program's difficulties, rather than generate public and legislative distrust with misleading reports, it would be better if the facts, grim or good, were dealt with frankly before the American people. Absent that, decisions will be made on the basis of factual errors, which is no way to run a government.

Relevant Readings

Cordesman, Anthony H. "Afghanistan and the Uncertain Metrics of Progress: Part Six: Showing Victory is Possible." Center for Strategic and International Studies (2011), http://csis.org/publication/afghanistan-and-uncertain-metrics-progress-part-six-showing-victory-possible.

Corn, David. *Blond Ghost.* New York: Simon and Schuster, 1994, 282–93.

Davis, Daniel L. "Truth, Lies, and Afghanistan: How Military Leaders Have let us Down." *Armed Forces Journal* (2012) http://www.armedforcesjournal.com/2012/8904030.

Fall, Bernard B. "The Theory and Practice of Insurgency and Counterinsurgency." *Naval War College Review* 51 (1998): 46–56.

Felbab-Brown, Vanda. *Aspiration and Ambivalence: Strategies and Realities of Counterinsurgency and State-Building in Afghanistan.* Washington: Brookings Institute Press, 2012.

Fore, Henrietta, Robert Gates, and Condoleeze Rice. *U. S. Government Counterinsurgency Guide. United States Government Interagency Counterinsurgency Initiative.* Washington, D.C.: Department of State, 2009, 13–21.

Olson, Eric T., James N. Mattis, and Michael G. Mullen. "Irregular Warfare: Countering Irregular Threats, Joint Operating Concept: Version 2.0." Washington: Department of Defense (2010):11–24.

Nine

The Soldiers They Send

Vietnam, 1969

I was sitting in a small sampan being poled along by a Vietnamese man standing in its stern. The boat was nearly three feet in the beam and about ten feet stem to stern. It was a very common, shallow-draft kind of craft found throughout the Mekong Delta, a sort of family car for a world where there were many creeks and canals but few roads. That size of sampan could easily carry three or four Vietnamese, but with the poleman in the stern and an armed Vietnamese officer in the bow, I was the big American sitting amidships feeling pretty cramped and exposed.

I was in the boat being poled up a creek because that day one of my teammates and I were scheduled to accompany a combat patrol working out of a remote militia outpost. In fact, it was sufficiently remote that after several months of my being on the job this would be my first visit. The outpost had been established to protect a small hamlet far up a creek that wound it way to the main canal running through our district. At the last minute, my teammate, one of our weapons specialists, had been needed to accompany another team member to go out with our local unit. No one had been available to fill in with me, but since plans had been made for us to visit the outpost and since I had never even been in that out-of-the-way hamlet, I thought it was important to get out there and evaluate both the place and its militia platoon. A shortage of hands on the team was a common problem and it couldn't be allowed to bring things to a halt. Someway or another, the job had to get done.

The only way that was going to happen in this case was if I violated the rule of pairs. The rule of pairs said that advisors should never go out alone. They should always go in pairs. That way, if something bad happened, each American would have another there to have his back. That was a common sense precaution, but on this particular day I decided that the contact with the hamlet and its militia platoon was important enough that I should go on even if I had to do it alone. That's what I did.

A Vietnamese officer from the district headquarters accompanied me and the two of us hitched a ride on in a large, engine-powered sampan heading in the right direction along our main canal. When we reached the place where the wandering creek entered the canal we thanked the owner of the large sampan and got off to find a small one that would take us up the creek to the militia outpost. Before long, we had found a villager who for a day's pay would take us where we needed to go in his small sampan. Now, here we were moving upstream under the pole power of the wiry Vietnamese man standing in the stern.

The hamlet we were going to was out there ahead of us along the narrow, wandering waterway. The main canal was behind us. Thickets of brush and reeds lined the creek banks. Banana trees and palms formed a canopy overhead with sunlight filtering down and speckling the water.

As we got away from the main canal the creek grew quiet. All you could hear was the singing of the birds and the slithing whisper of the water as the small sampan slid across its surface. The hamlet we were heading toward was still somewhere out in front of us, the jungle seemed to be closing in and I was beginning to think I shouldn't have come without a teammate. Maybe this wasn't such a bright idea. Who knows what's waiting around the next bend?

Still, I was fascinated by the experience. I was moving up that quiet creek in a sampan being poled by local villager. The trees, the sounds, the look of the black water dappled with sunlight were all interesting, and as we rounded a bend in the creek, a decrepit temple or shrine came into view. It had a tiled roof that had once been red but was now splotched with the dark mold and mildew of time. Otherwise, the building seemed to be made of wood, its weathered paint mostly green with red and yellow accents. It sat atop an earthen mound, likely to keep it above the flood waters that in most years came with the monsoons. A deck or small wharf at the water's edge

Nine. The Soldiers They Send

had steps rising to the temple's porch that was covered and looked out over the canal.

On the steps leading up from the waters edge sat two Buddhist priests or monks wearing loose robes of yellow cloth. Seeing us coming, they rose, and when the Vietnamese officer in the bow of the sampan told them who we were, they called for us to stop and have tea. I agreed for two reasons: First, I thought it was important to be polite to religious folks. Second, this place looked too interesting to pass without stopping.

The Vietnamese officer stepped onto the deck and tied the sampan to a post. Moving carefully so I wouldn't overturn the narrow boat, I stepped out and shook hands with the priests. They were all smiles and invited me to see their temple (or shrine, I was never sure which) while yet another of them prepared tea. I thanked them and agreed to look around while my Vietnamese colleague kept an eye on the back of the temple and our poleman watched the front.

The temple was old. Its interior paint, while not as faded and chipped as the outside, had worn away in many places. Wooden columns supported the tile roof, some of them carved with a winding figure, and over the entrance to the porch was a long wooden panel painted with a yellow dragon undulating across a red background, all of it darkened with mold. Smoke wafted upward from incense sticks and lent a cloying, sweet smell to the air. Figures had been carved into panels in the walls and a small Buddha statue of brass sat serenely on a platform. All of it was exotic to my eye, but my Vietnamese was not good enough to do more than express pleasure. A rifle or a bomb I could have asked about, but not Buddhist statues and carvings. All I could do was show I was impressed and give them my thanks.

After the tour, we sat on the floor of the porch and sipped tea as we looked out over the canal. I explained where I was from and what I was doing and they tried to explain what this building was doing out here in the middle of nowhere. I never did understand that, but I do remember sitting there looking out at the green surroundings and the still water and thinking, this is neat! The creek's black, glassy surface curved back through the overarching trees and reeded banks. Our small sampan was tied to a post at the dock of a Buddhist temple and there I was sipping tea on the porch. Everything seemed inordinately peaceful. In fact, there was no one else in sight but the two Buddhist priests, me, and the poleman still sitting in his sampan at the *dock.* This, I thought, *is a National Geographic moment, an experience that makes this job so interesting.*

After spending enough time at tea to be polite, I thanked the priests for their hospitality and said we needed to be on our way. There were smiles and handshakes all around and we reboarded the sampan and said goodbye. It wasn't long before tension set in again. Now the Vietnamese officer and I had our M-16s at the ready. Our eyes were on the canal banks ahead of us and I was asking myself if it had been wise to stop at the temple for even a few minutes. Had we delayed too long? Had the priests' hospitality been a delaying tactic? Had we been set up for an ambush?

No, it turned out, on all counts. Nothing happened along the way and before long we were pulling up to the militia outpost. The Vietnamese officer and I inspected the militia platoon then set off with them on the day's operation. It was a sweep of an area a few kilometers from the hamlet center, and it all went uneventfully perhaps because the platoon's pace was more an ambling walk than a determined patrol. Any enemy who might have been in the area had plenty of time to get out of the way and avoid contact. All in all, it wasn't a good showing, but at least things seemed correctable.

I had two counterparts that day, the officer from the district headquarters and the militia platoon leader. I had a session with the two of them suggesting to the platoon leader what he should do to improve his unit. I also promised that I and at least one my teammates would return in the near future to give a class and run demonstrations on small-unit maneuvers, all of which the platoon leader seemed to accept with good grace. When our critique session was over he insisted that we stay for the meal his unit's wives had prepared to celebrate our visit.

The food had been laid out on a long table under a bamboo thatch shelter. There were dishes of chicken, rat, and duck, all shared in common and eaten with steamed rice served in individual bowls. Nuoc mam, the pungent Vietnamese fish sauce, was in dipping dishes before each place and large brown bottles of Vietnamese beer were in ample supply not only for the meal but for the toasts that would have to be exchanged.

The Vietnamese district officer, the poleman, and I had to be careful about the amount of beer we drank because we still had to get back home. Somehow, we managed not to overdo it, at least in our own minds, and after the meal our poleman pushed us downstream back to the main canal.

Nine. The Soldiers They Send

There the Vietnamese officer and I hopped another large sampan for the trip back to the district town where we arrived just after sunset. My counterpart and I hopped off the sampan, waved our thanks to the owner, and chatted for a few moments before he left for his house and I walked back into my team's home fort.

I remember thinking what a great day it had been despite the poor showing of the militia unit. For a start, we had not been ambushed in an open sampan. That was good. On top of that I had experienced an interesting, perhaps unique interlude at the little Buddhist temple; I had gone on to do some practical advising; and I had had a great Vietnamese meal in a collegial atmosphere. A day in Vietnam could hardly get any better and good days in Vietnam were something I wanted to hold on to. I had had days of danger, frustration, dullness, weariness, sickness, and sadness; but I had had other good days, too, days like this one when I had been lucky enough to witness or participate in something unique, to conduct an operation with no casualties, to have a good Vietnamese meal, and to get home safely. Those were the days that made being an advisor a great experience.

In earlier parts of this book much was said about the uncertainties of counterinsurgency programs and the difficult realities that must be faced both by those who plan the programs in air-conditioned offices and by those who conduct them in the heat and confusion of the field. The uncertainties include the reliability of the host government, the virtues of its cause, and the tenacity of the insurgents. The difficult realities may also include the limited American interests at stake and the attitude of the American people toward the campaign being considered; but it is the advisor, the counterinsurgency operative out on foreign soil doing the job, who will almost always have to face difficult circumstances. There will be challenges, no question; still, on the good days it will be a fascinating job. It will provide an opportunity to do unique things, to see strange things, and to gain insights into a culture that few have opportunity to share.

Politicians or political appointees make the decisions whether or not to engage in a particular counterinsurgency campaign, but once a campaign is approved success becomes a matter of the intentions of the host government, the program design, and the quality of the advisors who pursue it. The host nation must be examined closely, a point made in Chapter One,

Counterinsurgency

for once the counterinsurgency program begins, that government can be advised, but not commanded. Program design is typically done in the offices of military and foreign policy leaders, but it is the soldiers they send to do the job who have their boots on the ground and it is they who must endure the difficulties of the counterinsurgency assignment.

In some cases, the advisor's job is to help defend a village at the same time he is to help build it. It is a special kind of challenge that requires a special kind of soldier to do it well. That soldier must have an I-can-do-this attitude without being arrogant, he must have a curiosity about lands and peoples not his own, and he must have the maturity, skills, and ability to make independent decisions and to act on those decisions.

I was a counterinsurgency advisor in Vietnam, likely not a very good one. Hindsight reveals much that at the time was either unnoticed or ignored, but while my time in the village and in combat was long ago, I am making comment now because the truth is that the fundamentals of insurgency/counterinsurgency have changed little. Technology changes; yesterday's booby trap sprung by a trip wire is today's improvised explosive device fired by a cell phone. Yesterday's guerrilla organization where communication was by personal contact, radio, or telephone and where higher authority was connected to lower through a pyramidal structure is today's insurgent cell communicating instantly via the internet to a relatively flat organization of collegial but not formally dependent units. The angers that impel insurgency have also changed; yesterday's communist radical is today's Islamic extremist; still, the most basic cause of insurgency is almost always the same: the failure of the government in power to care for its people.

That is what makes it so important for the U.S. to select its counterinsurgency partners carefully; not only is the task difficult and dangerous, but host nations are unlikely to be efficient partners. Further, some may turn out to be totally unreliable. If American lives and treasure are to be risked in a foreign adventure, that should be realized by all concerned from the beginning.

There is another element of counterinsurgency that affects advisors but has received little previous mention: it relates to the fact that American counterinsurgency operations have historically been conducted alongside major conventional American forces directed at defeating the enemy on the battlefield. Those conventional American soldiers and marines have

Nine. The Soldiers They Send

their battle buddies and their traditional regiments and divisions that give them identity and a sense of continuity with those who have struggled before them. They have the benefit of facing America's enemies *en bloc* where every American soldier feels bonded to thousands of others in a them-against-us atmosphere.

Advisors have a different kind of war. Depending on the specifics of the program, counterinsurgency advisors may operate in small teams living and working among people who may include numbers of the enemy. The number of true advisors, by which I mean those who train, live with, and fight along side their advisees, is typically small relative to the numbers of conventional soldiers engaged in the same conflict. This was true in Vietnam, Iraq, and Afghanistan. Their dispersion, their relatively small numbers, and their special tasks present counterinsurgency advisors with a different kind of war than the conventional soldier sees and the experience usually leaves them with a different set of memories and a different attitude about what they experienced.

An advisor who has spent a year in a village with a small team of other Americans has a different outlook and may develop different conclusions than an American soldier who spent that same year in that same theater but in a conventional army division with all of its logistical advantages, layered security, and combat support. The experiences advisors have can separate them from their more conventional colleagues in many silent ways and leave an influence on them that for decades to come will shape their views of what it means to do war in the village.

Vietnam, 1969

A Special Forces team stationed in our province capitol ran a Vietnamese Mobile Strike Force or "Mike Force" that had airboats armed with .30 caliber and .50 caliber machineguns. These boats could travel rapidly over very shallow water, so we often called on them to help us operate in remote areas of our district that offered the enemy sanctuary. We helped the SF team, as well, by letting them depot fuel and ammunition at our location for the operations they sometimes ran along the Cambodian border.

My team and the SF guys got on well together, so I suppose as an act of inter-team good will they handed us some of their Mike Force's tiger-stripe uniforms and Mike Force unit patches. Those were not regulation uniforms

Counterinsurgency

for American soldiers, but since we weren't with regular units, anyway, no one complained when we wore them. Advisors of the Vietnamese militias also wore the blue berets of their counterparts with their gold or silver crests and rank badges affixed. That was another departure from the standard U.S. Army uniform, but the point of those irregularities was to show a bond between us and the Vietnamese we were living with and fighting along side. The uniform irregularities were also an outgrowth of the feeling that we advisors were different from the GIs in the American units. To make that point, many of us didn't hesitate to blend our uniforms with those of our counterparts, not only for safety in the field, but to mark ourselves as being different from those other Americans.

Adding yet another irregularity, I had a tiger-stripe uniform with a patch sewed to the shirt pocket that showed the head of a snarling tiger. I told myself the snarling tiger was a display for the morale and confidence of the militiamen I was advising, but I think it was at least as much for me. The big cat was a talisman for combat aggressiveness. He was a totem for me much as a wolf or an eagle might have once been for an American Indian warrior or a lion or a cape buffalo might have been for an African. Wearing that tiger patch on my tiger-stripe uniform, I could inflate myself to being the Tiger of the Mekong. Yeah, boy.

I know, that sounds silly now; but in times of great stress people take their inspiration where they can find it. Today there are advisors working and fighting in totally different kinds of counterinsurgency situations than the one so many others and I faced in Vietnam. The components of the present insurgencies are different, the terrain is different and the people are different. The kinds and size of advisory teams that operated in Iraq and still operate in Afghanistan are also different from those in previous wars (Korea, Vietnam, El Salvador, etc.) and their degree of isolation may be different, as well; but counterinsurgency advisors still get their job done best when they live with, eat with, and operate with the indigenous forces or indigenous officials they are assigned to assist. Some of those advisors may search for their own iconic images to help boost their morale during difficult times. A counterinsurgency advisor in Iraq might have found inspiration by secretly thinking of himself as being the Lion of the Euphrates or an advisor in some remote stretch of Afghanistan may find the determination to once again defend a mountain pass or press forward building a school because he has made himself the Leopard of the Panjshir. Whatever image advisors can find to boost their energy and courage will be a help because they will surely have their days of exhaustion and frustration, of danger and difficulty, and, likely, even days of great disappointment. They will need all the support they can get from their military colleagues, their friends, their religion, and whatever totems they can find.

In the midst of all that trouble, most advisors will also have their days of bright insight, of energy and hope, and of revelation about something strange they would have never otherwise seen or done. Those are the days that make characters and change lives. They are the days that happen more often with proper advisor selection and proper counterinsurgency training. Importantly, they are the days that in the years to come will have those advisors thinking back to the time when they were the Lions of the Euphrates or the Leopards of the Panjshir, and in the fog of those distant years they will reflect that they were once called to serve their country under difficult circumstances. And they did.

Relevant Readings

Donovan, David. *Once a Warrior King.* New York: McGraw-Hill, 1985.
Metrinko, Michael. *Military Advisors.* Hauppauge, NY: Nova Science Publishers, 2009.

Bibliography

Andrade, Dale and James H. Willbanks. "CORDS/Phoenix: Counterinsurgency Lessons from Vietnam for the Future." *Military Review* March-April (2006): 9–26.
Brown, Donald M. *Vietnam and CORDS: Interagency Lessons for Iraq* (Fort Leavenworth, KS: School for Advanced Military Studies, 2008), 14–35; 41–44.
Cassidy, Robert M., "Back to the Street Without Joy: Counterinsurgency Lessons from Vietnam and Other Small Wars." *Parameters* 34 (2004): 73–83.
Coffey, Ross. "Revisiting CORDS: The Need for Unity of Effort to Secure Victory in Iraq." *Military Review* March-April (2006): 24–34.
Collins, James L. *Vietnam Studies: The Development and Training of the South Vietnamese Army, 1950–1972.* Washington, D.C.: Department of the Army, 1991, 68–122.
Cooper, Chester L., Judith E. Corson, Laurence J. Legere, David E. Lockwood, and Donald M. Weller. *The American Experience with Pacification in Vietnam.* Vol. 1. *An Overview of Pacification*. Arlington, VA: Institute for Defense Analysis, 1972, 1–61.
_____. *The American Experience with Pacification in Vietnam.* Vol 2. *Elements of Pacification*. Arlington, VA: Institute for Defense Analysis, 1972, 218–36.
Cordesman, Anthony H. "Afghanistan and the Uncertain Metrics of Progress: Part Six: Showing Victory is Possible." Center for Strategic and International Studies (2011). http://csis.org/publication/afghanistan-and-uncertain-metrics-progress-part-six-showing-victory-possible.
Corn, David. *Blond Ghost*. New York: Simon and Schuster, 1994, 282–293.
Corum, James. *Training Indigenous Forces in Counterinsurgency: a Tale of Two Insurgencies.* Carlisle, PA: Strategic Studies Institute. 2006.
Counterinsurgency Advisory and Assistance Team Special Report. "Partnering: a Counterinsurgency Imperative." *Small Wars Journal* 22 Nov (2010): 4–8.
Davis, Daniel L. "Truth, Lies, and Afghanistan: How Military Leaders Have Let Us Down." *Armed Forces Journal* (2012). http://www.armedforcesjournal.com/2012/8904030.
Donovan, David. *Once a Warrior King*. New York: McGraw-Hill, 1985.
Emerson, Gloria. *Winners an Losers: Battles, Retreats, Gains, Losses and Ruins From a Long War*. New York: Random House, 1978: 274–77.

Bibliography

Fall, Bernard B. "The Theory and Practice of Insurgency and Counterinsurgency." *Naval War College Review* 51 (1998): 46–56.

Felbab-Brown, Vanda. *Aspiration and Ambivalence: Strategies and Realities of Counterinsurgency and State-Building in Afghanistan.* Washington, D.C.: Brookings Institute Press, 2012.

Fitzgerald, David. *Learning to Forget: U.S. Army Counterinsurgency Doctrine and Practice.* San Francisco: Stanford University Press, 2013.

Fore, Henrietta, Robert Gates, and Condoleeza Rice. *U.S. Government Counterinsurgency Guide. United States Government Interagency Counterinsurgency Initiative.* Washington, D.C.: Department of State, 2009, 13–21.

Fox, J. and Dana Stowell. "Professional Army Advisors: a Way Ahead." *Infantry Bugler* Winter (2007): 8–13.

Galula, David. *Counterinsurgency: Theory and Practice.* New York: Frank A. Praeger, 1964.

———. *Pacification in Algeria 1956–1958.* Arlington: RAND Corporation, 1963.

Gardner, Lloyd C. and Marilyn B. Young. *Iraq and the Lessons of Vietnam or How Not to Learn from the Past.* New York: The New Press, 2007.

Gentile, Gian. *Wrong Turn: America's Deadly Embrace of Counterinsurgency.* New York: The New Press, 2013.

Grdovic, Mark. "The Advisory Challenge." *Special Warfare* 21 (2008): 22–28.

Heatherington, Richard H. "Foreign Military Advisor Proficiency: The Need for Screening, Selection, and Qualification." (Master Thesis, U.S. Army Command and General Staff College, 2009): 62–73.

Heiser, Joseph M. *Vietnam Studies: Logistic Support.* Washington, D.C.: Department of the Army, 1991, 229–42.

Helmer, Daniel. "Twelve Urgent Steps for the Advisor Mission in Afghanistan." *Military Review* July-August (2008): 73–81.

Henrickson, Thomas H. *Afghanistan, Counterinsurgency and the Indirect Approach.* MacDill Air Force Base, FL: Joint Special Operations University Press, 2010.

Hoffman, Bruce. "Insurgency and Counterinsurgency in Iraq" (an "Occasional Paper"). Santa Monica, CA: RAND Corporation, 2004.

Hoffman, Frank A. "New Principle of War: Understanding Must Take its Rightful Place. *Armed Forces Journal,* February (2012). www.armedforcesjournal.com/2012/02/8893629.

Hunt, Richard A. *Pacification: the American Struggle for Vietnam's Hearts and Minds.* San Francisco: Westview Press, 1995.

Jones, Robert A. "The Nationbuilder: Soldier of the Sixties." *Military Review* January (1965): 63–67.

Jones, Seth G. *Counterinsurgency in Afghanistan.* Santa Monica, CA: RAND Corporation, 2008, 106–33.

Kilcullen, David. *Counterinsurgency.* New York: Oxford University Press, 2010.

Kilner, Peter. "The Five Most Relevant Leader Attributes." *ARMY* January (2012): 57–60.

Lawrence, Thomas E. "Twenty-Seven Articles." *The Arab Bulletin* 20 August (1917).

Metrinko, Michael J. *The American Military Advisor: Dealing With Senior Foreign Officials in the Islamic World.* Carlisle, PA: Strategic Studies Institute, 2008.

———. *Military Advisors.* Happauge, NY: Nova Science Publishers, 2009.

Nagl, John. "Institutionalizing Adaptation: It's Time for an Army Advisor Command." *Military Review* September-October (2008): 21–26.

———. *Learning to eat Soup With a Knife: Counterinsurgency Lessons from Malaya and Vietnam.* New York: Praeger Publishers, 2002.

Bibliography

Nelson, Carl. *The Advisors*. Chula Vista, CA: New Century Press, 1999.

Olson, Eric T., James N. Mattis, and Michael G. Mullen. "Irregular Warfare: Countering Irregular Threats, Joint Operating Concept: Version 2.0." Washington, D.C.: Department of Defense (2010): 11–24.

Petraeus, David H., and John F. Amos. *Counterinsurgency; FM 3-24*. Washington, D.C.: Department of the Army, 2006.

Porch, Douglas. *Counterinsurgency: Exposing the Myths of the New Way of War*. New York: Cambridge University Press, 2013.

Ramsey, Robert D. *Advice for Advisors: Suggestions and Observations from Lawrence to the Present*. Fort Leavenworth, KS: Combat Studies Institute Press, 2006.

———. *Advising Indigenous Forces: American Advisors in Korea, Vietnam, and El Salvador*. Fort Leavenworth, KS: Combat Studies Institute Press, 2006.

Ricklefs, Norman. "Fourteen Rules for Advisors in Iraq." *Small Wars Journal,* August (2008). http://smallwarsjournalcom/jrnl/art/fourteeen-rules-for-advisors-in-Iraq.

Schwarz, Benjamin C. *American Counterinsurgency Doctrine and El Salvador: The Frustrations of Reform and the Illusions of Nation Building*. Santa Monica, CA: RAND Corporation, 1991.

Sepp, Kalev I. "Best Practices in Counterinsurgency." *Military Review*. May-June (2005): 8–12.

Silinsky, Mark. "An Irony of War: Human Development as Warfare in Afghanistan." *Colloquium* 3 (2010): 1–16.

Sorley, Lester. *Honorable Warrior: General Harold K. Johnson and the Ethics of Command* (Lawrence: University Press of Kansas, 1998): 227–58.

———. *The Vietnam Chronicles: The Abrams Tapes, 1968–1972* (Lubbock: Texas Tech University Press, 2004): 115.

"Special Forces Advisor Guide," (TC 31-73). Washington, D.C.: Department of the Army, 2008.

West, Francis J. *The Village*. New York: Harper and Row, 1972.

Index

Abrams, Creighton 157, 158, 161, 175, 190
advisors 65–84; characteristics of best 67–68; issues faced 75–81; selection of 67–75, 91; training of 73–74, 90–91; twelve rules for 92–108
advisory teams 160–162, 164–177; effectiveness of small 175–177; supply and sustenance of 171–175; within U.S. military culture 81–84
Afghanistan 6, 16, 20–24, 31, 49, 54, 60, 141–145, 152–54, 163, 168–170, 175, 179–181, 183, 192–195; absence of progress in 182–190
al-Qaida 23, 154
Arab Bulletin 85
Army of the Republic of Vietnam (ARVN) 158–159, 162, 176, 186
ARVN *see* Army of the Republic of Vietnam

Blond Ghost 191
brown water navy 74, 148

The Campaign 44–64
Central Intelligence Agency (CIA) 162, 170, 191
Chaumont-Guitry, Guy de 155
CIA *see* Central Intelligence Agency
Civil Operations and Revolutionary Development Support (CORDS) 30, 66, 67, 74, 152, 157, 158–165, 169–172, 176–177
Combined Arms Center 5

command influence 41–42
communication, preference for indirect 127
constabulary 32–33, 137; *see also* police
conventional forces 26, 32, 83, 90, 152, 158, 177
Cordesman, Anthony 194–195
CORDS *see* Civil Operations and Revolutionary Development Support
Corn, David 191
Corruption 33, 130, 171, 177; in host government 36–39, 55, 141, 160, 191–193
Counterinsurgency 9
"Counterinsurgency Guide" 183–185
counterinsurgency programs 29–43; effectiveness of 164–171; evaluation of 39–42; organization of 157–178; reasons for failure 134–156; rules for 87–92; *see also* Hamlet Evaluation System; Territorial Forces Evaluation System
counterparts, rules for relation with 106–114
cultural factors 114–132; *see also* culture shock
culture shock 70, 73, 77, 79
Cushman, John, Major General 68

Davis, Daniel, Colonel 192–194
Democracy 3, 16, 19, 20, 23, 145–146, 183
demographic control 136
Department of Defense 184, 180, 181, 183
Department of State 162, 181, 183

Index

development 2, 4, 30, 31–32, 66, 86, 137–138, 141, 63, 171, 192–193; as part of The Program 34–36
District Senior Advisor (DSA) 12, 40, 67, 89, 94, 162, 172, 187
district team 40, 67, 89, 162, 189
DSA *see* District Senior Advisor
dysgnosis 15, 68

El Salvador 6, 15, 29, 46, 179, 204

face *see* saving face
failure *see* counterinsurgency programs, reasons for failure
FM 3-07 180
FM 3-24 9
foreign policy 7, 9, 11, 15, 22, 24–25, 29, 65, 67, 83–84, 86, 92, 133, 160, 202

Hamlet Evaluation System (HES) 40–41, 162
HES *see* Hamlet Evaluation System
Hoa Hao 78–79
Hoffman, Frank 75
Honorable Warrior 155
host country 16, 23, 26–27, 36, 46, 55–57; American popular support for 23–29; government of 17; manpower resources and needs 34, 54–55; U.S. interests in 22; *see also* U.S. national interests
host government 14; ability to change 21–22; corruption within 36–39, 191–193; popular support for 17–20; willingness to change 20–21; *see also* corruption
Hunt, Richard 177

identification cards 136; *see also* demographic control
illiteracy, effects of 34, 36
insurgency 2, 11, 14, 17, 34, 42, 55, 65, 74, 80, 131, 135, 138, 146, 155, 204
intelligence 26–28, 39, 53, 136, 140, 170, 176, 185, 191; advisors role in 75, 92; objective reporting and hearing of 28
Iraq 6, 14–16, 20–25, 36, 39, 54, 64, 76, 141, 145, 152, 163, 175, 179, 181
irregular warfare 46, 82, 180–182, 187, 192–195

Johnson, General Howard 155–156
Jones, Seth 135
justice 39, 177; failure to achieve 137

Kilcullen, David 9

language 27, 75–78, 81, 102, 121, 182; fluency 25; training 74, 91, 165–169
Lawrence, T. E. 85, 110
leadership 9, 82–83, 110, 120; poor 32, 54
Learning to Eat Soup with a Knife 9
Lesson Learned 50–53, 60–63, 71–73, 87–90, 94–97, 101–105, 106–110, 110–114, 121- 124, 128–132, 148–152, 172–175, 187–191
lessons learned 8, 15; publications 6, 8
"light at the end of the tunnel" 186

MACV *see* Military Assistance Command Vietnam
MAT *see* Mobile Advisory Team
Military Assistance Command Vietnam (MACV) 50, 60, 66, 71, 87, 89, 94, 101, 106, 121, 128, 152, 157–158, 160–161, 165–166, 171–172, 175, 197–188, 190
Militia 2, 4, 12, 30, 32–33, 35, 37–41, 47, 56, 66–67, 79, 87–88, 107–108, 121, 140, 150, 155, 158, 162, 169–170, 172, 197, 198, 200, 201, 204
Mobile Advisory Team (MAT) 12, 30, 40, 44, 50, 87, 89, 101, 106, 116, 121, 157, 159–160, 162–176, 187; constitution of 66; duties of 66–67

Nagl, John 9
national borders, control of 32, 154–155
national executive, authority of 146–147
nationhood, weak sense of 177, 125

Once a Warrior King 4–5

Pacification: The American Struggle for Vietnam's Hearts and Minds 177
Pershing, Major John J. 15
personal space, concepts of 127
Petraeus, Lieutenant General David 2, 7
PF *see* Popular Forces
police 136–137, 140, 161; training and pay of 33–34
policy, counterinsurgency 13, 19, 42, 135
political process, failure of 138
Popular Forces (PF) 157–159, 162, 164–167, 171
popular support: degree of in America 23–24; degree of in host country 17–21
population, insurgents access to 32, 139–141

212

Index

Potemkin, Gregory 179–180
Potemkin village 179; avoiding 195; in counterinsurgency 180–185; decisions that lead to 185–192; in Iraq and Afghanistan 192–195
The Program 29–43; development in 34–36; government reform in 37–39; management of 30–31; progress evaluation 39–42; rules for 86–92
propaganda 138–139, 140, 161, 163
Province Reconstruction Team (PRT) 31, 163
Province Senior Advisor (PSA) 38, 41, 66, 97, 128, 162, 189
province team 66, 115–117, 162, 165, 172
PRT *see* Province Reconstruction Team
PSA *see* Province Senior Advisor
public utilities, improvement of 141

RAG *see* River Assault Group
rapport, development of 63, 76, 80, 93–94, 101, 108, 114, 121
Regional Forces (RF) 157–159, 162, 164–167, 171
religion 49, 54, 67, 78, 101, 109; importance of 98, 119–120, 127
RF *see* Regional Forces
River Assault Group (RAG) 110–112, 148–150
riverine forces 148, 150

Saigon Syndrome 22, 39, 90, 110
saving face 120–124
sectarian 16, 22, 54, 144–145
Security 2, 4, 16, 19, 21–22; general tasks of 32–33
Security Forces Advise and Assist Teams (SFAATs) 168–170
SFAATs *see* Security Forces Advise and Assist Teams
small war 11, 15, 25–26, 75, 83, 90, 135, 153, 155
Sorley, Louis 157
Special Forces 9, 90–91, 104, 128, 152–153, 159–160, 164, 168, 192; operation with 203–204
Special Operations Regiment, U.S. Marine Corps 167
Special Warfare School 66–67, 74, 121, 165
State Department *see* Department of State
Stationary Advisory Teams (STATs) 166

statistics 176
STATs *see* Stationary Advisory Teams
strategic terrain, control of 153–154
suffering, indifference to 52, 124–125

taboos, importance of 119–120
Taliban 14, 23, 154, 183, 193
TC 31–73 9
territorial forces 40, 158–159, 162, 171, 175–176; *see also* Popular Forces; Regional Forces
Territorial Forces Evaluation System (TFES) 40–41, 162
The Test 11–28
TFES *see* Territorial Forces Evaluation System
time, inattentiveness to 119; lack of 76
Tolstoy, Leo 134
tribal relationships, importance of 125
tribal rivalries 144–146
trust 57–63, 76, 94–97
Tung, Mao Tse 140
"Twenty-Seven Articles" 85

United States Agency for International Development (USAID) 131, 162
USAID *see* United States Agency for International Development
U.S. Army John F. Kennedy Special Warfare Center and School *see* Special Warfare School
U.S. national interests 14, 17, 22, 24, 45, 185, 196

VC *see* Viet Cong
VCI *see* Viet Cong Infrastructure
Viet Cong (VC) 14, 50, 52–53, 62, 122, 132, 148, 154–155, 159, 170
Viet Cong Infrastructure (VCI) 170, 176
The Vietnam Chronicles: The Abrams Tapes, 1968-1970 157
Vietnam, specific experiences in 12, 17, 30, 31, 34, 37, 40, 46, 55, 58, 66, 68, 78, 98, 115, 141, 197; *see also* Lesson Learned
Von Causewitz, Carl 11

War and Peace 134
Westmoreland, General William 77, 155, 157, 160–161
women: general, discussion of with counterparts 125–126; indigenous, contact with 125

213